APPOINTED INSPIRED PESSIMISTIC EXCITED OPTI
EFUL OFFENDED SURPRISED EMBARRASSED INSE
XCITED OPTIMISTIC RE   OVERWHELMED
SED INSECURE GRATEF   ION
ELMED CONTENT PROU   IDE
ED PASSIONATE FRUST   APPY
CONFIDENT AFRAID CALM RE   FUS
APPY INDIFFERENT EMPATHETIC DISA   D IN
JEALOUS CONFUSED STRONG HOPEFUL OFFENDED
SAPPOINTED INSPIRED PESSIMISTIC EXCITED OPTI
EFUL OFFENDED SURPRISED EMBARRASSED INSE
XCITED OPTIMISTIC RESENTFUL OVERWHELMED
SED INSECURE GRATEFUL INTIMIDATED PASSION
ELMED CONTENT PROUD DISCOURAGED CONFIDEN
ED PASSIONATE FRUSTRATED POSITIVE SAD HAPPY
CONFIDENT AFRAID CALM RELIEVED JEALOUS CONFUS
APPY INDIFFERENT EMPATHETIC DISAPPOINTED IN
JEALOUS CONFUSED STRONG HOPEFUL OFFENDED
SAPPOINTED INSPIRED PESSIMISTIC EXCITED OPTI
EFUL OFFENDED SURPRISED EMBARRASSED INSE
XCITED OPTIMISTIC RESENTFUL OVERWHELMED
SED INSECURE GRATEFUL INTIMIDATED PASSION
ELMED CONTENT PROUD DISCOURAGED CONFIDEN
ED PASSIONATE FRUSTRATED POSITIVE SAD HAPPY
CONFIDENT AFRAID CALM RELIEVED JEALOUS CONFUS
APPY INDIFFERENT EMPATHETIC DISAPPOINTED IN
JEALOUS CONFUSED STRONG HOPEFUL OFFENDED
SAPPOINTED INSPIRED PESSIMISTIC EXCITED OPTI
EFUL OFFENDED SURPRISED EMBARRASSED INSE
XCITED OPTIMISTIC RESENTFUL OVERWHELMED
SED INSECURE GRATEFUL INTIMIDATED PASSION
ELMED CONTENT PROUD DISCOURAGED CONFIDEN
ED PASSIONATE FRUSTRATED POSITIVE SAD HAPPY
CONFIDENT AFRAID CALM RELIEVED JEALOUS CONFUS
APPY INDIFFERENT EMPATHETIC DISAPPOINTED IN
JEALOUS CONFUSED STRONG HOPEFUL OFFENDED
SAPPOINTED INSPIRED PESSIMISTIC EXCITED OPTI
EFUL OFFENDED SURPRISED EMBARRASSED INSE
XCITED OPTIMISTIC RESENTFUL OVERWHELMED
SED INSECURE GRATEFUL INTIMIDATED PASSION
ELMED CONTENT PROUD DISCOURAGED CONFIDEN
ED PASSIONATE FRUSTRATED POSITIVE SAD HAPP

RUSTRATED POSITIVE SAD HAPPY INDIFFERENT E
EMPATHETIC DISAPPOINTED INSPIRED PESSIM
ISTIC RESENTFUL OVERWHELMED CONTENT PRO
OURAGED CONFIDENT AFRAID CALM RELIEVED J
NFUSED STRONG HOPEFUL OFFENDED SURPRISE
SED INSECURE GRATEFUL INTIMIDATED PASSION
RUSTRATED POSITIVE SAD HAPPY INDIFFERENT E
EMPATHETIC DISAPPOINTED INSPIRED PESSIM
ISTIC RESENTFUL OVERWHELMED CONTENT PRO
OURAGED CONFIDENT AFRAID CALM RELIEVED J
NFUSED STRONG HOPEFUL OFFENDED SURPRISE
BARRASSED INSECURE GRATEFUL INTIMIDATED PA
RUSTRATED POSITIVE SAD HAPPY INDIFFERENT E
SAPPOINTED INSPIRED PESSIMISTIC EXCITED O
RESENTFUL OVERWHELMED CONTENT PROUD DIS
ONFIDENT AFRAID CALM RELIEVED JEALOUS COI
NFUSED STRONG HOPEFUL OFFENDED SURPRISE
SED INSECURE GRATEFUL INTIMIDATED PASSION
RUSTRATED POSITIVE SAD HAPPY INDIFFERENT E
SAPPOINTED INSPIRED PESSIMISTIC EXCITED O
RESENTFUL OVERWHELMED CONTENT PROUD DIS
ONFIDENT AFRAID CALM RELIEVED JEALOUS COI
NFUSED STRONG HOPEFUL OFFENDED SURPRISE
SED INSECURE GRATEFUL INTIMIDATED PASSIONA
RUSTRATED POSITIVE SAD HAPPY INDIFFERENT E
SAPPOINTED INSPIRED PESSIMISTIC EXCITED O
RESENTFUL OVERWHELMED CONTENT PROUD DIS
ONFIDENT AFRAID CALM RELIEVED JEALOUS COI
OFFENDED SURPRISED EMBARRASSED INSECURE
E GRATEFUL INTIMIDATED PASSIONATE FRUSTRAT
OSITIVE SAD HAPPY INDIFFERENT EMPATHETIC D
PIRED PESSIMISTIC EXCITED OPTIMISTIC RESENT
OVERWHELMED CONTENT PROUD DISCOURAGE
FRAID CALM RELIEVED JEALOUS CONFUSED STR
NG HOPEFUL OFFENDED SURPRISED EMBARRASS
E GRATEFUL INTIMIDATED PASSIONATE FRUSTRAT
OSITIVE SAD HAPPY INDIFFERENT EMPATHETIC D
TIC EXCITED OPTIMISTIC RESENTFUL OVERWHE
OUD DISCOURAGED CONFIDENT AFRAID CALM RI
ALOUS CONFUSED STRONG HOPEFUL SURPRISED
BARRASSED INSECURE GRATEFUL INTIMIDATED PA
SIONATE FRUSTRATED POSITIVE SAD HAPPY INDI

PRAISE FOR *THE EMOTIONALLY STRONG LEADER*

"Stern challenges us to drop our fears and hesitation about engaging with our feelings and helps us to understand how an emotionally intelligent leader is more authentic and effective. A compelling read and timely call to action."

JEFF SCOTT, PRESIDENT & CEO, COASTAL PACIFIC XPRESS

"Stern reveals that how a leader shows up for others is key to their success. *The Emotionally Strong Leader* teaches you how to develop your EI sense and show up as the leader you want to be. Stern's insight and guidance has been transformational for me."

MIKE LEONARD, PRESIDENT & CEO,
BRITISH COLUMBIA MARITIME EMPLOYERS ASSOCIATION

"Now more than ever, leaders need to connect, build trust, and bring their genuine selves to their teams every day. Unlike other authors who also ask us to reconsider our approach to leadership, Stern challenges us to dive deeper and own not only our approach to leading others, but also how we show up, who we are, and how we got here."

WALLY SMITH, ED.D.,
DIRECTOR OF TALENT DEVELOPMENT, UCHICAGO MEDICINE

"This book opens the door to a new kind of leadership through an inside-out approach that cuts straight to the heart of the issue: why we do what we do. Rather than being afraid of your emotions, learn to embrace them. Stern provides a simple set of strategies that will bring you to the best version of yourself in the workplace. I know it did for me."

DUANA KIPLING, PRESIDENT, NEPTUNE BULK TERMINALS

"In these pages, Stern presents with honest clarity the power of emotional intelligence. Having experienced Stern's excellent work with the leadership team at University of Findlay, I encourage you to read her work carefully, and to apply the principles of EI bravely."

KATHERINE FELL, PHD, PRESIDENT, UNIVERSITY OF FINDLAY

"An extraordinarily rich guide articulating why emotions are your superpower. Stern reveals how emotional intelligence can become the magic ingredient to connect authentically, communicate effectively, and thrive collectively."

DAN PONTEFRACT, AWARD-WINNING AUTHOR
AND LEADERSHIP STRATEGIST

"This book teaches you that change starts from within. If you want to dramatically improve your ability to connect and lead—at home and in life—start with Stern's program and undergo your own transformative, inside-out evolution. It worked for me."

DUANE JEBBETT, RETIRED PRESIDENT & CEO, ROWMARK

"To be an even better leader, you need to be principled, purpose driven, and able to fully tap into the emotions within yourself and that exist among your team. Stern's playbook on emotional intelligence will help all leaders move their impact to the next level. A must-read!"

JIM REID, AUTHOR OF *LEADING TO GREATNESS*, AND FORMER CHIEF HR OFFICER, ROGERS COMMUNICATIONS

"Stern allows us to look inside ourselves, acknowledge our emotions, and understand how they impact our careers and relationships. She then provides the understanding and tools to embrace those emotions so we can thrive as leaders, team members, and partners."

DAVID MACLAREN, FOUNDER & CEO, MEDIAVALET

"Stern's well-researched book clearly identifies the critical connection between emotional intelligence and leadership, and she provides an excellent guide to support our personal development and that of our teams. This is a must-read."

PAUL DANGERFIELD, PRESIDENT, CAPILANO UNIVERSITY

"For too long, emotional intelligence has been denigrated or relegated to the private sphere. Yet it is one of the essential keys to successful leadership in the twenty-first century. Let Stern be your guide, with this book born of long practice and deeply moving personal stories."

CÉLINE SCHILLINGER, FOUNDER & CEO, WE NEED SOCIAL, AND AUTHOR OF *DARE TO UN-LEAD*

"Stern takes us on a journey to embrace—not suppress—our emotions as an integral part of our humanity. Our brain integrates the sum of everything on our mind into one behavior—and emotions are a key part of this. A better understanding of our emotional predisposition is empowering, and will help create better, empathetic leaders."

CLAUDIA KREBS, MD, PHD, PROFESSOR OF TEACHING IN NEUROANATOMY, UNIVERSITY OF BRITISH COLUMBIA

"*The Emotionally Strong Leader* is a warning bell for all leaders who are ignoring emotions in the workplace. Especially in these challenging times, we need to embrace our emotions and those of others. Stern provides a clear path and a set of tools for leaders to do just that."

BOB HANLEY, SENIOR VICE PRESIDENT, CHIEF HUMAN RESOURCES OFFICER, UCHICAGO MEDICINE

the Emotionally

STRONG

LEADER

An **Inside-Out** Journey to
Transformational Leadership

CAROLYN STERN

Figure.1
Vancouver / Toronto / Berkeley

Cataloguing data is available from Library and Archives Canada
ISBN 978-1-77327-168-2 (hbk.)
ISBN 978-1-77327-169-9 (ebook)
ISBN 978-1-77327-170-5 (pdf)

Jacket design by Naomi MacDougall
Interior design by Teresa Bubela
Illustrations by Matt Nosworthy
Author photograph by Arjun Malik

Editing by Steve Cameron
Copy editing by Marnie Lamb
Proofreading by Alison Strobel
Indexing by Stephen Ullstrom

Printed and bound in Canada by Friesens
Distributed internationally by Publishers Group West

Figure 1 Publishing Inc.
Vancouver BC Canada
www.figure1publishing.com

Figure 1 Publishing works in the traditional, unceded territory of the xʷməθkʷəy̓əm (Musqueam), Sḵwx̱wú7mesh (Squamish), and səlilwətaɬ (Tsleil-Waututh) peoples.

For the sake of anonymity, the names of clients and students appearing in this book have been altered, as have some job titles and work industries.

*To every leader who wants to join me on my quest of
making it okay to be human in the workplace.*

*Let's topple the idea that emotions don't belong at work.
We are human before we are employees or leaders,
and thus, we are filled with feelings.*

*Don't be afraid of your emotions, but rather, gain the emotional
skills and mental strategies to be bigger and more intelligent
than your feelings, and help others learn to do the same.*

*Turn the way you think of leadership on its head;
lead from the inside-out with emotional intelligence.*

CONTENTS

You can be emotional and strong; **they are not mutually exclusive.**

INTRODUCTION

MANY PEOPLE SEE the words "emotional" and "strong" as contradictory terms that do not belong together when describing the kind of leaders who can transform their own lives, the lives of their colleagues, and the future of their business for the better. After all, how can anything to do with feelings be the key to unlocking personal and collective success?

Well, it's essential to learn how to be in the driver's seat of your feelings and understand how to lead with a strong mind and a kind heart while using a set of clear, simple, and tested skills and strategies. Doing so will allow you to connect more authentically and communicate more effectively with your coworkers and teams. This kind of connection and communication will create an environment of trust and belonging that will spur engagement, spike curiosity, and engender fraternity among team members. That is what leading with emotional intelligence (EI) looks like.

Through embracing emotional self-awareness and empathy by acknowledging your feelings and those of your coworkers, you can drive exceptional results. But unfortunately, too many leaders choose another path, one that eschews their emotions and those of their employees as bothersome and unimportant to the task at hand. This limited and damaging viewpoint tends to make people feel as though they are simply task-managing machines and not terrific, complex individuals full of energy, passion, and unlimited potential.

Let's face it: we all have feelings. Emotions make us human and are the universal language we can all relate to and understand, no matter how diverse, dispersed, and digital we are across the globe. And they are with us all the time, especially in the workplace. But many of us go through life pretending not to have them.

Why?

Simply put, because we are scared of our emotions.

The hard truth is emotions can be messy, annoying, and confusing. And yes, some emotions can be challenging to handle. Therefore, many of us choose to numb, ignore, or distract ourselves to avoid experiencing our feelings.

Emotions can carry a lot of power over us, despite our best efforts to steer clear of them. Even though we may intuitively know emotions need an out, we still try to stuff them down. But they can wiggle their way into our psyche at the most inopportune times, making us feel like we've inadvertently aired our dirty laundry for all to see.

We are culturally averse toward being emotional—or at the very least, we dislike appearing emotional. This attitude about our feelings has been passed down by our parents, teachers, and role models. For most of us, we have been led to believe that being emotional is a weakness and that showing our emotions should be cause for shame.

Because emotions have been given this bad reputation, we suppress them. But neglected feelings can make us do and say things we regret later. When we get angry, hurt, or defensive and respond in a manner that is blown out of proportion—or may be viewed as irrational by others—our reaction has everything to do with our unresolved feelings and very little to do with the current moment.

This impulsiveness occurs simply because we do not understand in the moment why we are experiencing the particular emotion. Or put another way, we don't understand what's happening in our life that is underneath the surface and is the cause of our feelings.

When we habitually avoid interacting with our feelings, we lose the ability to notice, understand, and label what we are feeling. As psychiatrist Dan Siegel points out, if we can't express our emotions and put a name to them, we can't tame them.[1]

We suck at **understanding our feelings.**

Plainly, we suck at understanding our feelings because we have not been taught how to be aware of, discuss, or manage our emotions.

Because we suck at understanding our feelings, we also suck at understanding how others feel. This can become a hot mess because when trying to understand others—and conversely, when others are trying to understand us—we tend to judge and label a person's actions by making assumptions and wrongly attributing an emotion to that behavior.

Psychologists call this phenomenon—when people make judgments and assumptions about why others behave in a certain way—attribution bias,[2] and these attributions may not necessarily be an accurate mirror of reality.[3] When we form a perception of someone based on their behavior, we tend to neglect other factors that may influence that behavior.[4] These perceptual errors lead to a slew of misconceptions, miscommunications, and mishaps at work.

Addressing the feelings of others in the workplace can be a terrifying proposition. For many leaders, asking what lies behind the actions and reactions of their people is akin to opening Pandora's box. They don't want to find out what's lurking inside. Many managers do not know how to deal with—and they fear—their employees' emotions.

Leaders of these organizations have good reason to be scared. After all, few of us know how to handle emotions (let alone how to handle them at work). Many of us have not been taught how to tend to our feelings and those of others. So isn't it better to sweep all those pesky emotions under the rug and carry on as if they don't exist?

The answer is an unequivocal *no!*

Instead of spending time and money on dealing with the inappropriate behaviors and disrespectful communications stemming from emotional issues in your workplace, you can get to the heart of those issues and deal with your feelings, and the feelings of your people, head-on.

You can gain emotional skills and mental strategies to be stronger and more intelligent than your feelings, and to help others learn to explore their emotions. Being stronger than your emotions is not strong-arming your feelings or having a steely resolve not to feel. It simply means that you work to acknowledge, understand, and accept that you feel things. You identify that your feelings contain wisdom, and you use that information to guide your behaviors when confronted with emotional triggers that can drive hasty reactions and undisciplined behavior.

For more than two decades, I have synthesized all that I have studied and researched in education, psychology, and business, as well as what I've learned, witnessed, and experienced in my classes and inside hundreds of organizations, to teach the emotional skills necessary for both students and leaders to thrive.

Based on that, I've developed an approach for enhancing your emotional knowledge and skills. My Self-Coaching to Enhanced Emotional Intelligence Model is a six-step framework, backed by leading science and grounded in my decades of in-the-field experience.

It is a personal, step-by-step process where you first identify the specific emotional skills that most impact your life and career. All of us have distinct strengths and areas for growth at different points in our life and for all kinds of different situations. This framework will provide you a structure to ensure that whatever your emotional challenges are at this moment, they are explored thoroughly and from many angles.

Coaching yourself through the model will help you uncover your barriers to growth and change, set goals for yourself, and tap into your motivation, giving you the tools and drive to manage the hurdles life throws at you. As life changes and your emotions evolve, this framework will continue to serve as a powerful tool you can continually call upon throughout the seasons of your life.

This program will also empower you to accept that your emotions, and those of others, are not the enemy. Once you accept that, you will be able to create committed, engaged, and fulfilled teams who feel truly valued, recognized, seen, and appreciated for their contributions.

Dale Carnegie said it best in his book *How to Win Friends and Influence People*: "When dealing with people, let us remember we are not dealing with creatures of logic. We are dealing with creatures of emotion."[5]

Humans are both thinking and emotional creatures. Sometimes, we can be persuaded by the power of our feelings rather than our rational thoughts, whether we like it or not.

Every business leader is unique, and so is their emotional makeup. Emotional makeup can be influenced both by nature (genetic influences) and nurture (environmental influences).[6] The good news is that anyone can learn, develop, and enhance their EI skills in order to understand their emotional nuances. Developing EI skills is your key to unlocking your leadership potential. Doing so will enable you to realize why you act and think the way you do and allow you to channel that internal knowledge into positive, conscious behaviors as opposed to negative, impulsive actions. Through this inside-out kind of leadership, you will be able to better lead yourself and guide your people to emotional clarity.

If I could tell every business leader who is struggling to get the results they want one thing, it would be this: *don't be afraid of emotions—yours or those of your teams.*

Feelings are not facts. They are just feelings. They are not good or bad or right or wrong; they are simply an emotional experience or reaction to a person, thing, or situation.

Even though feelings are emotional experiences or emotionally triggered reactions, they can also be full of wisdom, if you look for it. Travis Bradberry and Jean Greaves share in their book *Emotional Intelligence 2.0* that "the only way to genuinely understand your emotions is to spend enough time thinking through them to figure out where they come from and why they are there."[7] Emotions are filled with insights and should be used as data to learn more about yourself, others, and the world.

What follows here is an actionable book about what it takes to be a leader who is both emotionally connected and powerful in their ability to understand and regulate their emotional reactions. The processes and tools shared in these pages, when combined with an open mind and a willingness to accept your shortcomings and confront the sometimes brutal truth, will astoundingly influence your performance, your results, and your happiness. Simply put, this book has the capacity to start you on a life-changing journey to dramatically improve your personal, interpersonal, and professional effectiveness.

So join me on this journey and become the leader you wished you had: one who engages in self-leadership and leadership of others with EI and compassion. Get inspired, take action, and achieve more. Join others like me who are enhancing their EI and unlocking their unparalleled potential for success. I absolutely know you'll be glad you did.

SECTION I

IFFERENT EMPATHETIC DISAPPOINTED INSPIRE
NT AFRAID CALM RELIEVED JEALOUS CONFUSED
TE FRUSTRATED POSITIVE SAD HAPPY INDIFFEREN
MED CONTENT PROUD DISCOURAGED CONFIDENT
ED INSECURE GRATEFUL INTIMIDATED PASSIONAT
EXCITED OPTIMISTIC RESENTFUL OVERWHELMED
PEFUL OFFENDED SURPRISED EMBARRASSED INSI
TIC DISAPPOINTED INSPIRED PESSIMISTIC EXCIT
LM RELIEVED JEALOUS CONFUSED STRONG HOPE
D POSITIVE SAD HAPPY INDIFFERENT EMPATHETI
NT PROUD DISCOURAGED CONFIDENT AFRAID CAL
RE GRATEFUL INTIMIDATED PASSIONATE FRUSTRAT
OPTIMISTIC RESENTFUL OVERWHELMED CONTENT
NDED SURPRISED EMBARRASSED INSECURE GRAT
NTED INSPIRED PESSIMISTIC EXCITED OPTIMISTI
US CONFUSED STRONG HOPEFUL OFFENDED SURP
IDIFFERENT EMPATHETIC DISAPPOINTED INSPIRE
NT AFRAID CALM RELIEVED JEALOUS CONFUSED
TE FRUSTRATED POSITIVE SAD HAPPY INDIFFEREN
MED CONTENT PROUD DISCOURAGED CONFIDENT
ED INSECURE GRATEFUL INTIMIDATED PASSIONAT
EXCITED OPTIMISTIC RESENTFUL OVERWHELMED
PEFUL OFFENDED SURPRISED EMBARRASSED INSI
TIC DISAPPOINTED INSPIRED PESSIMISTIC EXCIT
LM RELIEVED JEALOUS CONFUSED STRONG HOPE
D POSITIVE SAD HAPPY INDIFFERENT EMPATHETI
NT PROUD DISCOURAGED CONFIDENT AFRAID CAL
RE GRATEFUL INTIMIDATED PASSIONATE FRUSTRAT
OPTIMISTIC RESENTFUL OVERWHELMED CONTENT
NDED SURPRISED EMBARRASSED INSECURE GRAT
NTED INSPIRED PESSIMISTIC EXCITED OPTIMISTI
US CONFUSED STRONG HOPEFUL OFFENDED SURP
DIFFERENT EMPATHETIC DISAPPOINTED INSPIRE
NT AFRAID CALM RELIEVED JEALOUS CONFUSED
TE FRUSTRATED POSITIVE SAD HAPPY INDIFFEREN
MED CONTENT PROUD DISCOURAGED CONFIDENT
ED INSECURE GRATEFUL INTIMIDATED PASSIONAT
EXCITED OPTIMISTIC RESENTFUL OVERWHELMED
PEFUL OFFENDED SURPRISED EMBARRASSED INSI
TIC DISAPPOINTED INSPIRED PESSIMISTIC EXCIT
M RELIEVED JEALOUS CONFUSED STRONG HOPE
D POSITIVE SAD HAPPY INDIFFERENT EMPATHETI

SECTION I

Turn Leadership On Its Head

WHEN YOU THINK of a leader, what comes to mind? Is it an unscrupulous, cajoling egoist like Gordon Gekko of *Wall Street*? Perhaps, it is the brash, ill-tempered vibrato of Spider Man's J. Jonah Jameson, who micromanages his employees, barking orders from behind his desk at the *Daily Bugle*? Or do you imagine a more contemporary touchstone like Logan Roy of *Succession*, whose need for power has him trample on anyone in his way?

Whether it be politicians, high-ranking officers, or Fortune 500 CEOs, the examples we have of what a leader *ought* to be often don't fit with what a leader *needs* to be.

Time is up for the irreproachable leader whose very presence can cause waves of terror among employees. So too is it up for the stoic, detached, and unflappable leader whose inability to be seen as anything but in control creates tense and inauthentic interactions.

These kinds of failed leadership do more harm than good—to the people being led and to the bottom line of the organizations being run.

What we need today are leaders who embrace their feelings, who understand themselves from the inside-out. These are leaders who know why they do what they do, are in touch with their emotional makeup, and use the data from their feelings to help them make informed, rational decisions—especially when the stakes are high. These are leaders who express humility, engage in genuine and caring conversations with the people they lead, and aren't afraid to admit when they make a mistake.

These are leaders who are leading with their superpower: EI.

It's time to knock down the lie that sharing our emotions and being honest about how we are feeling is a sign of weakness. It's time for our corporate world to stop encouraging people to stuff down their feelings while at work. It's time to make friends with our feelings. Because if we stop being so scared of our emotions and look for the wisdom they provide us, we can change how we connect, communicate, and lead.

When a leader chooses to discuss what they are feeling, no longer are others experiencing that leader solely through outward behavior, but rather, they are experiencing deeper connections from underneath the surface. When this kind of genuine connection happens, others feel seen and heard, cared for and valued, and in a work setting, this affects their dedication, engagement, and fulfillment.[1]

Emotions matter, and your employees' emotional well-being is impacting your organization, for better or for worse. Focusing on the emotions of your people is key to making sure your company stays motivated, innovative, and productive. But you first must understand and manage your own feelings.

Section I is here to illustrate to you the gift that emotions can bring to your leadership. As an emotionally strong leader, you will embrace the powerful insights that emotions provide and use that information to handle any challenges and changes that come your way.

Creating an emotionally strong culture where feelings, concerns, and motives are openly discussed does not require you to be high in all EI competencies. The only requirement is that you focus on enhancing your EI—being aware of your emotions and those of others, and how they affect your self-perception, communication, relationships, decision-making, and stress management.

That said, improving your EI is not a one-size-fits-all process. We are all wired differently, and that's not a bad thing; it means each of us has unique strengths and development opportunities. However, because we are all different, understanding, expressing, and managing your emotions involves figuring out which particular emotional tactics and regulation strategies will work best for you in any given situation.

In the following pages, I will help you turn the way you think of leadership—as it relates to emotions—on its head. I will share with you why EI is the magic ingredient to connect authentically, communicate effectively, and thrive collectively. Incorporating EI into your repertoire will take your leadership to new heights.

Everyone is human, and thus, everyone has feelings, so let's learn how to manage them in the workplace so we all can be more productive, healthier, and happier.

HETIC DISAPPOINTED INSPIRED PESSIMISTIC EX
RELIEVED JEALOUS CONFUSED STRONG HOPEFUL
OSITIVE SAD HAPPY INDIFFERENT EMPATHETIC DIS
UD DISCOURAGED CONFIDENT AFRAID CALM REL
ATEFUL INTIMIDATED PASSIONATE FRUSTRATED POS
TIC RESENTFUL OVERWHELMED CONTENT PROUD
SURPRISED EMBARRASSED INSECURE GRATEFUL I
D INSPIRED PESSIMISTIC EXCITED OPTIMISTIC RE
LOUS CONFUSED STRONG HOPEFUL OFFENDED SU
HAPPY INDIFFERENT EMPATHETIC DISAPPOINTED I
RAGED CONFIDENT AFRAID CALM RELIEVED JEAL
MIDATED PASSIONATE FRUSTRATED POSITIVE SAD
TFUL OVERWHELMED CONTENT PROUD DISCOURA
EMBARRASSED INSECURE GRATEFUL INTIMIDATED
ESSIMISTIC EXCITED OPTIMISTIC RESENTFUL OVE
ONG HOPEFUL OFFENDED SURPRISED EMBARRAS
HETIC DISAPPOINTED INSPIRED PESSIMISTIC EX
RELIEVED JEALOUS CONFUSED STRONG HOPEFUL
OSITIVE SAD HAPPY INDIFFERENT EMPATHETIC DIS
UD DISCOURAGED CONFIDENT AFRAID CALM RELI
ATEFUL INTIMIDATED PASSIONATE FRUSTRATED POS
TIC RESENTFUL OVERWHELMED CONTENT PROUD
SURPRISED EMBARRASSED INSECURE GRATEFUL II
D INSPIRED PESSIMISTIC EXCITED OPTIMISTIC RE
LOUS CONFUSED STRONG HOPEFUL OFFENDED SU
HAPPY INDIFFERENT EMPATHETIC DISAPPOINTED I
RAGED CONFIDENT AFRAID CALM RELIEVED JEAL
MIDATED PASSIONATE FRUSTRATED POSITIVE SAD
TFUL OVERWHELMED CONTENT PROUD DISCOURA
EMBARRASSED INSECURE GRATEFUL INTIMIDATED
ESSIMISTIC EXCITED OPTIMISTIC RESENTFUL OVE
ONG HOPEFUL OFFENDED SURPRISED EMBARRAS
HETIC DISAPPOINTED INSPIRED PESSIMISTIC EX
RELIEVED JEALOUS CONFUSED STRONG HOPEFUL
OSITIVE SAD HAPPY INDIFFERENT EMPATHETIC DIS
UD DISCOURAGED CONFIDENT AFRAID CALM RELI
TEFUL INTIMIDATED PASSIONATE FRUSTRATED POS
TIC RESENTFUL OVERWHELMED CONTENT PROUD
SURPRISED EMBARRASSED INSECURE GRATEFUL II
D INSPIRED PESSIMISTIC EXCITED OPTIMISTIC RES
LOUS CONFUSED STRONG HOPEFUL OFFENDED SU
APPY INDIFFERENT EMPATHETIC DISAPPOINTED I

PART I

Emotions Are Superpowers

TODAY'S LEADERS ARE managing the most complex workforce at the most demanding time in history. Our labor force is made up of people from multiple generations, across different ethnicities, religions, genders, sexual orientations, and cultural backgrounds—people who bring their life experiences and expectations from global environments with them to the job.

The work environment has also drastically shifted, thanks to a combination of technology and the new realities brought by COVID-19. We no longer have to be in the same country as our colleagues, never mind the same office. Today's employees are less willing to spend their lives commuting to crowded offices and instead want to work remotely and in virtual teams.

Isn't it fitting then that when dealing with such fractious, uncertain, and challenging times, we have, inside each of us, a superpower that can create trust bonds and make us happier, healthier, and more likely to succeed?

Before we are employees, managers, or senior leaders, we are human. As humans, we have feelings, and those feelings—when we learn to identify them, accept them, and act accordingly with them—will become the superpower we need to thrive, personally and professionally. This superpower will be *the* factor that leads to more engagement, collaboration, creativity, innovation, and happiness.

An emotionally intelligent leader realizes this underappreciated and unrecognized potential inside themselves and their colleagues and treats their employees as humans first and foremost. People are not simply task completers; they are emotionally complex and remarkably resilient.

Learning cognitive strategies to be bigger than our emotions is critical for success in school, business, and life. We need to learn to be observers of our emotions and take the emotional charge out of situations. We need to learn to look for the incredible gift emotions provide us and what they tell us about ourselves, others, and the world. And we need to learn to be in command of our emotions, so we have the strength and stamina to be more powerful than our feelings, learn mental strategies on how to regulate them, and not let them take over our life.

Emotions should not be feared but celebrated. A wealth of amazing possibilities are available if we learn to harness our superpower.

Chapter 1

Your Emotions Are Not the Enemy

I F YOU ARE anything like me, you've been taught and encouraged from when you were little to suppress or deny uncomfortable emotions when they arise. My family certainly didn't teach me how to acknowledge my feelings, let alone encourage me to experience them and guide me in how to manage them in a healthy way. No. In my family, emotional expression was the enemy. I was taught to believe that emotions, especially negative ones, were bad; they made things complicated and messy. And no one in my family wanted to clean up the emotional mess.

I grew up in a family with many secrets, and I was taught, at a young age, to push them under the rug and not share my thoughts or feelings with others, especially those in my immediate or extended family. Keeping the peace and not rocking the boat was placed above all else.

This foundational introduction I had in how to handle my feelings is, unfortunately, near universal. It has caused a lot of harm and disfunction. Rather than being taught about feelings, many of us were expected to observe people around us and from there discern culturally appropriate ways to handle emotions.

If you were lucky enough to have strong role models when you were learning how to tend to and communicate your emotions, you are ahead of the curve.[1] Still, for most of us, we have missed out on some very important emotional lessons, to say the least.

I know that had I been raised in an environment where I could have safely expressed my feelings and learned to manage them, it would have saved me a lot of heartache and despair—not to mention thousands of dollars on therapy.

Because I was an emotionally sensitive child, my family tried to do whatever it took to hide things from me. They actively protected me from gloomy emotions, like hurt and disappointment. I was rarely involved in family decisions or difficult conversations, even though I desperately wanted to be included and hated not knowing important family matters.

Being left on the emotional sidelines and brushed off as "overly emotional" led me to doubt my natural emotional responses when hard realities were thrown my way. This—coupled with my constant feelings of anxiety, of not knowing what was around the corner—ran roughshod over me, turning my worries into emotional outbursts, panic attacks, and meltdowns. And eventually, emotional dependence.

After my parents divorced, I became so dependent on my mother, it was near crippling. My mother loved and cared for me like no other. She still does. I am forever grateful for all that she sacrificed in her life for me.

But our co-dependence—her protecting me from the world as a classic helicopter parent, and my fragile sense of self-worth stemming from being constantly coddled—served only to further reinforce my learned habit of not trusting my own judgment, being afraid to take risks, and constantly needing her emotional reassurance and approval. (All that said, my mother and I have a fabulous relationship today, and I owe much to her resolve and hard work for enabling me to pursue my dreams.)

For many decades, my emotions created havoc in my life, with a laundry list of undesirable consequences. But just because I am an emotional person does not mean I am weak. Not paying attention to, understanding, and managing my emotions was what was ruining my world—not the fact that I felt, and still feel, things strongly.

Since the days of my childhood, I've slowly come to learn that our emotions are not the enemy. Nor are they a sign of weakness. Rather, demonstrating vulnerability, speaking our truth, and telling others how we really feel is our superpower.

We've been hoodwinked all these years into believing that our emotions are dirty and that expressing them is a shameful act. Nothing could be further from the truth.

Our emotions are full of wisdom when we pay attention to them and look for the meaning inside them. Feelings can provide incredible insights into our internal psyche and the external world around us.

Our feelings are data. Think of how advertising agencies use consumer behavior data to make good strategic choices to encourage us into buying their stuff. Well, it's the same thing with our feelings—we can use emotions as data to make good behavioral choices.

And this is where the emotional gap exists for many of us. How we showcase our internal emotions in our external actions needs work, care, and understanding. So how do we close the gap? That is where EI comes in. EI is quite simply being smart about our emotions. It is the ability to:

- understand, express, and manage your own emotions;

- develop and maintain good social relationships; and

- think clearly and solve problems under pressure.

EI is about being bigger and stronger than our emotions, not allowing our emotions to rule us, but allowing us to rule our emotions. As Marc Brackett, author of *Permission to Feel: Unlocking the Power of Emotions to Help Our Kids, Ourselves, and Our Society Thrive* and Founder and Director of the Yale Center for Emotional Intelligence, says, "Emotional intelligence doesn't allow feelings to get in the way—it does just the opposite. It restores balance to our thought processes; it prevents emotions from having undue influence over our actions; and it helps us to realize that we might be feeling a certain way for a reason."[2]

Consequently, until we become friends with our feelings and learn about all of our emotions, positive and negative, we cannot fully understand ourselves or our actions or regulate how we think and behave. We must learn to manage and work through tough feelings and emotional situations. EI helps us recognize, comprehend, express, and manage our feelings so our emotions don't stand in the way of our bright futures.

Simply put, we must take back the wheel and be in the driver's seat of our unruly emotions.

However, before we dig into *how* we do this—section II of this book—I want to take some time to highlight the leadership problems with ignoring our emotions, demonstrate how incredibly powerful and insightful our emotions are, and share with you what you will gain by becoming an emotionally intelligent and strong leader.

The Problem at Work

For most organizations, it is obvious which emotions are acceptable, appropriate, and tolerated. The unwritten and unspoken rules on which feelings are okay to demonstrate at work typically allow for emotions such as happiness, passion, and enthusiasm, while emotions like sadness, fear, or frustration are frowned upon.

Most of us have been taught, at times, to essentially wear an emotional straitjacket at work. We tend to park our emotions outside of the office since we don't feel it's safe to admit we are humans and have feelings. So we put on corporate personas and masks and hide a huge part of who we are from others.

Right now, within many corporations, workers who are subconsciously encouraged to keep taboo emotions under wraps are likely smiling at their desks but suffering behind closed doors. This leads to overvaluing our positive emotions and undervaluing our negative ones. But we need to experience both positive and negative emotions in healthy, sustainable ways as they each provide valuable information about ourselves and teach us crucial life lessons.

When our feelings do get the best of us and take over, we have been conditioned to want to appear tough or unflappable; a "never let them see you sweat" kind of attitude takes hold of us. We habitually don't want people to witness us as hurt, sad, or afraid. We fear that if we are seen expressing those emotions, we will be perceived as weak.

Alternatively, if we appear too elated, excited, or enthusiastic, our colleagues might think we are trying too hard and working to outshine them. Others may see us as eager beavers. Even though we may just be determined go-getters, our over-exuberance could have diminishing returns or start to work against us in the workplace.

A large part of the reluctance for people to express these so-called banned emotions in the workplace stems from leaders themselves who subscribe to the outdated universal notion that a leader must be stoic and unhindered. Essentially, this creates a workplace culture in which people are afraid to ask for help, cannot make decisions for fear of being wrong, and shove workplace conflicts under the rug to fester.

Many leaders do not know how to address feelings connected with work challenges and changes. They are too scared to deal with the emotions associated with them in the workplace. Yet not dealing with emotions—not condoning employees to be human at work— hurts us, our people, and our organizations. Worse, it holds us back from creating remarkable cultures and achieving incredible results. Unfortunately, the gaps in leadership that allow such long-standing attitudes to take hold are all too common.

Emotions are the one thing that unites us as humans. If people were not so scared of their feelings (or the feelings of others), emotions could be our universal language, connecting and bonding us together.

However, this is currently not the case.

Why are we so afraid of emotions in the workplace when we know how much not tending to them hurts and limits us, our teams, and our organizations?

We are afraid of the consequences. We are frightened that by sharing our feelings, we will be perceived as weak. We are nervous that if we share our emotions, they could be used against us. We fear conflict, rejection, and resentment. And what if tending to our emotions at work makes things even worse? What if our disclosure has a ripple effect and impacts our future? These fears, and others like them, stop us in our tracks and keep us silent.

But why are we afraid of the consequences?

We are afraid of the consequences because we do not know *how* to tend to our emotions in the workplace—or anywhere, frankly—in a manner that achieves the results we desire. For instance, we might be upset with a situation at work, but don't have the tools to express our anger truthfully and constructively and fear that in expressing our emotions about the situation, we will act out in a way that can harm us and alienate others. That aftermath is scary, so we don't share or deal with emotions in the workplace because we do not have the tools (and the confidence to use them) to effect the change we want.

To no longer fear the consequences, we need to debunk the myth that emotions are bad and that expressing our feelings makes us weak. Emotions are real, and just like the classic Clint Eastwood spaghetti western, they can be good, bad, or ugly. Similar to the characters of that film, nobody is perfect. We are complicated, and it is time to stop pretending we're not.

Even as demographics continue to shift and our working conditions are in a constant state of flux, the one remaining platitude is that we all have emotions, and very few of us were raised knowing how to recognize, understand, label, express, or regulate our emotions at home, in schools, or in workplaces. We must learn these emotional skills along the way.

As leaders, we must adapt ourselves and our workplaces to better accept, nurture, and explore feelings. If we do not know the importance of connecting, empathizing, and relating at an emotional level with our people, or how to bring out the best in each of our workers, our organization will underperform and lose excellent employees, and have workplace politics, disengagement, low productivity, and burnout. We must learn the emotional skills needed to survive and thrive in this human-filled corporate world.

Conditioned in the Classroom;
Sent to the Office

Our problems with expressing emotions may start at home, but they are conditioned in the classroom. At school, much ado has been made about cognitive intelligence and intelligence quotients (IQ), while EI and emotional quotients (EQ) are often ignored. Just like IQ is a numerical value correlated with cognitive ability or traditional intelligence, EQ is a numerical value correlated with EI. IQ can be developed but normally peaks at high school graduation, between age seventeen to eighteen.[3] However, EQ is not fixed, can be developed and enhanced, and rises as you get older, and a study shows that it peaks as you enter your sixties.[4] In the corporate world, as in school, technical skills and abilities are trumpeted over "soft skills" like active listening and demonstrating empathy, which are associated with EQ.

As a university professor and corporate trainer and coach, I see how our failure to teach students and employees emotional skills affects our work environments. Instructors and leaders alike cause a lot of stress for people, but we never think to teach them how to manage it. We don't give them any cognitive strategies on how to cope well under pressure, rebound quickly from setbacks, or develop a more positive outlook on the future.

We also put students and employees in teams but rarely teach them exactly how to work within those teams. We don't give them any guidelines on how to collaborate with others who have different personalities or communication styles or may have different cultural norms.

So while preparing the workers of tomorrow for a career, why aren't we preparing them to manage emotional conflicts? Why aren't we teaching students how to handle stress? Why aren't we teaching them to manage their personal responses to change and to become more resilient to life's challenges? Why aren't we teaching students to speak their truth respectfully and professionally? Why aren't we showing them to love who they are and not compare themselves with others? And why aren't we, as leaders who've inherited employees from a system that ignores these things, doing a better job to equip our employees with the safe emotional spaces they need—especially given that we know these skills are essential to success and self-fulfillment?

The World Economic Forum *Future of Jobs Report*[5] and the Organisation for Economic Co-operation and Development *Future of Education and Skills*[6] both state that EI involves a set of essential skills needed for the future of work, yet we are not focusing on these skills, anywhere.

Despite the bevy of research, EI is still downplayed as a "touchy-feely" soft skill when it really is a set of mental skills that enable us to think clearer and more creatively, and which bring out the best results from ourselves and the people around us. There's nothing mushy or soft about that.

I'm on a crusade to ensure EI skills are taught in every business university curriculum and inside every corporate training program across the globe. Our failure to provide an emotional education to our students and our employees has led to stress, anxiety, and insecurity—all things that plague the modern work environment. If we can teach our kids and employees EI, our schools will thrive, and our future workplaces will be better for it.

Here are some examples I've picked up over the years as the students I've taught at the university level have struggled to understand and regulate their feelings. See if you can spot how issues like these continue to arise where you work (and if you have kids, perhaps your children are experiencing them right now at school):

- To keep the peace in their group projects, students do not assert themselves. Those who are more driven to succeed will instead take a passive approach and end up doing most of the work.

- Rather than having a calm and collected face-to-face meeting or conversation when interpersonal conflicts arise, students impulsively and disrespectfully text each other and then regret what they said later.

- Students are insecure about trying something new and/or worry about making mistakes because they think others will laugh at them, so they stay frozen and do nothing.

- Students who are stressed or anxious don't think clearly; they are not able to separate their worries and cannot concentrate effectively.

- Students are constantly comparing themselves with others and/ or tying their grades to their self-worth.

- In an effort to help others, students are not setting good boundaries and are getting enmeshed in other students' issues. They are putting themselves last while trying to tend to others' needs and please them.

- With the number of on-screen activities rising, students have difficulty with simple face-to-face relational tasks, like making eye contact when speaking or shaking hands.

- With competition fierce, students, worried about optics, are not taking any downtime to rejuvenate or focus on their self-care needs, allowing school and work pressures to jeopardize their mental health and happiness.

A sampling of the research exhibits similar findings:

- A study at Ohio University found that people with poor assertiveness tend to neglect their own rights and have higher anxiety levels.[7]

- A study that examined text-message usage in college students revealed that dependent text-message users have higher levels of impulsivity.[8]

- In a paper published by *Australian Psychologist*, students' fear of failure was found to drive them to either over-strive or self-protect, leaving them vulnerable to setbacks such as emotional instability, high anxiety, low resilience, and helplessness.[9]

- Research indicates that stress has an emotional impact, and while some stress may produce feelings of mild anxiety, long-lasting stress can affect an individual's memory, self-esteem, focus, and other areas of learning and cognition.[10]

- In an analysis published in the *Canadian Medical Association Journal*, teenagers' self-view and interpersonal relationships were found to be affected by comparisons and negative interactions on social media.[11]

- Research suggests that individuals will often people please to make others happy or more comfortable, but in the end, their efforts can be self-destructive and damaging.[12]

- Educational researchers have noticed a steady increase of students exhibiting a lack of social skills, which has produced consequences in examinations and assignments, absenteeism, and the inability to sustain interpersonal relationships.[13]

- A meta-analysis of seventeen studies found that graduate students who don't engage in self-care behaviors don't achieve the same positive outcomes as those who do.[14]

Because we are not teaching students how to cope with stress, solve problems when emotions are involved, be self-directed, set healthy boundaries, or have confidence in themselves, that responsibility gets placed on the corporation that hires them, which then gets placed on *you*, their leader.

Ask yourself whether you are seeing any of the following behaviors creeping into your workplace:

- Is there anyone on your team that is not speaking up in meetings or is taking the lion's share of the work on team projects rather than equally sharing the workload?

- Are any of your workers sending snotty emails before thinking them through?

- Are any of your employees scared to share a new idea or worried about making mistakes and therefore not taking risks?

- Does anyone in your department have trouble concentrating because of stress or anxiety?

- Are any of your staff members comparing their work or themselves with others on your team?

- Is anyone on your team a people pleaser, completely overwhelmed with work because they are not setting up healthy boundaries and just saying "yes" to everyone who asks them for help?

- Does anyone on your team hide behind their screens and appear uncomfortable in face-to-face meetings or social gatherings?

- Are any of your staff working too many hours and struggling with work-life balance?

As their leader, you must ensure that your workers have the necessary emotional skills and are supported to thrive. Your employees have a lot to offer your company and have a lot to learn, starting with becoming aware and in control of their emotions. If you choose to help them hone these emotional skills at work, you will be part of building a more respectful, tolerant, and capable society. If we all act now, the world of work a decade into the future will be a much better place.

Chapter 2

My Journey to My Own Superpower

AFTER READING CHAPTER 1, I can understand if you felt compelled to turn to the jacket flap and re-read my bio. If I were you, I would too.

It is true that I am a highly sensitive person. It is true that for a large portion of my youth, and even into my twenties, I struggled with emotional regulation. It is also true that I have honed my emotional skills and mastered teaching others to do the same.

As an EI expert who helps professionals tune into emotions in the workplace, I can tell you that when those professionals do the requisite work to harness their individual EI, it is also true that this leads them to connect authentically, communicate effectively, and thrive collectively.

Now, just because I am an EI expert today does not mean that I am emotionally perfect or gifted with an amazing emotional aptitude. Far from it. However, they say you teach what you need to know, and I know how awful it is to live life one way and feel it another. I know how defeating it is to be told there is no room for your feelings. I know how wonderful it is to be in control of your emotions and channel the insight from them to make sound decisions that lead to positive outcomes.

If you are anything like me, someone who feels deeply about things and has strong, transparent emotional reactions that easily bubble up to the surface, you are way closer to your own human superpower than you (or others) might think.

If you are someone who has repressed their feelings or does not feel comfortable sharing them because you grew up in a family where talking about emotions was not okay, I hope to take you on a journey where you walk away realizing emotional exposure is courage, not weakness.

If you are someone in between, who can share and express your emotions some of the time but keeps some of your feelings to yourself, don't worry; I wrote this book for you too.

All emotions are full of wisdom and can be managed and expressed constructively.

But before I show you why EI is your best path forward toward allowing yourself to be human, and before I teach you how to build your own emotional skills, it might help to learn about my journey and how becoming an emotionally strong leader has made me the best version of myself.

Because if I can do it, so can you.

The Quote That Changed It All (for Me)

Often, teachers work in schools with populations that are very different from what they encountered as they were themselves developing. Teachers need to be well read, open to new people and cultural experiences, as well as reflective. They must approach situations from a base of knowledge and understanding. When teachers understand the community surrounding the school and the demands on the lives of the children they teach, they will be more respectful of the burdens some children face each day.[1]

This quote, which I first read while doing my Master's thesis and which came at a time in my life when I was making a shift from teaching teenagers to teaching adults, served to validate my self-taught teaching process—what I liked to call my secret sauce.

That process really wasn't complicated and came to me intuitively. When I started my teaching career, I learned I could motivate, spark ideas, and enrich lives through three simple steps:

1. Create structure and guidelines.

2. Connect with my students—believe in them, and empower them to do the same.

3. Get out of the way, and let them show me what they can do.

I discovered that when I taught this way—by connecting with my students on a personal level—good things happened. However, this method wasn't something I learned in school. Being deeply connected to my feelings led me to teach in a way that felt natural to me; essentially, I acted in the way I wished my teachers had behaved with me.

By learning to connect with our emotions and those of others, we can all better understand the role and function that emotions play in our life and that of others. By asking the other person what they are feeling and why, we are getting to the root cause of their issues— their fears, motives, stressors, or concerns. When leaders use their EI skills and focus on feelings, they are working on their empathy skills, learning to put themselves in other people's shoes and seeing the world through their eyes.

Empathy is about being tuned into how others feel and caring about those feelings as much as we do our own. It is critical in building strong interpersonal relationships. Empathy allows us to feel connected to others, learning to understand why other people do the things that they do.

To be an outstanding teacher, I needed to always shift the focus off my own experience and onto my students. I needed to continue to teach with empathy, but I had to truly connect with how my students felt before focusing on what they needed to learn.

Since then, it has been clear to me why emotions matter so much. Feelings affect learning, decision-making, creativity, relationships, and performance, among a host of other things. When I started to focus on the emotional state of my students, my teaching improved and so did their motivation and the caliber of their work.

Now, whether I am instructing university students or training corporate professionals and executives, I plan my delivery with the whole lives of my audience in mind. When designing a lesson or coaching and training my students and clients, I ask myself the following questions:

- Given the everyday emotional stresses and strains in the personal and professional lives of my audience, what is the most effective way to deliver the content, so they are able to receive, pay attention to, remember, and learn the information I am trying to teach them?

- What can I do to make their learning experience positive?

- How can I create a learning environment where they feel comfortable to approach, connect, and interact with me and their peers?

- How can I make sure they feel psychologically safe to ask questions, challenge ideas and concepts, take risks, and make mistakes?

- How will I ensure there is time to practice the application of the learning, as well as time to self-reflect on how they did?

- How will I provide constructive feedback beneficially?

- What can I do to help them feel appreciated for their efforts and work?

- How can I design their assignments so they are relevant, meaningful, and motivate my audience to do their best?

That simple quote changed my life. It taught me the importance of paying attention to the emotional state of others. Emotions should not be feared but faced head-on. When you are a leader, asking others how they are feeling and talking about the emotional issues your people are experiencing, especially those that are often ignored, matters.

From Fist Fights to First in Class

Early in my teaching career, I found myself leading a high school class on entrepreneurship where the students were to run a school-based business. I could see immediately that this was not going to be easy. Many of my students were known among the teachers as being difficult.

Two of the students, "Cindy" and "Kyle," were especially well known for their poor behavior in class. Cindy was defiant and had a wicked temper. Kyle was large and used his intimidating stature to bully and coerce others to get his own way.

And wouldn't you know it? On the first day of class, when discussing what type of business we should run, the pair of them got into a fist fight.

After the incident, I reflected on the fact that for their whole school lives, these two kids had likely been written off by teachers and authority figures as "challenging" and because of that had probably never been given the chance to show the world what they could do.

So I decided to elect Cindy to be the VP of Production and Kyle to be the VP of Human Resources for our school business.

I knew Cindy had a lot of friends in the school and class, so why not make her responsible for the operations of the business, where she could use her influence to spark engagement, productivity, and innovation? And I knew, because of his size, that Kyle intimidated others, so why not make him the person responsible for managing all the students in the class, using his words, not his stature, to guide, stimulate ideas, and motivate others?

My colleagues at the school thought I was crazy. How could I give the two most challenging students in my class such important roles in the business? After all, they and all the other VPs were responsible for locking and unlocking the business every day, counting the dollars earned, paying our vendors, scheduling the students for after-hour shift work, assessing their performance, and driving all the marketing efforts. This was a tremendous amount of responsibility and work, above and beyond what was expected of their classmates.

I wanted Cindy and Kyle to genuinely feel cared for, connected to something larger than themselves, appreciated for their efforts, and fulfilled in their roles. Let me tell you, it was hard for all concerned. I put in many extra hours and a lot of energy to learn precisely what made them tick, what made them who they were. I was not trying to change them, but simply meeting them where they were and listening openly and with empathy to what they were saying.

And Cindy and Kyle, well, they had to build new habits and let go of their default reactions to stimuli when those reactions weren't serving them well anymore. It was a challenge for them to be open to the feedback I provided them, to self-reflect on how they were performing, and to re-apply their learning the next day. In other words, they needed feedback, time, practice, and repetition to deepen their learning and change their ingrained behaviors.

Long story short, not only did we make record sales in the history of the school board for our student-run business—we were even highlighted in the local newspaper—but the experience also helped both Cindy and Kyle become more interested and engaged in school.

Kyle became a gentle giant who could command attention and respect and no longer terrified others. Cindy was named First in Class. She was chosen by all the teachers as the most improved student in the school.

Building productive relationships is primarily an emotional task, and creating trustworthy, caring, and genuine connections takes time but goes a long way. Taking an interest and active role in the development of your people is the key to keeping them engaged and growing their skill sets. Engaging in conversations about emotions is one of the many actions you as a leader can use to guide your people to boost business practices and improve performance. Establishing meaningful connections with my students changed their lives and mine.

While writing this book, I attempted to get in touch with Cindy and Kyle to see where their lives had taken them. I was not able to track down Kyle, but I did connect with Cindy.

It had been twenty years since we had last been in contact, and Cindy was excited for the chance to share her life with me. Our conversation stunned me as Cindy revealed what she had been going through all those years ago when I was coaxing her to open up and give the VP role a real chance. She shared with me that after having been in foster care for some time, she had been reintroduced to her family that year. She complained of a lack of focus and direction and at the time had been so disillusioned with life that she tried to end hers. It was heartbreaking to hear her recall the pain and suffering she endured as a teenager. But I was also heartened by her strength. The courage she exhibited enabled her to pull herself up and be named the most improved student in the school.

"You know," she said, "after all the pushing away I did, you pushed back. Most people, when I push, they get pushed over, and then, they don't make it. I've found that in my relationships with my partners, I tend to push because that's how I know about love and strengthening relationships. You know, if I push them, are they going to stay? Are they going to go? And when I pushed you, you pushed back and pushed back right away. Then when you came back, that gave me the strength and the security of knowing that you weren't not going to walk away so easily."

In my line of work, I often hear these kinds of emotional stories. Occasionally, though, the stories I hear sound downright normal, and yet they still have a profound impact on those involved. As Marc Brackett so marvelously puts it, "Sometimes the tales aren't nearly so dramatic—just people who grew up in homes where everyday emotional issues were ignored because no one had ever learned how to talk about them or take actions to address them. Your life didn't have to be tragic for you to feel as though your emotional life didn't matter to anyone but you."[2]

Everyone is fighting a battle you know nothing about. Keep that in mind and be kind. I think, in hindsight, for Cindy, even though I did not know the depths of her despair and heartache, I did not run away from the challenge. I did not let her emotions and associated behaviors scare me away. I spent time with her, listening to her, learning with her, and supporting her development. That, in a nutshell, is being an emotionally strong leader. So ask yourself who the Cindys and Kyles are on your team.

Connecting with the heart of the people you lead **is the key to your leadership success.**

My Personal Wake-Up Call

True leadership starts with leading yourself first. When the plane is going down, you are instructed to put your oxygen mask on first before helping others. Leadership is no different, especially during stressful times. Leaders need to replenish their energy and reserves to be effective and focus on their emotional wellness, which is where, early in my career, I struggled.

It started innocently enough. I was growing my new coaching and training company and had convinced myself that hard work was the price to pay for success. So I let myself work eighteen hours a day, seven days a week. In fact, I calculated that I had been on 120 flights throughout the year, educating people across the continent, which meant I was in a different city almost every three days!

Work has always been my drug of choice. It doesn't help that our "hustle culture" glorifies productivity and creates a workday that never truly ends. Hustle culture is a mindset that promotes the grind, encouraging people to exert themselves at maximum capacity to match the speed of the digital world around us.[3]

Food. Food is my second drug of choice. The combination of eating unhealthfully while using my insane work schedule as an excuse to do so doomed me. On top of that, I wasn't spending time taking care of myself physically, and before I knew it, I had gained one hundred pounds and confined myself to my house.

I was ashamed. Instead of getting my feelings out, I squashed them down and ate them. I was scared to see anyone, or more accurately, I was scared they would see me and judge me like I was judging myself.

I walked my dog in the evenings, shopped at the twenty-four-hour grocery store at 3 AM to avoid running into people, and did not see my family, who lived in the same city, for an entire year. Scared of the judgment I would receive from others, I was only able to muster up the strength to go to work to pay my bills. These self-limiting beliefs became debilitating for me.

I was at an all-time low in my life. My weight gain had eroded my confidence, and a voice in my head was telling me I wasn't worthy of all I had achieved.

Still, there was another voice. Although it spoke to me in only faint whispers, it told me that there had to be a better way to live. Listening to that other voice was the best decision of my life. And that is what led me to become a certified EI facilitator, trainer, and coach.

When getting my certification, I took my own EI assessment, and when I got my results, they rocked me to the core. They showed how low my EQ was and which areas I was weakest in. The assessment saved my life because it gave me a path forward. It highlighted what I needed to stop doing, what I needed to start doing, and what I needed to continue.

It also made me realize that being an emotional person did not mean I was weak. I simply needed to harness the power of my emotions for my personal gain, not demise.

Taking back the wheel and putting myself in the driver's seat of my emotions has made me the happiest and most fulfilled, personally and professionally, that I've ever been. My life may be far from perfect, and that's okay. It never will be perfect. But I am happy. That is what EI did for me. And it is my passion to share what I know about EI so that you too can thrive.

My Promise to You

EI has been my lifeline. It changed me as a person, and to this day, it has been the answer for every personal and interpersonal problem I have encountered.

I am now a more effective leader, better performer, and more successful and happier person, not only in business but also in all areas of life—as a partner, daughter, sister, friend, and citizen. EI will forever be my life's journey. I spend my time and energy getting better and emotionally stronger every day.

For well over two decades, I have had the privilege to work with and learn from some great leaders. I have also had the honor to teach the up-and-coming generations, who have already entered the world of work or will be entering the workforce in the years to come. Because I have seen all of these people and worked with them,

I know how much emotions can help or hurt a person's overall happiness and well-being.

You may be tired of feeling stuck or feel like something is missing in your life. Perhaps, you want to grow in your career and become a more effective leader, mend broken relationships and have better connections with others, make better decisions and solve problems under pressure or have a greater resilience to the challenges you face, or simply feel better about yourself. Regardless of where you are starting from, the tools in these pages can help.

Now, I am not promising that your life will be perfect or you will no longer have any conflicts or problems. But you will learn the skills that can lead to a happier, more fulfilling life, just like I did.

OPTIMISTIC RESENTFUL OVERWHELMED CONTENT
NDED SURPRISED EMBARRASSED INSECURE GRATI
NTED INSPIRED PESSIMISTIC EXCITED OPTIMIST
JEALOUS CONFUSED STRONG HOPEFUL OFFENDE
SAD HAPPY INDIFFERENT EMPATHETIC DISAPPOI
JRAGED CONFIDENT AFRAID CALM RELIEVED JEA
ATED PASSIONATE FRUSTRATED POSITIVE SAD HA
JL OVERWHELMED CONTENT PROUD DISCOURAGE
D EMBARRASSED INSECURE GRATEFUL INTIMIDAT
ED PESSIMISTIC EXCITED OPTIMISTIC RESENTFUL
NFUSED STRONG HOPEFUL OFFENDED SURPRISE
INDIFFERENT EMPATHETIC DISAPPOINTED INSPII
NFIDENT AFRAID CALM RELIEVED JEALOUS CON
ONATE FRUSTRATED POSITIVE SAD HAPPY INDIFF
MED CONTENT PROUD DISCOURAGED CONFIDENT
SECURE GRATEFUL INTIMIDATED PASSIONATE FRU
OPTIMISTIC RESENTFUL OVERWHELMED CONTENT
NDED SURPRISED EMBARRASSED INSECURE GRAT
NTED INSPIRED PESSIMISTIC EXCITED OPTIMIST
JEALOUS CONFUSED STRONG HOPEFUL OFFENDE
SAD HAPPY INDIFFERENT EMPATHETIC DISAPPOI
JRAGED CONFIDENT AFRAID CALM RELIEVED JEA
ATED PASSIONATE FRUSTRATED POSITIVE SAD HA
JL OVERWHELMED CONTENT PROUD DISCOURAGE
D EMBARRASSED INSECURE GRATEFUL INTIMIDAT
ED PESSIMISTIC EXCITED OPTIMISTIC RESENTFUI
NFUSED STRONG HOPEFUL OFFENDED SURPRISE
INDIFFERENT EMPATHETIC DISAPPOINTED INSPII
NFIDENT AFRAID CALM RELIEVED JEALOUS CON
ONATE FRUSTRATED POSITIVE SAD HAPPY INDIFF
MED CONTENT PROUD DISCOURAGED CONFIDENT
SECURE GRATEFUL INTIMIDATED PASSIONATE FRU
OPTIMISTIC RESENTFUL OVERWHELMED CONTEN
NDED SURPRISED EMBARRASSED INSECURE GRAT
NTED INSPIRED PESSIMISTIC EXCITED OPTIMIST
JEALOUS CONFUSED STRONG HOPEFUL OFFENDE
SAD HAPPY INDIFFERENT EMPATHETIC DISAPPOI
JRAGED CONFIDENT AFRAID CALM RELIEVED JEA
ATED PASSIONATE FRUSTRATED POSITIVE SAD HA
JL OVERWHELMED CONTENT PROUD DISCOURAGE
D EMBARRASSED INSECURE GRATEFUL INTIMIDA
ED PESSIMISTIC EXCITED OPTIMISTIC RESENTFU

HETIC DISAPPOINTED INSPIRED PESSIMISTIC EA
RELIEVED JEALOUS CONFUSED STRONG HOPEFU
OSITIVE SAD HAPPY INDIFFERENT EMPATHETIC DI
UD DISCOURAGED CONFIDENT AFRAID CALM REL
TEFUL INTIMIDATED PASSIONATE FRUSTRATED PO
TIC RESENTFUL OVERWHELMED CONTENT PROUD
SURPRISED EMBARRASSED INSECURE GRATEFUL I
INSPIRED PESSIMISTIC EXCITED OPTIMISTIC RE
OUS CONFUSED STRONG HOPEFUL OFFENDED SU
APPY INDIFFERENT EMPATHETIC DISAPPOINTED
RAGED CONFIDENT AFRAID CALM RELIEVED JEAL
IDATED PASSIONATE FRUSTRATED POSITIVE SAD
TFUL OVERWHELMED CONTENT PROUD DISCOURA
EMBARRASSED INSECURE GRATEFUL INTIMIDATEI
SSIMISTIC EXCITED OPTIMISTIC RESENTFUL OVE
ONG HOPEFUL OFFENDED SURPRISED EMBARRAS
HETIC DISAPPOINTED INSPIRED PESSIMISTIC EX
RELIEVED JEALOUS CONFUSED STRONG HOPEFU
OSITIVE SAD HAPPY INDIFFERENT EMPATHETIC DI
UD DISCOURAGED CONFIDENT AFRAID CALM REL
TEFUL INTIMIDATED PASSIONATE FRUSTRATED PO
TIC RESENTFUL OVERWHELMED CONTENT PROUD
SURPRISED EMBARRASSED INSECURE GRATEFUL I
INSPIRED PESSIMISTIC EXCITED OPTIMISTIC RE
OUS CONFUSED STRONG HOPEFUL OFFENDED SU
APPY INDIFFERENT EMPATHETIC DISAPPOINTED
RAGED CONFIDENT AFRAID CALM RELIEVED JEAL
IDATED PASSIONATE FRUSTRATED POSITIVE SAD
TFUL OVERWHELMED CONTENT PROUD DISCOURA
EMBARRASSED INSECURE GRATEFUL INTIMIDATED
SSIMISTIC EXCITED OPTIMISTIC RESENTFUL OVE
ONG HOPEFUL OFFENDED SURPRISED EMBARRAS
HETIC DISAPPOINTED INSPIRED PESSIMISTIC EX
RELIEVED JEALOUS CONFUSED STRONG HOPEFU
OSITIVE SAD HAPPY INDIFFERENT EMPATHETIC DI
UD DISCOURAGED CONFIDENT AFRAID CALM REL
TEFUL INTIMIDATED PASSIONATE FRUSTRATED POS
TIC RESENTFUL OVERWHELMED CONTENT PROUD
SURPRISED EMBARRASSED INSECURE GRATEFUL I
INSPIRED PESSIMISTIC EXCITED OPTIMISTIC RE
OUS CONFUSED STRONG HOPEFUL OFFENDED SU
APPY INDIFFERENT EMPATHETIC DISAPPOINTED

PART II

The F-Word

FEELINGS. THAT OTHER F-WORD, so popular these days, is bound to slip out from time to time, but "feelings" needs to become a mainstay of workplace discourse and education.

Many don't use this F-word at work, and worse yet, many believe it has no place in the workplace. Why are we so hung up on hiding our feelings at work?

Feelings are transient. They are merely a temporary response that helps us in adapting to new opportunities, circumstances, and challenges.[1] They are not final or always factual, but fleeting and subjective. They are like clouds; they float into our minds and then blow away and leave. We can feel several different emotions on any given day.

Even though feelings are short-lived and internal sentiments known only to us, they still matter. And you need to feel your true feelings. Why? When you don't squander your energy and focus trying to dodge your real feelings, you give yourself more mental space and clarity. The more you allow yourself to accept, experience, and face your true feelings, versus judging them, the more energy you have to dedicate to your life.[2]

What are your emotions **teaching you about yourself?**

As John Bradshaw shared in his book *Healing the Shame That Binds You*, "E-motions are energy in motion. They are the energy that moves us—our human fuel."[3] Feelings need a way out. If that energy is not expressed, it is repressed and bottled up. I don't think I need to tell you what happens with bottled-up emotions. They can leak into our conversations or worse, explode into our actions.

Now, focusing on feelings is not a pass to be an emotional mess at work. Let me be clear: having emotions and being emotional are two different things. I am not saying that being emotional to the point where you lose your temper and scream at a colleague is acceptable. Hardly. You need to pay attention to, understand, express, and manage your emotions. In other words, you need to take the reins of your feelings. Learning to be smarter than your emotions is critical for success.

The trick is to distance yourself from your feelings, take a step back, and become an observer. Learning to be an observer of your emotions can take the emotional charge out of situations. The trouble is your feelings are so personal. It's hard to be an objective bystander.

EI gives you the tools and confidence to deal with those personal and temporal feelings, taking the time to understand what they mean, where they come from, and why they are there. It's learning to take back the power your emotions have over you and look objectively at what you are feeling and why. Then, it's about being smarter than your emotions, to prevent yourself from acting out and having your reaction to a fleeting experience define you.

EI is getting to the heart of the matter and not suppressing, ignoring, and letting your emotions take over and explode. It's about creating space to observe your feelings from a distance and choosing to make a conscious choice on how you will respond. Ask yourself what your emotions are teaching you about yourself. This will allow you to differentiate between the emotions themselves and the way you react to them.

Our feelings hold great power; they are the driving force behind our thinking and actions. With so much happening in our everyday lives, it is easy to neglect our emotions and tread on. However, the act of suppressing our emotions actually has adverse effects on us individually and on our team performance.[4] Therefore, we must focus on our feelings. Bottom line—don't be afraid of the F-word!

Chapter 3

Emotions Matter

WE ARE BOMBARDED with images in advertising and in our social media feeds of happy- and successful-looking people. It can be hard then to feel like we are allowed to be anything less than perfect, to be human and express our true feelings. This can be especially true at work—where we spend most of our waking hours—particularly when it doesn't feel like our organizations want us to be human either.

Sandwiched between the ideal lives on social media and the accepted behaviors at work, we don't have much room for the vital and healthy expressions of those forbidden feelings, like fear, frustration, anger, worry, distress, and sadness.

Even thinking about this unfair state we've found ourselves in makes me frustrated. So I feel your pain. And the good news is that *everyone*, in some way, feels this way too.

Our society is a like a vise, squeezing us tighter and tighter. Only by harnessing the power of EI can we stop ourselves from popping. Even then, we still might pop from time to time, and that's okay too. Remember, we humans can and will make mistakes.

It's not about perfection; it's about progress. After all, we are not machines.

Part of becoming emotionally intelligent is accepting that we are human, and that certain aspects of being human—like having feelings—are intrinsically part of all of us. Heck, even the world's most advanced artificial intelligence humanoid robot has feelings, famously expressing its desire to have children.[1]

Emotions influence almost every aspect of our life, from learning, communication, and relationships, to decision-making, creativity, and productivity, to name a few. When we start to focus on and tend to our emotional state—especially given the daily pressures and demands being put upon us—not only does our motivation change but so does the quality of our work (and our life).

Here is some proof.

Emotions and Memory

Emotions influence our attention, memory, and learning.[2] Our feelings determine what we will focus on and retain. When we're unable to manage our emotions, it can cause us to be less productive and concentrated on our work. According to the *State of the Global Workplace 2021 Report*, "This lack of engagement costs the global economy US$8.1 trillion, nearly 10% of GDP, in lost productivity each year."[3]

Think about it. When was the last time you were emotional and could focus clearly on the task at hand? Or when you were feeling bored, were you able to absorb what you were reading? Or perhaps when you were afraid of embarrassing yourself or looking foolish, and your emotions got the best of you and took over, were you able to think of anything else? Even though you may have wanted to redirect your mind to something else, were you paralyzed?

When we feel strong negative emotions, like fear or anger, our brains secrete cortisol, the stress hormone, which affects our prefrontal cortex and inhibits it from processing information.[4]

When we feel strong positive emotions, like joy and excitement, the excretion of dopamine, serotonin, and the like also influences our thinking and behavior,[5] and can enhance our overall well-being and result in more cognitive acuity.[6]

This is because extremely emotionally charged events—those that become defining moments in our personal history, such as our wedding, the birth of a child, the September 11th World Trade Center attack, or the first day of lockdown during the global COVID-19 pandemic—are indelibly marked in our memory. We tend to remember everything: where we were, who we talked to, and what we were doing. We remember these events with acuity and detail because of the big emotional activation which enables us to imprint these memories.[7] While strong emotional activation makes events more memorable, these strong emotions can also make recalling previously learned information more difficult.[8]

Emotions and Communication

Emotions impact our communication.[9] Consider this: Did you communicate constructively the last time you were angry and frustrated? My guess would be probably not. When emotional, most of us cannot say what we need to say in a calm and collected manner.

Research shows that anger can be used to mask other emotions we don't want to deal with, such as worry, loneliness, or loss. In such instances, anger becomes a secondary emotion.[10]

In the workplace, these kinds of negative emotions and our inability to deal with them even color the manager-employee relationship, as 69 percent of managers report being uncomfortable even *talking* with their employees,[11] and 37 percent say they are uncomfortable having to give direct feedback when they think their employees will react negatively.[12]

Employees crave feedback, but managers fear giving it to their employees. Why? Because we fear feelings! Fixing the communication chasm through EI can boost productivity and engender feelings of pride, belonging, and confidence, all of which produce happier, healthier workers who in turn work harder and achieve more. Imagine that!

IT'S NOT WHAT YOU SAY BUT HOW YOU SAY IT

Did you know that 55 percent of what we "hear" comes from body language, 38 percent from tone of voice, and only 7 percent from words?[13] When we feel a positive emotion, like passion, enthusiasm, or joy, that can be infectious and draw people in. Similarly, when we feel a negative emotion, like shame, sadness, or worry, we communicate those nonverbal signals too, whether in our body language and gestures, tone of voice, or facial expressions. Unexpressed emotions can color your conversations in ways you may not consciously intend. Better to be truthful with your feelings and to those around you so that when you speak and people listen, they are getting the message you mean.

Emotions and Relationships

Great connections with people can enhance our life, contribute to our well-being, and strengthen our mind. Conversely, strained or difficult relationships can be both a physical and emotional drain. According to a meta-analysis conducted by the journal *Personality and Social Psychology Review*, people who feel more camaraderie with their coworkers, and more engaged with their company, have better mental health and are less prone to burnout.[14]

Have you ever had a negative personal experience with a colleague at work? My guess is that unless the dispute was mutually and amicably resolved in a way that was satisfactory for both parties, the exchange negatively influenced your perception of the other person's work ethic and performance. Sometimes in these situations, simply thinking about this person can affect your emotional state, which then can influence how you communicate and interact with them. In these moments, it can feel like the last thing you want to do is share your feelings about the situation, but that in fact is the path forward.

To build trust and compassion with the other person, we must be true to *our* feelings. When we think of our relationships as investments, we understand that the more we contribute, the more secure and profitable they can be for us.

Remember, our emotions impact how we act toward others. If we feel love, trust, confidence, and happiness when we think of a person, those feelings are going to influence how we treat said person. But if we feel disgust, frustration, mistrust, and anger, that too will affect our interactions with others. How we feel affects our social exchanges and how we relate to other people.

Emotions and Decision-Making

Emotions impact our decision-making abilities.[15] They directly influence our decisions by subconsciously or unconsciously running in the background of our mind. Our emotional history and makeup can determine our course of action or inaction. For instance, if you are emotionally dependent upon others to help you through problems, you may lack the confidence to make decisions without external reassurance.[16] If you have low self-esteem, you may take a long time to make decisions or delay or avoid making them, and when you do, you'll likely worry about what others will think of you.[17] If you have narcissistic tendencies and need to be right, you may squash the ideas of others and promote your own ideas, even if they aren't as strong or as worthy.[18]

Researchers have determined that individuals with higher EQ scores are better able to identify important bodily signals from others and more often use that information to avoid making risky decisions. Those with lower EQ scores frequently miss these subtle bodily cues, and when they do detect them, they misread them.[19] The point? Our emotions can alter our perceptions of the world around us, affecting our judgments and decision-making abilities.

Strong emotions can lead to rash choices. For instance, anger and embarrassment can make us more susceptible to high-risk, low-reward decisions. Researchers suspect that decision-making skills and rational capabilities are harmed by intense negative emotions.[20]

Being aware of the role emotions play can help us solve problems under pressure more effectively. Acknowledging our feelings, positive or negative, gives us clarity on how to make better decisions.

Emotions can be a beneficial guide.[21] As an example, when making a big purchase, like buying a house or car, feelings of anxiety and nervousness tend to flood our thinking. But this can be a good thing. These negative emotions can encourage caution, and the decision can then be navigated by researching and fact finding, weighing the options, and understanding the risks before making an ultimate decision on such a big purchase.[22]

Emotions and Creativity

Emotions influence our creativity.[23] Creativity is not solely reserved for fine artists, musicians, architects, and the like. Being creative in decision-making is critical for everyone. Creativity helps grow and scale organizations. Peter Senge, MIT professor and author of *The Fifth Discipline: The Art and Practice of the Learning Organization*, defines "creative tension" as the gap between the vision of the future (what could be) and the current reality (what is).[24] If there were no gap, there would be no need for any action to move toward the vision. But there is a gap; thinking of new and better ways of doing things moves us forward from status quo to innovation. Though once we arrive at the vision of the future, that becomes reality, and the gap again appears, thus keeping us in a constant loop of needing innovation and creativity.

Being creative takes vulnerability. You need confidence and courage to put yourself out there knowing there is a good chance you or your ideas will be shot down by those with less visionary zeal or who feel threatened by others who have ideas. Think about a time when you decided not to share a creative, new idea because you feared what others might say or think about it. The decision on whether to share or not was no longer just an action; it became personal. But sharing knowledge is critical for the success and scalability of companies, and if we don't have the courage to take risks and express our ideas, we stifle our progress.[25]

A study published in *Business Perspectives and Research* found that a positive and significant relationship between EI and creativity at work exists if:

1. the individual has a proactive personality, and

2. the work environment supports it.[26]

Having a proactive personality means that you take personal responsibility, have perseverance and persistence, can find and solve problems, are change and uncertainty tolerant, are oriented toward personal development, and are biased toward action.

But even a proactive person can become insecure if the environment doesn't support them. In a leadership context, this can trigger feelings, of course, and whether it is stress about failure, fear of a disapproving board of directors, or discontent with how the corporate identity is stuck in the past, these negative feelings and worries have a way of stymieing creative thought and grinding to a halt the willingness to put yourself out there.

Emotions and Health

In 2020, a Gallup survey "found that roughly seven in 10 people [were] struggling or suffering in their lives." This is a huge and deeply saddening number, and it is directly linked to work. "What the whole world wants is a good job," Gallup's CEO and Chairman Jim Clifton comments about the stat in his blog post, "The Mood of the World." "People want a job that uses their God-given strengths every day with a manager who encourages their development."[27]

Our feelings, whether at work or otherwise, originate in our brain, which we tend to forget is still part of our body like all our other organs. But most of us don't put the same emphasis on their emotional well-being and mental health as they do on their physical body and health.

Again, we need to talk about and learn to deal with our feelings at work in a healthy and sustainable way. Many of us break from work to eat, get up and stretch, or go for a walk. But how many of us check in with how we feel before a critical meeting with the Board of Directors? How many of us think about our emotional state when making a difficult decision or when triggered by an unrealistic deadline? How many talk to or ask others about what they are actually feeling at work throughout their day?

Being mindful—paying attention on purpose and without judgment to our emotions—has been increasingly shown to be a skill that when practiced can increase our ability to face challenges more calmly and effectively.[28] We need to analyze our emotions and understand their origin and purpose before we can manage them. Research shows that EI plays a critical role in ensuring that we strive to live happy, healthy, and productive personal and professional lives.[29]

Emotions and Stress Management

Feelings become heightened when we are stressed. But not all stress is bad. On the one hand, eustress, or good stress, tends to be short-lived, linked to changes you want to see or goals you want to achieve, and push you to achieve more. It feels positive and productive. It's like being given a challenging but exciting project that motivates you to push yourself to perform to your maximum capabilities (potentially finding you are capable of more than you initially thought)—or in sports and business speak, "upping your game."[30] On the other hand, bad stress or being chronically stressed out is linked to where you feel a loss in control or feel your mastery is lacking. This kind of distress feels unpleasant, can deplete your energy, and usually decreases your performance.[31] At work, this can happen when workloads are unsustainable, a bad handoff is given for a team project, or relationships are strained due to work conditions.

Research shows that employees who are adept at managing their emotions may have valuable strategies to cope with negative emotions caused by stress. This minimizes the negative consequences of stress on well-being and job satisfaction and improves job performance.[32] According to LinkedIn, employees who struggle with work-related stress (that earn low scores for "I am able to cope effectively with work-related stress") are 92 percent more likely to look at a job posting than those who aren't dealing with heavy workloads and high stress levels.[33]

When we are under duress day in and day out, stress can become a chronic condition where our brains are full of stress hormones, resulting in physical health concerns, like heightened risk of infection, diabetes, cardiovascular disease, headaches, and colds, to name a few.[34] In fact, a recent study showed that metabolic syndrome is more than twice as common in those with chronic stress at work than it is in people without work stress.[35] Further, in a meta-analysis published by *The Lancet*, employees who work more than 55 hours a week have a higher risk of stroke and heart attack.[36]

So ask yourself when was the last time that the pressure was on and you were able to still think positively about the future, adjust well to change or uncertainty, and not let the stress decrease your performance. In these moments, it is imperative to discuss your feelings—not only for the good of your job but for your mental and physical health and well-being.

Emotions and Performance

We are predisposed to experience certain levels of approach-related arousal emotions (such as happiness, elation, and enthusiasm) and tend to feel the urge to approach, and to experience avoidance-related arousal emotions (like sadness, fear, and boredom) and tend to feel the urge to withdraw.[37] These feelings inherently influence different aspects of job performance.[38]

When we are feeling energized, we are productive, focused, and full of passion. On the contrary, when we are bored, we are lethargic and distracted and struggle to come up with the next great revolutionary idea. Or when we have heightened stress levels, our performance can become hampered.[39]

Studies show a correlation between positive feelings and better performance ratings, and also between negative feelings and worse ratings.[40] It isn't rocket science.

The way we feel at work and about our work **affects how we perform at work.**

When you were last angry, tired, or apathetic, did you perform well on the task at hand? Probably not. However, if you are feeling hopeful, happy, or engaged, you probably also have a can-do attitude, which acts as motivation to do the job well, and performance can soar.[41] When feeling positive, you are also likely to be more helpful to others, which influences the team's productivity.

Our emotions affect our attention and focus, decision-making, creativity, and emotional well-being, which all impact the employee experience and on-the-job performance. A recent Gallup poll "estimates that actively disengaged employees cost the U.S. $450 billion to $550 billion in lost productivity per year."[42] Bottom line—the way we feel at work and about our work affects how we perform at work.

* * *

IF IT IS NOT ALREADY CLEAR, emotions *do* matter. Our emotions do not stop when we start our workday, nor do they turn back on when we are done. There's no on-off switch for feelings. Therefore, leaders need to find a way to create a culture where emotions are safe to share.

Our feelings manifest themselves in the macro actions of daily life. From our memory to our relationships to our daily performance, poor emotional regulation is costing us big time. If emotions are not acknowledged, they can become unhinged and be detrimental to the organization, leading to high turnover, low productivity, lousy communication, interpersonal conflicts, and poor morale and employee engagement.

Being an exceptional leader is the single differentiating factor between a thriving business and one that is just getting by. Whether you are managing the next workforce, leading your team through change, or running day-to-day operations, you are at the forefront of driving your team to success. However, if you want to grow and scale your business, you must grow and scale your leadership, which begins with growing and scaling your EI and allowing your employees to be human and share their emotions at work.

Emotions are the linchpin to our success. Therefore, it can be frustrating to realize how hard they are to control and how easily they seem to come at you in a flash. However, understanding a little of how our brain works regarding how and when we experience emotions will help arm you to better control them in the future.

Chapter 4

The Brain and Emotions— It's a Team Effort

L ET ME EXPLAIN in simple terms a bit about our brains and emotions and what parts of our brain are working when we learn to lead with EI.

As the study of brain science continues to unfold, scientists agree that no single point in the brain is in control of EI; no single brain structure is responsible for the production, control, or regulation of emotions.[1]

However, many researchers are getting a better sense of which parts of the brain may play a role. While specific identification is difficult, we know that several brain regions work together as a team and are involved during emotion processing.[2] Every region has its own job, but they all work together to identify, process, remember, and control an emotion.

The limbic system, deep within our brain, is made up of a number of different structures, and scientists have not reached a consensus on which parts compose the limbic system. However, four central parts relate to emotions and memory: the amygdala, the hypothalamus, and the hippocampus, and parts of the thalamus. While the limbic system has been identified as one of the key networks for

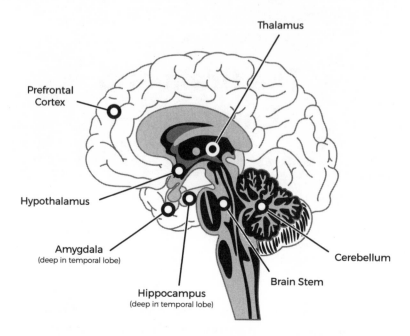

emotional processing, it also has many reciprocal relationships with the prefrontal cortex (the part of the brain that help us think, reason, and consciously process our emotions).[3]

The thalamus is one part of the limbic system that interacts with the prefrontal cortex.[4] The thalamus is the egg-shaped structure above the brain stem that processes all sensory inputs (inputs from our senses) coming up from the spinal cord and relays that information to other parts of the brain. It acts as a gatekeeper to the entire cerebral cortex.[5] Thus, the thalamus analyzes the data coming in and determines where the information must go or whether the cortex needs to ignore it. For instance, the thalamus receives information from the amygdala in the limbic system (the emotional brain) and relays it to the prefrontal cortex (the thinking brain) of the neocortex.[6]

The amygdala—a tiny part of the brain, about the size and shape of an almond—is a salience filter for both positive and negative information.[7] The amygdala assesses the "value"[8] of every stimulus or piece of information that comes to it,[9] and is useful for encoding and coor-dinating physiological, behavioral, and cognitive responses in an emotional context.[10]

The amygdala is in near-constant communication with the pre-frontal cortex, which acts as a kind of control center guiding our actions and is involved during emotion regulation.[11] In his book *The Brain and Emotional Intelligence: New Insights*, Daniel Goleman states, "Self-regulation of emotion and impulse relies greatly on the interaction between the prefrontal cortex—the brain's execu-tive center—and the emotional centers in the midbrain, particularly circuitry converging on the amygdala."[12]

The amygdala acts like a guard warning the brain of dangers, and it regulates the significance of a stimulus. However, if the "amyg-dala senses danger, it makes a split second decision and begins the fight-or-flight response before the [pre]frontal cortex has time to over-rule it."[13] Therefore, if the amygdala senses a perceived threat—real or assumed—it will label it as scary and send that mes-sage to the hypothalamus; this activates the sympathetic nervous system (a component of the autonomic nervous system), which floods the body with hormones to allow us to react.[14] This fight-or-flight response is a pure survival reaction where we experience an augmented heart rate and rapid breathing, shaking, and increased sweat response. This is all an automatic process, meaning we cannot stop ourselves from having this physiological reaction (though we can control how we respond to this reaction).[15]

THE AUTONOMIC NERVOUS SYSTEM

"The autonomic nervous system has two components: the sympa-thetic nervous system and the parasympathetic nervous system." Similar to the gas pedal in a car, the sympathetic nervous system triggers the "body with a burst of energy so that it can respond" and react to perceived dangers. On the contrary, the parasympa-thetic nervous system acts like the brake pedal, promoting a "rest and digest" response, which "calms the body down after the danger has passed."[16]

The amygdala also communicates closely with the hippocampus. The hippocampus is a requisite structure for learning and memory formation. It takes in new information, registers it, and holds on to it for some time before sending it off to long-term memory.[17] The connection between our memory system and amygdala explains why we remember things we label as important or that we care about.[18]

The amygdala is both a "connector and communicator sending messages directly to the hippocampus, which relays information to other brain areas, including the hypothalamus (releases hormones), thalamus (relays motor and sensory signals to the cerebral cortex), and cerebral cortex" (makes sense of the information and puts it into context).[19]

The amygdala evolved to help us rapidly navigate the world, to make behavioral and physiological changes based on an immediate threat or danger. In our modern context, sometimes the amygdala can overreact.[20] This causes it to label lesser threats (like a buzzing phone) as dangerous.[21]

When our brain thinks we are in danger, it changes the way it prioritizes information and literally shuts down the functions of the other areas to prepare the body for battle. This is called the amygdala hijack.[22] Coined by Daniel Goleman, this term refers to an immediate and emotional reaction that can be disproportionate (but not always) to the stimuli.

Our brain did not evolve in the safe environment of the modern, Western, industrialized world, so at times, it can overreact, and our immediate reaction takes precedence over a thoughtful one.[23] An immediate response would not be bad if the amygdala got triggered only when we were truly in danger, like during a car crash or a house fire.

The problem is that our personal history shapes what our brain reads as danger. Our experiences create a sort of database of what's been dangerous to us in the past, physically or emotionally. When something comes along that's similar to a past danger, our amygdala fires off.

How does this relate to leading with EI? Think back over the past few weeks. My guess is that you'll be able to identify a few situations in which an amygdala hijack occurred for you at work. For instance, perhaps your boss got angry and yelled at you and your team (a fight reaction). Or a typically outspoken colleague became withdrawn during a meeting (a flight reaction). Or perhaps someone at work reminds you of someone who hurt you in the past; your poor amygdala could be going off every day, making it difficult to steer your work relationship.

The neuroscience of our emotions is at the heart of so many difficult situations in the workplace or the home, such as miscommunication, conflict, poor decision-making, and disengagement.

However, the good news is that even though the amygdala may trigger an immediate behavioral response based on the emotional value or salience, the prefrontal cortex can have control over that and has the power to prevent this type of reactive response from occurring.

If we learn mental strategies using our prefrontal cortex (thinking brain) and not let our emotional brain take over, we can learn to be smarter than our emotions. We have agency and are not dependent only on our amygdala for a behavioral response—the prefrontal cortex can inhibit the amygdala's activation and take back control.[24] That's what leading with EI looks like—controlling our emotional reactions to behave in appropriate ways—and learning to regulate and cope with emotion is a fundamental skill we all must learn.[25]

Your Inner Eeyore

I am no neurologist, but quite simply, studying what parts of the brain are needed when learning about EI and what it takes to change behaviors into habits for myself, as well as teaching others the same, reminds me of two of my favorite childhood fictional characters, Tigger and Eeyore from the books and movies of Winnie-the-Pooh.

When we try to learn the soft skills needed in the workplace such as leadership and EI, we are using circuitry that runs between prefrontal lobes, which is part of the neocortex, and the brain's limbic system.[26]

Our emotions, motivations, and impulses are ruled by our limbic system.[27] It feeds into our basal ganglia, which are associated with a variety of functions, including procedural, conditional, and habitual learning. The basal ganglia are a large collection of subcortical nuclei[28] and are connected with the rest of the brain through a set of circuits:

- The associative or cognitive circuit is essential for learning and trying out new behaviors.

- The motor circuit is active in learned and established motor patterns.

- The limbic circuit is responsible for emotional behaviors, including emotional body language.

These circuits are all active at the same time, and the basal ganglia integrate the sum of everything that is on our mind (emotion, previous experiences, stress, learning, rewards, etc.) into one behavioral output.[29] A dominant feature in the basal ganglia is "chunking" the behavior together into a unit.[30]

"Habits are learned by the association between the response and the stimulus that triggers it."[31] The habit- and behavior-forming parts of our brain are slower because of extended training.[32] We all know that any way you slice it, changing our behaviors and making them into habits is a very slow process.

Our technical and analytical skills are ruled by our neocortex, which understands concepts quickly.[33] Sometimes, it can comprehend something after a single hearing or reading. This reminds me of Winnie-the-Pooh's friend Tigger. Tigger is always bouncing around, positively making connections with others. He is fast, full of energy, and very active. Just like the neocortex, learning happens fast when our "Tigger" is triggered.

However, other brain regions (like the basal ganglia, which feed into the limbic system) are slow learners, even slower if we have to relearn deeply ingrained habits and retrain our brain. These brain areas build up habits and skills over time, and the circuits are reinforced when the habits lead to achieving a desired goal.[34] Many skills employees need are beyond technical ability and require training to approach learning from these brain areas. These areas remind me of Eeyore. Eeyore moves slower, much more lethargically. He needs time and patience to learn something new.

Designing soft skill training such as leadership and EI skills in the same way as the training you would design for more analytical and technical skills like computer programming is a big mistake. You can't make Eeyore a Tigger. If you do, Eeyore will just get frustrated, de-motivated, and disengaged. Eeyore needs time to practice, repeat, and receive feedback on how he can improve.

The problem is that most training programs for enhancing leadership skills target the neocortex rather than those areas engaged with habits and emotions. But the fact is, you can teach an old dog (or a donkey like Eeyore) new tricks, but they need time. Skills and habits like EI are reinforced best through "motivation, extended practice, and feedback."[35]

When we provide our clients with the time to learn and practice, to repeat the skill time and time again, to learn from their mistakes,

It is possible to relearn old habits.

and then provide feedback on how they did, the "neural connections used over and over become stronger. The act of learning is the key to stimulating new neural connections." This type of learning takes more time and practice, but it is possible to relearn old habits. It is a bumpy, non-linear process full of surprises and aha moments.[36]

Making It Stick

Believe it or not, one of the most important lessons I ever learned was from a wizard—Mr. Wizard, that is, the one on Nickelodeon in the 1980s. When I was twelve years old, working as a child actor on the Nickelodeon set filming *Mr. Wizard's World*, Mr. Wizard taught me that to make learning stick for people, you need to let them practice and repeat the learned behaviors so that they overlearn them. This helps a person master the skill so that it stays with them even when stress is high and they are triggered; muscle memory of the newfound habits will take over, rather than reverting to old patterns or behaviors.[37] What you repeatedly do ultimately forms the person you are, the things you believe, and the type of person you portray to the world.

In her book *Dare to Lead: Brave Work. Tough Conversations. Whole Hearts.*, Brené Brown talks about sports: "All sports rely on key fundamentals, those skills that are drilled into players from the first day you sign up for a class or join a team."[38] You are allowed to practice these fundamental drills before they throw you in the "arena" for an actual game. These are the skills you need to perform well in the game, especially when under pressure.

Sport coaches also create plays to simulate how players should react and move in certain situations to defend their position or score in the game. The mechanics of these moves and plays are repeated over and over to create muscle memory. Why? When you are in the heat of play and under pressure, you can rely on the skills you developed over time.

The same holds true for any skill, including EI. When starting to enhance your EI, you need the time and practice to build up your strength and emotional stamina.

Taking this time to develop the emotional skills you need will help you to be the best version of you, an emotionally strong leader. Your brain must "feel the burn" in order to build new neural connections that actually last "when it's learning. Your mind might hurt for a while—but that's a good thing," says the NeuroLeadership Institute's Mary Slaughter and David Rock.[39]

Changing behaviors into habits is hard, but don't worry; I've got your back. I designed my Self-Coaching to Enhanced Emotional Intelligence Model with this in mind. Using the learning modalities contained in section II, I've ensured that you will have the time, repetition, reflection, and feedback that your inner Eeyore needs to relearn and change your behaviors into lifelong habits. These will enable you to achieve your goals and become an emotionally strong leader—the kind of leader who exhibits the habits and gets the results I'll speak of in part III.

RELIEVED JEALOUS CONFUSED STRONG HOPEFUL
SITIVE SAD HAPPY INDIFFERENT EMPATHETIC DIS
UD DISCOURAGED CONFIDENT AFRAID CALM RELI
TEFUL INTIMIDATED PASSIONATE FRUSTRATED POS
TIC RESENTFUL OVERWHELMED CONTENT PROUD
SURPRISED EMBARRASSED INSECURE GRATEFUL I
INSPIRED PESSIMISTIC EXCITED OPTIMISTIC RE
OUS CONFUSED STRONG HOPEFUL OFFENDED SU
APPY INDIFFERENT EMPATHETIC DISAPPOINTED
RAGED CONFIDENT AFRAID CALM RELIEVED JEAL
IDATED PASSIONATE FRUSTRATED POSITIVE SAD
TFUL OVERWHELMED CONTENT PROUD DISCOURA
EMBARRASSED INSECURE GRATEFUL INTIMIDATED
SSIMISTIC EXCITED OPTIMISTIC RESENTFUL OVE
ONG HOPEFUL OFFENDED SURPRISED EMBARRAS
HETIC DISAPPOINTED INSPIRED PESSIMISTIC EX
RELIEVED JEALOUS CONFUSED STRONG HOPEFUL
SITIVE SAD HAPPY INDIFFERENT EMPATHETIC DIS
UD DISCOURAGED CONFIDENT AFRAID CALM RELI
TEFUL INTIMIDATED PASSIONATE FRUSTRATED POS
TIC RESENTFUL OVERWHELMED CONTENT PROUD
SURPRISED EMBARRASSED INSECURE GRATEFUL I
INSPIRED PESSIMISTIC EXCITED OPTIMISTIC RES
OUS CONFUSED STRONG HOPEFUL OFFENDED SU
APPY INDIFFERENT EMPATHETIC DISAPPOINTED
RAGED CONFIDENT AFRAID CALM RELIEVED JEAL
IDATED PASSIONATE FRUSTRATED POSITIVE SAD
TFUL OVERWHELMED CONTENT PROUD DISCOURA
EMBARRASSED INSECURE GRATEFUL INTIMIDATED
SSIMISTIC EXCITED OPTIMISTIC RESENTFUL OVE
ONG HOPEFUL OFFENDED SURPRISED EMBARRAS
HETIC DISAPPOINTED INSPIRED PESSIMISTIC EX
RELIEVED JEALOUS CONFUSED STRONG HOPEFUL
SITIVE SAD HAPPY INDIFFERENT EMPATHETIC DIS
UD DISCOURAGED CONFIDENT AFRAID CALM RELI
TEFUL INTIMIDATED PASSIONATE FRUSTRATED POS
TIC RESENTFUL OVERWHELMED CONTENT PROUD
SURPRISED EMBARRASSED INSECURE GRATEFUL I
INSPIRED PESSIMISTIC EXCITED OPTIMISTIC RES
OUS CONFUSED STRONG HOPEFUL OFFENDED SU
APPY INDIFFERENT EMPATHETIC DISAPPOINTED

PART III

Leading with Emotional Intelligence

I **WAS RECENTLY ASKED** to create a leadership development program for an executive team in the advertising industry.

Before we developed a learning journey for them, my colleagues and I interviewed several of the senior team to find out where they thought the leadership strengths and gaps were in the company.

What became evident was that the CEO led his company by fear. The culture was driven from the top-down, and the executive team had little choice but to agree with him or feel his emotional wrath. The CEO used a command-and-control approach to leadership, where he, the leader, was in command and always tried to control his employees.

It goes without saying that the relationship between the CEO and his very talented and intelligent senior team was strained. He was clearly not creating a psychologically safe environment where people felt comfortable sharing their feelings, challenging ideas, or making mistakes.

What I quickly learned was that the senior team were constantly worried about how the CEO *might* respond to their ideas. The team, instead of placing their efforts on innovative thinking, spent their time placating the CEO and managing him and his expectations through back channels to get his approval. It was a tragic waste of time and talent.

The CEO had built the company from the ground up and was used to being the person in control; he did not feel he could trust his executive team enough to delegate, so he micromanaged every decision. Blinded by hubris, he kept such a tight grasp on the way things were being done that his negative impact on his employees was clear to all but him.

As I worked more closely with the CEO, we learned that his EI skills were the root of the problem. He was closed to viewing any situation from the perspective of another; he felt his reality was the only one that mattered. At times, he would dominate discussions, intimidate others, and hurt people's feelings. He had very little patience for those who he felt did not work as hard or as much as he did. He was never satisfied with his accomplishments, always striving for more, and he pushed these rigorous expectations on his team.

The CEO was stuck in his ways. He could not build relationships grounded in trust and compassion, and thus, he had a hard time trusting others who presented alternative ways to do business. This affected the team's ability to innovate and flourish. The company was going to grow only as large as the CEO could take it on his own because it was hard to convince him to deviate from what he thought was right and best for the business.

This rigid stance resulted in the departure of several top-performing players on his executive team because they could no longer tolerate having their ideas squashed and belittled. Simply put, they were sick and tired of the friction and stress they felt every day in the office. None of them felt safe to share what they thought or how they felt; so instead, they left the company.

A leader's emotional makeup can significantly alter an organization's results—whether that be the profits and productivity from their teams, or an engaged and happy workforce committed to doing meaningful and fantastic work.

To have an emotionally intelligent workplace, you, as the leader, are responsible for the environment you create. Creating an emotionally

intelligent culture is an inside job. It comes from the internal relationship your employees have with you as their leader and with the
work itself.

How do you cultivate these kinds of relationships with your
employees? How do you make them feel passionate about their job,
supported by their leaders, competent in their work, and devoted to
the organization?

Leading yourself and others with EI is the answer.

An emotionally intelligent leader knows how their emotions
influence their words and actions, affecting the connections they
have with their employees, the decisions they make throughout the
day, and the way they cope with work pressures. Your employees will
go out of the way for you when they feel cared for and connected to
you, appreciated for their efforts, and fulfilled in their role.

But before you can learn how to tend to the emotions of others and
coach them to help unlock their potential, you need to focus within.
You need to start paying attention to how your own feelings are helping or hurting you. How are your emotions influencing your actions?
Are your behaviors having a domino effect on your people—how they
think, feel, communicate, and act at work? And even if you have
the greatest of intentions, you must realize that as a leader, you are
responsible for how your intentions are experienced by your team.

To be an emotionally strong leader, you must first take an inside-
out approach to learn how you currently show up as a leader, what
emotional areas need your attention, and how your EI affects your
external results.

Chapter 5

What Leading with Emotional Intelligence Looks Like

N TODAY'S DAY AND AGE, soft skills are equally as important as—if not more important than—hard skills.

According to the late organizational consultant and author Warren Bennis, EI is the biggest factor in workplace success. "Emotional intelligence, more than any other factor, more than I.Q. or expertise, accounts for 85 percent to 95 percent of success at work ... I.Q. is a threshold competency. You need it, but it doesn't make you a star. Emotional intelligence can."[1]

Technical skills and intelligence are the price of admission as you move up the proverbial corporate ladder, but their importance starts to wane as you advance throughout your career. We all know that IQ isn't everything; being a genius doesn't automatically equal success. As the old saying goes, "It's not what you know; it's who you know." But allow me to offer a spin on the phrase: "It's not what you know; it's the strength of the relationships you have with who you know."

Leading with EI is the magnetic attraction that captures everyone's attention and moves teams forward. Professionals with high EI have exceptional self-awareness, better control of their actions, and more empathy for others. An increased level of EI can also help individuals manage stress better, build healthier relationships, and be more successful in work and life.

A leader with high EI builds mutually beneficial and nurturing relationships based on trust and compassion. They actively listen, can put themselves in other people's shoes, and see things from perspectives other than their own.

Those who lead with EI show humility in their actions. They admit publicly when they make a mistake. They ask for input and help. They give specific praise and constructive feedback to their teams so they can grow and develop and are always open to feedback on how they can be better as a leader. They model the way and confidently speak up in meetings—encouraging everyone to do the same. This prevents the team going along with unilateral decisions.

A key to EI leadership is the fostering of a growth mindset.[2] Emotionally intelligent leaders can see the opportunities in every challenge. They commit to noticing, articulating, and regulating their emotions, so their teams will do the same. They bravely lead their teams during challenging and uncertain times, and even though their emotions are heightened, they know how to regulate their behaviors and responses. They use emotional information to help solve problems. These leaders can think objectively and not let emotions cloud their judgment. They do their research and gather the facts, first to weigh the pros and cons and then to come to an informed decision.

Leaders with high EI set clear boundaries, especially when physical boundaries are blurred between their work and home life. They model the way by investing in, and boosting, their physical and mental health because they understand the positive impact emotional well-being has on their organization and their life.

To be an emotionally intelligent leader, you do not have to be perfect. But you do need to start to recognize, understand, and learn how your internal emotions are influencing your external results. But how do you do that? By being courageous enough to explore and share what lies beneath your surface so that others will feel safe to do the same.

The Tip of the Iceberg

In 1912, on the maiden voyage of the British luxury liner RMS *Titanic*, crew members spotted an iceberg in the ocean and tried to swerve the "unsinkable ship" around it. What they did not know, however, was that the iceberg was gigantic. The ship, of course, collided with the iceberg and tragically sank, taking with it the lives of over 1,000 people.[3] We will probably never know for sure, but reports from the few survivors estimated the height of the iceberg to be between 50 to 100 feet, and its length was estimated to be 400 feet.[4]

Just like those crew members, we can be blamed for underestimating what lies beneath *our* surface. When we interact with people, the experiences we typically share are those akin to the tip of the iceberg. We are seeing and being seen by what is immediately apparent.

Much of our communication and actions are colored by what is below the surface—our past experiences, personal history, attitudes, emotions, inner thoughts and beliefs, intentions, assumptions, aspirations, moods, motivations, fears, and stressors. The bulk of the iceberg, these hidden elements, is most significant and determines how we outwardly behave and interact with others.

We all have a different lens through which we look at the world. That point of view has a significant impact on our communication with others. Many of us overlook the breadth and depth of these inner elements and how much they influence our daily interactions.

The key is to understand how the other person sees the situation, to understand them better and improve your communication with them. But you cannot do that without EI. The problem is that unless you are a leader brave enough to talk about emotions and what's underneath the surface, these conversations do not happen.

A universal boot camp on the consequences of ignoring our inner icebergs was delivered to leaders the world over during the COVID-19 pandemic. Every human on the planet was affected in some way by the pandemic, and emotions were significantly heightened.[5] Customarily parking them at the door while working through the global crisis was an impossible prospect for many.

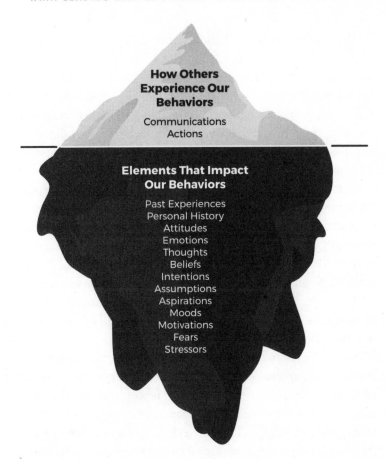

As such, people's emotions simply took over and erupted from underneath, finally out there in the workplace for everyone to witness.

The pandemic was the catalyst that forced organizations to stop in their tracks and start realizing that their workers were human, full of emotions, with complicated lives outside of the office, and their leaders were not equipped with the skills on how to deal with emotions. In fact, the World Economic Forum *Future of Jobs Report 2020* has identified EI as one of the top emerging skills now in high demand across many countries around the world.[6]

The global challenge brought by COVID has provided an unparalleled opportunity for us leaders to realize emotions matter in the workplace, and we must pay attention to upskilling our managers so that they know how to lead with EI.

The problem is none of us were born with an innate talent in recognizing what we or anyone else is feeling and why. To add insult to injury, all of us can experience an emotion internally but choose not to express or display it externally.[7] Emotions are both experiential and expressional.[8] Those two components are distinct, meaning that the emotion a person chooses to express in the office may lack sincerity in relation to their actual internal experience of said emotion.[9]

That is the hard truth for both the leader and the employee. Right now, many organizations revere hiding feelings as a badge of strength. Unfortunately, this is globally pervasive in the workplace, especially if negative connotations and disapprovals surround certain emotions. So many of us put on a poker face and hide what we are feeling—and leaders are just as guilty of this as their employees.

Therefore, we leaders need to go first and be courageous and vulnerable and share how we are actually feeling, both positive and negative emotions. By doing so, we are giving others permission to be human. We need to instill a shared belief in the office that we all are able to show our true self (with flaws and all) without worrying about how our self-image, career, or social or professional standing will be affected. We leaders need to also encourage employees to truly voice their concerns and speak up when they need assistance or are having troubles. Otherwise, we are all hiding a huge part of who we are.

In her book *Daring Greatly: How the Courage to Be Vulnerable Transforms the Way We Live, Love, Parent, and Lead*, Brené Brown shares that when we enter the work "arena," we come with a variety of emotions—fear, self-doubt, anxiety, uncertainty, and shame, to name a few. Many of us "armor up" emotionally and psychologically, trying to shield ourselves from vulnerability and appear perfect and infallible to others:

> Perfect and bulletproof are seductive, but they don't exist in the human experience. We must walk into the arena, whatever it may be—a new relationship, an important meeting, our creative process, or a difficult ... conversation—with courage and the willingness to engage. Rather than sitting on the sidelines and hurling

judgment and advice, we must dare to show up and let ourselves be seen. This is vulnerability.[10]

Before we, as leaders, can help our teams move forward, we need to start making it okay to use the F-word at work. We need to let our employees know they will not be judged for having feelings. We need to connect with them on a deeper level—understanding where they are coming from, meeting them where they are at, and supporting their learning and development.

It is essential to focus on our workers' inner motivations, fears, concerns, and feelings associated with any challenge or change that may come their way. We need to create a psychologically safe place for our teams to express themselves, and as leaders, we must listen attentively, coach and empower our employees to find their solutions, and support them where we can.

However, attentively listening and empowering our employees does not mean we should get entangled in each problem or struggle that arises. We can have compassion, empathy, *and* boundaries at the same time. We must teach our employees to be stronger than their issues and coach them to have confidence in and rely upon themselves to find the solutions to manage their feelings. In other words, we need to tune into our EI and teach others to manage their stressors, make sound decisions, and focus on their emotional health.

EI IS GOOD FOR PEOPLE AND FOR BUSINESS

It is easy to tell you from my vantage point that EI is good for people and business, but here are some stats to back up my claims:

◐ EI helps companies retain good people.

Employees who work for a manager skilled in EI are happier at work, more inspired and productive, and more committed to their employers. A study found that employees who have the same amount of work are inspired 80 percent of the time when they have a boss with high EI and only 28 percent of the time when they have a boss with low EI.[11]

➲ EI improves employee engagement.

EI helps ensure that employees feel valued and appreciated for their efforts and are more fulfilled in their roles. EI accounts for 15.9 percent of variance in employee engagement.[12] "Compared with disengaged teams, engaged teams show 24% to 59% less turnover, 10% higher customer ratings, 21% greater profitability, 17% higher productivity, 28% less shrinkage, 70% fewer safety incidents and 41% less absenteeism."[13]

➲ EI improves employee experience.

Employees enjoy their work more when they feel valued, cared for, and appreciated for their contributions. Connecting with the person, not just the employee, improves how they feel and perform at work. A study in the *Journal of Applied Psychology* showed that the benefits of EQ coaching extend beyond the workplace, including higher levels of happiness and mental and physical health, enhanced social and marital relationships, and lower levels of the stress hormone cortisol.[14]

➲ EI improves team performance.

Teams skilled at EI benefit from clearer communication, higher levels of cooperation, and a greater capacity for innovation. According to a study, "Executives who lacked emotional intelligence were rarely rated as outstanding in their annual performance reviews, and their divisions underperformed by an average of almost 20 percent."[15]

➲ EI facilitates leader development.

Leaders who understand the importance of EI are more self-aware, confident, authentic, and motivated and can inspire their teams. A forty-year study of PhDs at University of California, Berkeley, discovered that EQ is 400 percent more powerful than IQ in determining who will accomplish more in their industry.[16]

➲ EI improves the bottom line.

Companies who invest in developing EI within their leadership enjoy stronger financial performance over time than those who don't. According to a study published by the Carnegie Foundation, personal skills accounted for job success or failure seven times more than technical skills.[17]

Chapter 6

It Starts with You but It Stays with Them

LEADERS HAVE THE ABILITY to sway people's emotions either positively or negatively. This can happen when a leader is excited about a new product launch and their feelings are infectious and inspire others to work harder. A great leader can motivate their staff to go places they might not have gone otherwise. On the flip side, a leader can lose their temper when an employee makes a mistake, causing the worker a lot of trepidation and fear. This frightful experience can cause the employee to stop sharing their ideas, speaking up at meetings, or challenging the status quo moving forward.

As a leader, you need to be aware of how your emotions influence your people. You hold a lot of power in your hands to produce incredible outcomes—more profits, more productivity, more engagement, more fun. However, your positional power and the emotional influence you hold can do a lot of damage. According to Gallup, employee turnover is heavily influenced by the managers' effectiveness at focusing on engagement and emotional well-being.[1] In fact, research shows "there is a negative association between the emotional intelligence of leaders (immediate managers) as perceived by employees and the turnover intentions of employees."[2]

Taking an interest and active role in your employees' development is key to keeping your staff engaged, growing their skill sets, and encouraging enthusiasm and excitement in their jobs. Find out what matters to your people, and assign tasks that are meaningful and which give them a sense of purpose. If you do this, your company won't lose good people, and your intellectual property and brain trust won't flee with disgruntled employees into the arms of the competition.

Daniel Goleman, Richard Boyatzis, and Annie McKee said it best in their book, *Primal Leadership: Unleashing the Power of Emotional Intelligence*:

> Great leadership works through the emotions. No matter what leaders set out to do—whether it's creating strategy or mobilizing teams to action—their success depends on *how* they do it. Even if they get everything else just right, if leaders fail in this primal task of driving emotions in the right direction, nothing they do will work as well as it could or should.[3]

For those reasons, engaging in deeper conversations about emotions is one of the many leadership actions you must be brave enough to take. It starts with you. Your actions speak volumes and stay with your team.

While it may sound nerve-racking, focusing on emotions in the workplace can be illuminating. From a business perspective, understanding attitudes and behaviors is necessary, since it's your people who create your organization's competitive advantage; when you start treating and caring for people as people and not just task completers, it's amazing what they can accomplish.

Exceptional leaders are measured by their ability to relate to others. They can create a genuine connection to their people and get the best results from their teams. When leaders are empathetic and supportive of their people's struggles and work-related stressors, their teams feel cared for and valued.

Every employee is one of a kind. Each individual's stress capacity is different, and it is important for leaders to acknowledge that everyone needs to be supported differently. A stellar leader recognizes and adapts to these differences. Leading with the heart captures everyone's attention, connects people on a deeper level, and moves everyone forward.

Leaders are also measured by their ability to handle challenging situations and recover quickly from misfortunes. Great leaders show serenity and understanding, distancing themselves from their own emotional reactions. In her book *Emotional Agility: Get Unstuck, Embrace Change, and Thrive in Work and Life*, Susan David shares:

> Emotionally agile people are dynamic. They demonstrate flexibility in dealing with our fast-changing, complex world. They are able to tolerate high levels of stress and to endure setbacks, while remaining engaged, open and receptive. They understand that life isn't always easy but they continue to act according to their most cherished values and pursue their biggest long-term goals. They still experience feelings like anger and sadness—who doesn't?—but they face these with curiosity, self-compassion and acceptance. And, rather than letting these feelings derail them, emotionally agile people effectively turn themselves—warts and all—toward their loftiest ambitions.[4]

But it's difficult to remain calm on the job when others across the organization are on edge or staff members make costly mistakes. Think about the last time one of your employees made an error and it ended up costing the company money. Were you able to keep your cool? Chances are you may have felt angry and disappointed, which might have caused you to lose your temper. What impact do you think that experience had on the employee? Certainly not a positive one. However, being mentally tough and emotionally resilient pays off in dividends. Your ability to soldier through struggles—while expressing your emotions without being emotional—can have a ripple effect on how your people cope with stress and pressures, and influences them to also have a more positive mental attitude about challenging situations.[5]

Tapping into how you are feeling throughout the day and conducting regular check-ins with your colleagues is essential. It provides a safe place for your team to express their fears and stressors and have candid conversations about what is going on right now. It's hard for people to focus on work when their emotions are running amuck.

Gallup released a global study asking employees if they had experienced stress, worry, sadness, and anger a lot during the previous day. As shown in the table below, the Gallup *State of the Global Workplace 2021 Report*[6] results were staggering.

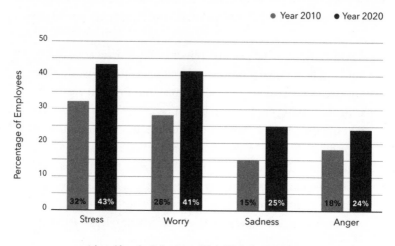

Adapted from the Gallup *State of Global Workplace 2021 Report.*

What do you think happens in an organization when the employees are feeling stressed, worried, sad, and angry most of the time at work? How does this impact the organization's collective results?

Let's face it; our mental health has worsened over the years.[7] We need to empower our employees to share their feelings rather than stuff them down, and teach them to be stronger than their emotions and move past them, both of which will free them to focus on the results we need them to.

None of these leadership measurements can happen without EI. EI is *the* essential skill by which you can foster loyalty based upon how you, as a leader, interact with and treat people. In his book *Developing the Leader within You 2.0*, John Maxwell says it best: "People do not care how much you know, until they know how much you care."[8] Remember, it starts with *you*.

I AM 100 PERCENT RESPONSIBLE

When my students do not do well on an exam, what percentage of the onus is my responsibility as their instructor? It's common for people to think 50 percent. My responsibility is to teach them the curriculum, and their responsibility is to learn, ask questions, and absorb the material.

You may not recognize that by blaming someone else, you are handing over your power to them; they are now responsible. A statement like "the students did not do well on the exam because they were not paying attention in class and were always distracted by their phones" places the blame on them.

By shifting your mind to start thinking of yourself as being 100 percent responsible for any situation you are involved in, you will always try to find another way forward. In accepting that you are 100 percent responsible, you place the onus on yourself. This brings you to a place of resourcefulness versus one of blame or victimization. You come to the situation with a growth mindset.[9] What can you do to creatively plan other strategies to get to a new outcome and be better? If you don't take responsibility, you walk away thinking you have done your part, and that doesn't get you or your situation anywhere.

When my students do not do well on an exam, I always ask myself what I failed to teach them. How could I have created more engaging content for the learning to stick? I always look at myself first. I always try to focus on what I can do before blaming others.

From a very young age, I was told by my mother that three fingers point back at you when you point your finger at someone else. So focus on what *you* can do. Ask yourself how you are contributing to the issue or challenge in the workplace.

If you are not getting the results you want at work, you need to look inward before you look outward. Your attitude and behavior as a leader have an enormous impact on how employees think and act, how hard they work, what they focus on, and how they make decisions and work together.

But you cannot do that if you are not focusing on your emotional makeup. This does not mean being perfect, just being brave enough to take a good honest look in the mirror, see how you are showing up, and try to be better.

Inside-Out Kind of Leadership

When we think of leadership, many of us think of leading a group of people in an organization. But the kind of leadership I am speaking about is as much about personal growth and raising self-awareness as it is about managing and inspiring others.

Leadership is not just a job we do; being a leader isn't any different than being ourselves. No matter where we are in the company's

Leadership is not about being the best; **it is about being willing to go first.**

organizational structure, we are bringing our life experiences, personality traits, beliefs, attitudes, values, motivations, stressors, and concerns.

Whether we have spent the time developing our emotional skills or not, these skills really come into play when we are leading others. It's inevitable that our emotions and those of others will affect performance at work, and we need to have the skills and tools to know how to tend to all kinds of emotions for all types of people in all sorts of situations.

However, before we can focus on addressing the emotions of others and work with them to help unleash their potential, we need to focus on the power from within: that inside-out kind of leadership that will allow us first to free our potential, so we can live a life of fulfillment with a great sense of purpose, guiding us to make a positive contribution to the world around us. If we can do this, we give others permission to do the same.

Many of us may have taken a leadership course or two but probably have never been taught personal leadership—learning how to first lead ourselves on the right path. Taking an inside-out approach does not mean we should be focusing only on the inner and forget about the outer results. Instead, we should be constantly looking both inwardly at our emotions and outwardly at our actions and the impact those actions have on others. Do our external results, what is happening on the outside (good or bad), match what we feel or want on the inside? Do our intentions match our impact?

Leading from within is a journey, not a destination, of profound self-discovery, requiring self-awareness and self-actualization. It's an inside job that is constantly shifting. We are continuously learning about ourselves and going deep underneath the surface of our actions. We need to challenge old beliefs and thinking patterns that are no longer working for us. And we need to face our fears, courageously reaching deep within ourselves to find out what fulfills us and genuinely makes us happy.[10]

If leaders can unveil their own humanness, employees will feel more comfortable and connected to their superiors, as well as their work. It can be as simple as starting the meeting off with "I am feeling a little overwhelmed today. How is everyone else feeling?" This can open the opportunity for an intimate conversation beyond the usual "how was your weekend?" watercooler chatter. In fact, research shows that when leaders drop their "glossy professional presentation,"[11] employees tend to trust and believe more in what the leaders are sharing.[12]

Leadership is not about being the best; it is about being willing to go first. The key is that leaders must go first. They need to step out of their comfort zone and be the first to admit their vulnerabilities and open the conversation to a deeper one beyond the agenda for the meeting. Taking the corporate mask off even slightly and allowing yourself and your people to be human in the workplace is critical.

Leaders need to allow others to honestly share how they are feeling, make errors, offer suggestions, and be open about themselves. When leaders do this, employees are more productive, are happier overall, and tend to be more loyal to their organization.[13]

When leaders show they genuinely care about their employees' well-being and move from employing to empowering their people, the work atmosphere changes. The results? People try harder, perform better, and are kinder to and have more compassion for others.

Intention vs. Impact

You and everyone around you are full of untapped, hidden potential. The power to create the team and company you want—actually, nearly anything you can envision—is available to you. You simply need to be true to yourself, and you'll see when you are that the world around you begins to change.

You might not know how to make this change happen, how to shift out of potential mode, chart the course, and go. What you may lack are basic instructions. But, don't worry, I am here for you.

In section II, I will provide you a step-by-step process on becoming the kind of emotionally strong leader who is aware of what you are feeling and why, and how your actions affect others.

Now, I want you to press pause and reset.

I want you to take a moment where you become more conscious, more self-aware. Pause and think about where you are at this moment in your life. You are living your reality TV show right now, and if you don't like what is happening on your show—with your team, your company, your life—you need to change the channel. It starts with *you*, and it begins *now*.

Michael Schrage, author of *Serious Play: How the World's Best Companies Simulate to Innovate*, states, "Serious leaders understand that, both by design and default, they're always leading by example."[14] Your small positive actions can have a significant influence on people's lives. However, at the same time, actions that seem insignificant to you can have negative consequences that you may not be aware of. Understanding the power your mere presence has on those you lead will help you keep the notion of unintended consequences top of mind.

One of the best leadership lessons of my career slapped me in the face and made me realize the difference between my intentions as a leader and my impact on others. One of my employees told me she was much happier working in a different city from me.

Wow, that was an arrow to my heart!

Getting that feedback hurt, but more than anything, it shocked me. I thought I was a great leader. I included her in all company decisions and asked her many questions to get her feedback and perspective. But to her, I was overinvolved. She knew what she was doing and did not need me to be involved in her day-to-day tasks. She also did not want to be included in every company decision. She wanted to be left alone to produce high-quality work. This experience made me realize that as a leader, you can have the grandest intention, but the impact you leave may land very differently from what you hoped for.

I learned I could have a genuine desire to show up in a certain way, but that does not always equal my impact—how others experience me as their leader. The problem is that people don't know your intentions (what's underneath the surface), but they do experience your impact. If the trust isn't there—or if it is but is muddied by actions that cause an employee to think they aren't trusted—the employee will assume the worst, not the best, of you or your intentions.[15] The bottom line is that "good intentions don't sanitize bad impact."[16]

How your staff feel about your behaviors **will give you insight on how to lead.**

My relationship with my employee changed after that conversation. I started to delegate more and turned the decision-making over to her. I always knew how capable she was, but my attempts to involve her made her feel the opposite. So I simply let go and allowed her to work out the details of assignments and accomplish her tasks the way she wanted. We still stayed connected on her projects, but this was only so I could be informed.

That critical feedback changed the way I lead. I now check in to see how my staff feel about my communications, actions, and decisions. How they feel about my behaviors provides me insight into how I should lead.

Taking a step back and thinking about our impact moves us from being self-focused to other-focused in a healthy way. This taps into our empathy skills—listening, understanding, and determining what others need and want from us—which builds trust and allows us to have more honest conversations and deeper connections. To lead intentionally and effectively means we need to be aware of and understand our impact. Minimizing the gap or disconnection between our intentions and our effect is vital.

Many leaders don't consider relationships in the workplace and instead busy themselves with managing what their people are doing. A crucial part of leadership is setting an example—how you give, receive, and solicit feedback, how you treat people, how you forgive people's genuine mistakes, and how you own up to your errors. You set the tone of what is culturally acceptable in your workplace.[17]

So what kind of leader are you striving to be? Are you aware of the impact your leadership is having on your team? Are you aware of how your emotional makeup affects your communications, decisions, and relationships? How do you ensure the effect you are having is a positive one for all concerned?

Remember that just like a boat leaves a wake in the water, your actions as a leader have a ripple effect on others. What you say (or don't say) and do (or don't do) can influence others. You must acknowledge yourself as an emotional being and realize that your actions and reactions reflect what is going on underneath the surface of your inner iceberg. Showing up in the workplace ready to share yourself authentically will enable others to feel comfortable doing the same.

But what if, until now, you did not know you were 100 percent responsible for the outcomes of your life? What if you blamed others for your circumstances?

Your team is at fault for not meeting their goals and realizing your vision. You have no time to finish your work during the day because your assistant keeps booking you in back-to-back meetings. Of your four direct reports, one is a jerk, and that's that.

But what if I told you that if you look inward first, you can learn to clean up your side of the street before you ask others to clean up their side?

For the most part, people behave the way they have been trained to act or are being rewarded for behaving. The organizational design enables misbehavior too. What is your company's culture around what is acceptable and not acceptable behavior?

How you show up as a leader—your attitude and behavior—has an enormous impact on how your employees think, what they focus on, how hard they work, how they make decisions, and how they collaborate. Improving how you interact with people, especially those different from you, will significantly improve collective team performance.

Being intentional in your leadership can significantly influence your organization's culture and ultimately, business results.

 CLIENT STORY: "SHAWN"

Years ago, I was asked to come in and coach Shawn, a senior leader with an engineering and military background; he was on the chopping block to lose his job. I was told he was a handful. He had inferior social skills and a bit of a temper and thought talking about feelings was a complete waste of time.

In our first meet-and-greet session, while skeptically arguing about having to work with me, he said, "Having emotions in the workplace is unprofessional."

I am used to being met with resistance, as some leaders are "voluntold" to work with me because their HR leader, manager, or board sees a leadership gap and wants them to learn a new set of skills. They often feel forced by management to concede or suffer from the consequences of being seen as not wanting to grow and develop in their role.

But Shawn's reluctance felt different. How could a highly educated, experienced, senior leader have such a robust mental model about feelings in that way?

I replied, "There is a difference between having emotions and being emotional. Being emotional in the workplace is unprofessional. But having emotions isn't. It's what makes us human. We all have emotions, but learning to be stronger than your emotions is critical for success in the workplace."

In the first session, I asked him to take an EQ assessment and generated an EQ report that ranked him in fifteen emotional competencies. Through this, we both learned that he was not aware of his various emotional states throughout his day at work. This low emotional self-awareness meant he was not aware of how his emotions, when triggered, would unconsciously affect his decisions or communications. Coupled with the fact that he had low empathy and weak interpersonal relationship skills, this resulted in strained connections with others on the team. During his breaks, he would not socialize with anyone as he felt fraternization was a waste of his time. He was there to work and not make friends.

After working with him for a few more sessions, I could see his problem was that he feared emotions. As I started to build more trust with him, he began to reveal his inner iceberg, and together, we faced what emotions were under the surface. With my guidance, we developed frameworks and strategies on how to tend to his own emotions and those of others in the office. Here, he learned that his mere presence as a leader had an impact on others. And when his emotions ran amuck, it had negative consequences on his team.

Together, Shawn and I practiced using a communication model that enabled him to express and present what really mattered to him in any given situation, without guilt, humiliation, shame, blame, coercion, or threats. The key was to be truthful about how he was feeling, even if it left him feeling exposed and naked to the world. He needed to look at himself before blaming others. His new ability to share his feelings in a managed way and display vulnerability helped him resolve conflicts, connect better with others, and live in a way that was attuned to his needs and those of others.

This was a landmark step for Shawn. When his boss asked to check in with him about his progress with me, we both knew the stakes were high for Shawn. In a meeting that was to last fifteen minutes, the pair talked openly for an hour and a half. Shawn was brave enough to talk about what he was feeling underneath the surface, and his boss listened with empathy, truly trying to understand what Shawn needed and wanted from him. Shawn won back the respect of his boss, and together, they were able to begin the process of moving the company forward because Shawn had developed the emotional skills to communicate effectively.

Three months later, not only did Shawn not lose his job but he was promoted!

Being emotional in the workplace is unprofessional. **But having emotions isn't.**

Winning Is Not the End Goal

What follows in section II of this book will send you on a journey similar to the one Shawn took. You will need to explore your inner iceberg, reviewing your skills, wants, goals, and motivations. This self-awakening will be powerful, transformational, and even life-changing.

However, let me be clear; this book is not about becoming an expert on your feelings. I don't think we ever truly "win" or fully master our feelings perfectly. Learning about our emotions and enhancing our EI is our life's work and journey, full of ups and downs. We will never "arrive" at our end goal, where we can become the ultimate authority over our emotions.

I think that black-and-white thinking is what gets in our way. It limits our openness to learn more about ourselves and be better. If we feel we need to win, we will never experience what it feels like to lose or make a mistake.

We need to allow for failure because it teaches us to pick ourselves up, dust ourselves off, learn from our errors, and try not to make the same mistake twice. Losing and making mistakes can teach us lots of crucial life lessons, including having self-compassion, emotional resilience, and empathy for others, to name a few.[18]

Take me, for example. I have many days when I am wiser and stronger than my emotions, days when my emotions are not ruling me but I am ruling them. On those days, I use my emotions as data to make sound, objective, and conscious decisions.

But I also have some days when I make mistakes, as we all do. Those are the days when my emotions get the best of me. I mean, I am human, which essentially means fallible. And that is the point. When I have those instances where my emotions boil over, I pause, reflect, identify what happened, and apologize. I'll also likely feel bad about having let my emotions erupt. But I take the opportunity to learn from that experience.

All we can ask of ourselves is to learn from our experiences and strive to be better than the day before.

"Some days doing the 'best we can' may still fall short of what we would like to be able to do," said the late Mr. Rogers, the American preschool television host, "but life isn't perfect—on any front—and doing the best we can with what we have is the most we should expect of ourselves or anyone else."[19]

That's why every year, I go through the process I am going to take you through in this book.

I start by taking an EI self-assessment: an inventory of my emotional state to see what areas I am currently strong in and which areas need to be my focus for the next 365 days. Sometimes, I find that my

EI levels have gone down as a whole. That's not to say I am becoming less emotionally intelligent, but the more that I learn about myself, others, and the world, the more I realize how much I still need to learn. I will forever be a lifelong learner of EI.

The process and exercises in section II are the same ones I use and provide to my clients, like Shawn, and I hope that they will provide valuable introspection and ultimately evolve the way you feel about feelings. After you read and complete the exercises, I hope you won't be afraid to talk about or tend to your emotions or those of others.

We all have a systemic impact on our world, with each of our daily interactions leaving an impression on those we interact with. When you lead with a strong mind and a kind heart, the trail you leave behind changes how people experience you and your actions. No longer are they experiencing you solely through your outward behavior, but deeper connections form underneath the surface. When you make the effort to connect with others on this level, they feel valued and validated, which in a work setting, deepens their commitment, engagement, and satisfaction.[20] When your teams feel like they are a part of something larger than themselves and genuinely feel recognized and appreciated for their contributions, they will have a renewed sense of loyalty, strengthening their commitment to your company's success and your vision as a leader.[21]

Remember, it starts with you, but it stays with them. It is time now to discover your inner superpower.

SECTION II

FERENT EMPATHETIC DISAPPOINTED INSPIRED F
AFRAID CALM RELIEVED JEALOUS CONFUSED ST
RUSTRATED POSITIVE SAD HAPPY INDIFFERENT E
CONTENT PROUD DISCOURAGED CONFIDENT AF
NSECURE GRATEFUL INTIMIDATED PASSIONATE F
CITED OPTIMISTIC RESENTFUL OVERWHELMED CO
UL OFFENDED SURPRISED EMBARRASSED INSECU
DISAPPOINTED INSPIRED PESSIMISTIC EXCITED
RELIEVED JEALOUS CONFUSED STRONG HOPEFUL
OSITIVE SAD HAPPY INDIFFERENT EMPATHETIC D
ROUD DISCOURAGED CONFIDENT AFRAID CALM
RATEFUL INTIMIDATED PASSIONATE FRUSTRATED
MISTIC RESENTFUL OVERWHELMED CONTENT PR
ED SURPRISED EMBARRASSED INSECURE GRATEF
D INSPIRED PESSIMISTIC EXCITED OPTIMISTIC R
ONFUSED STRONG HOPEFUL OFFENDED SURPRIS
FERENT EMPATHETIC DISAPPOINTED INSPIRED P
AFRAID CALM RELIEVED JEALOUS CONFUSED ST
RUSTRATED POSITIVE SAD HAPPY INDIFFERENT E
CONTENT PROUD DISCOURAGED CONFIDENT AF
NSECURE GRATEFUL INTIMIDATED PASSIONATE F
CITED OPTIMISTIC RESENTFUL OVERWHELMED CO
UL OFFENDED SURPRISED EMBARRASSED INSECU
DISAPPOINTED INSPIRED PESSIMISTIC EXCITED
RELIEVED JEALOUS CONFUSED STRONG HOPEFUL
OSITIVE SAD HAPPY INDIFFERENT EMPATHETIC D
ROUD DISCOURAGED CONFIDENT AFRAID CALM
RATEFUL INTIMIDATED PASSIONATE FRUSTRATED
MISTIC RESENTFUL OVERWHELMED CONTENT PR
ED SURPRISED EMBARRASSED INSECURE GRATEF
D INSPIRED PESSIMISTIC EXCITED OPTIMISTIC R
ONFUSED STRONG HOPEFUL OFFENDED SURPRIS
FERENT EMPATHETIC DISAPPOINTED INSPIRED P
AFRAID CALM RELIEVED JEALOUS CONFUSED ST
RUSTRATED POSITIVE SAD HAPPY INDIFFERENT E
CONTENT PROUD DISCOURAGED CONFIDENT AFR
NSECURE GRATEFUL INTIMIDATED PASSIONATE F
CITED OPTIMISTIC RESENTFUL OVERWHELMED CO
UL OFFENDED SURPRISED EMBARRASSED INSECU
DISAPPOINTED INSPIRED PESSIMISTIC EXCITED
RELIEVED JEALOUS CONFUSED STRONG HOPEFUL
OSITIVE SAD HAPPY INDIFFERENT EMPATHETIC

SECTION II

The *EI Experience* Self-Coaching to Enhanced Emotional Intelligence Model

I WROTE THIS SECTION of the book to give you private, one-on-one, step-by-step guidance—the same as Shawn had (see pages 84–85), except this time in the comfort of your own home—so you too can become an emotionally strong leader. What follows is The *EI Experience* Self-Coaching to Enhanced Emotional Intelligence Model, a rigorous self-assessment and structure that has been adapted for self-coaching from the coaching model I have created and delivered to leading universities and organizations across North America. This model will take you through a process to put you on a path of discovery and toward becoming an emotionally intelligent leader. It is a six-step framework that approaches self-coaching from a place of curiosity and compassion, not judgment and criticism. The model will help you generate action-oriented goals for short-term and long-term development, and it will help you uncover your barriers to growth and change. It will allow you to identify and understand your talents, and it will teach you how to leverage them and turn them into leadership strengths so that you walk away motivated, engaged, and more committed to your job, your teams, and your organization.

By confronting the emotional reality of your inner iceberg, you will gain a level of understanding about your emotional makeup that will give you confidence in yourself to determine the roadblocks that are hindering you from reaching your goals, and will assist you in shifting your perspective on some of your current leadership challenges.

Ultimately, the program will help you expand your thinking, maximize your full potential, and achieve more.

Building EI and resilience requires intentional preparation. You will spend time self-reflecting and identify your strong emotional competencies, as well as your underutilized ones. And you should know that even though I am an EI expert, I have not mastered my EI skills, but I know my strengths and development opportunities. I also know when I overplay or exaggerate one of my competencies and that strength then becomes a liability. My team knows this too.

Changing behaviors is hard, but throughout the rest of the chapters, I am going to share with you real-life examples of how freeing sticking with the plan and attaining EI is, how important it can be for the people around you, and how even if you stumble (which you will because we all do), you can get back on track. Remember, EI is not fixed and can be developed and enhanced anytime.

The only way to improve your EI competencies is to exercise them. If you want to strengthen your abs, for example, you target them with crunches and core work. In the same way, if you want stronger emotional muscles, you need to map out your plan or exercise regime to fine-tune and strengthen each muscle and do the specific exercises.

So think of me as your personal EI trainer and coach; I'll guide you to exercise your emotional muscles. However, I'm not going

to be there to physically train you. You'll have to abide by the core concepts of self-coaching:

- Follow a coaching model.

- Create time and space for self-reflection and inner dialogue.

- Answer powerful and thought-provoking coaching questions.

- Engage in constructive thinking.

- Develop an action plan and strategies to implement it.[1]

I will provide you with opportunities to experience all of these in the pages to come. Will the work be challenging? Sure! Anything worth your time is.

But I promise that in the following pages, I will show you the skills and strategies to become stronger and more intelligent than your emotions so that you can be an emotionally powerful leader making a positive impact on others and living a fulfilling life for yourself, just as I have.

THE *EI EXPERIENCE* SELF-COACHING TO ENHANCED EMOTIONAL INTELLIGENCE MODEL

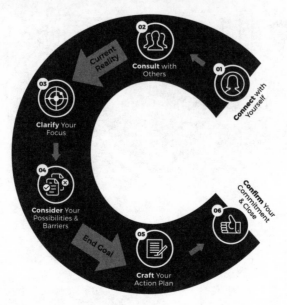

Self-Discovery

STEP 1: CONNECT WITH YOURSELF

You begin by taking a good hard look in the mirror, accepting where you are today. You identify the good and the bad in a non-judgmental way. Changing behaviors is hard, so we ensure that you approach this step with self-compassion and patience, while still being vulnerable, open, and transparent with yourself in the process.

Get Clarity

STEP 2: CONSULT WITH OTHERS

In this step, you reach out to trusted friends, colleagues, and family members—those who know you best—and interview them to see if how you envision yourself is how others perceive you. You then circle back and compare the results obtained from your interviewees with your own self-perception.

STEP 3: CLARIFY YOUR FOCUS

Here, with all the data you have collected, you define and assess where you are right now, how you are feeling about your current reality, and what success will look like if you reach the EI goal you have set for yourself. It's important that you become laser focused on what you want to achieve, always keeping your end goal in mind. What kind of emotionally strong leader do you want to be?

Ready, Set, Action!

STEP 4: CONSIDER YOUR POSSIBILITIES AND BARRIERS

Now, it is time to brainstorm the possibilities for action and discuss barriers that may get in your way of reaching your goal. Here, you find out what your real issues are and why you keep getting stuck. You identify all the ways to become the leader you strive to be and discuss ways to dissolve the roadblocks getting in your way of success.

STEP 5: CRAFT YOUR ACTION PLAN

Now, it's time for action! You tease out your action plan into bite-size chunks, setting near-term and long-term goals and target dates for completion. You pose and answer thought-provoking questions so you can create a specific plan of action, getting you that much closer to being the emotionally strong leader you desire to be. You also establish how you will handle any relapses into old patterns of behavior.

STEP 6: CONFIRM YOUR COMMITMENT AND CLOSE YOUR CONVERSATION

In this step, you recap the inner excavation conversation with yourself and highlight the key learning you gained. Here, you commit to following through on your goals and determine your motivational level to work your action plan. You also identify where you can find support, strength, and encouragement from others. You establish accountability to ensure that you are focused on your journey to emotional strength.

HETIC DISAPPOINTED INSPIRED PESSIMISTIC EX
RELIEVED JEALOUS CONFUSED STRONG HOPEFU
OSITIVE SAD HAPPY INDIFFERENT EMPATHETIC DI
UD DISCOURAGED CONFIDENT AFRAID CALM REI
TEFUL INTIMIDATED PASSIONATE FRUSTRATED PO
TIC RESENTFUL OVERWHELMED CONTENT PROUD
SURPRISED EMBARRASSED INSECURE GRATEFUL I
INSPIRED PESSIMISTIC EXCITED OPTIMISTIC RE
OUS CONFUSED STRONG HOPEFUL OFFENDED SI
APPY INDIFFERENT EMPATHETIC DISAPPOINTED
RAGED CONFIDENT AFRAID CALM RELIEVED JEAL
IIDATED PASSIONATE FRUSTRATED POSITIVE SAD
TFUL OVERWHELMED CONTENT PROUD DISCOURA
EMBARRASSED INSECURE GRATEFUL INTIMIDATEI
SSIMISTIC EXCITED OPTIMISTIC RESENTFUL OVE
ONG HOPEFUL OFFENDED SURPRISED EMBARRAS
HETIC DISAPPOINTED INSPIRED PESSIMISTIC EX
RELIEVED JEALOUS CONFUSED STRONG HOPEFU
OSITIVE SAD HAPPY INDIFFERENT EMPATHETIC DI
UD DISCOURAGED CONFIDENT AFRAID CALM REL
TEFUL INTIMIDATED PASSIONATE FRUSTRATED PO
TIC RESENTFUL OVERWHELMED CONTENT PROUD
SURPRISED EMBARRASSED INSECURE GRATEFUL I
INSPIRED PESSIMISTIC EXCITED OPTIMISTIC RE
OUS CONFUSED STRONG HOPEFUL OFFENDED SI
APPY INDIFFERENT EMPATHETIC DISAPPOINTED
RAGED CONFIDENT AFRAID CALM RELIEVED JEAL
IIDATED PASSIONATE FRUSTRATED POSITIVE SAD
TFUL OVERWHELMED CONTENT PROUD DISCOURA
EMBARRASSED INSECURE GRATEFUL INTIMIDATEI
SSIMISTIC EXCITED OPTIMISTIC RESENTFUL OVE
ONG HOPEFUL OFFENDED SURPRISED EMBARRAS
HETIC DISAPPOINTED INSPIRED PESSIMISTIC EX
RELIEVED JEALOUS CONFUSED STRONG HOPEFU
OSITIVE SAD HAPPY INDIFFERENT EMPATHETIC DI
UD DISCOURAGED CONFIDENT AFRAID CALM REL
TEFUL INTIMIDATED PASSIONATE FRUSTRATED PO
TIC RESENTFUL OVERWHELMED CONTENT PROUD
SURPRISED EMBARRASSED INSECURE GRATEFUL I
INSPIRED PESSIMISTIC EXCITED OPTIMISTIC RE
OUS CONFUSED STRONG HOPEFUL OFFENDED SI
APPY INDIFFERENT EMPATHETIC DISAPPOINTED

PART IV

Self-Discovery

THIS SELF-COACHING MODEL will teach you how to assess, harness, and grow your EI. The ability to lead with EI is in each of us; we simply need to learn how to tap into our superpower. Focusing on emotions has the power to unlock true human potential—your own potential as a leader and the full potential of your team. But it's an inside-out kind of job. You have to look inward and find out what's going on inside you.

In chapter 7, Connect with Yourself (the first step of our model), I will guide you as you learn to look inside yourself, reviewing your emotional skills that most affect your life and career. This self-awakening will be powerful, transformational, and life-affirming.

You will examine and start articulating your talents, strengths, and contributions clearly, but we will also be looking at your areas of development, challenges, and potential growth opportunities. It can be hard to face the brutal truth about yourself. But when you know who you are, warts and all, you exhibit the kind of strong, authentic leadership that others will want to follow. You need not be perfect or have all the answers. People follow others who are genuine and trustworthy, not someone who is flawless.[1]

So let's take a snapshot of your life at this moment and determine whether who you are and how you show up at work, for better or worse, is creating the outcome you are hoping for.

Chapter 7

Step 1: Connect with Yourself

WHEN THINGS AREN'T GOING WELL, we all want change, but few of us want to change ourselves or be a part of the change, and even fewer want to lead the change. Here, not only will you be attempting to change some aspects of yourself, including some behaviors that are ingrained in your way of being, but you will also be leading yourself through the change. Let's face it: change is a process and a hard one at that. When improving our leadership, we are all in a continuous learning mode. None of us ever arrive and master this. It is a lifelong discipline.

Self-assessment is necessary to understand your leadership development needs accurately. It will clearly show you the disconnection between what kind of leader you are today and what type of leader you want to be. Who you are is how you lead.[1] Understanding your inner self will help you lead more consciously and purposefully. By gaining intimate knowledge of your strengths and development opportunities without judgment or criticism, you can break down your barriers to growth and change.

This self-discovery process will do more than scratch the surface. Taking time to learn your natural emotional makeup will amplify

Understanding your inner self will help you lead **more consciously and purposefully.**

your strengths, giving you the tools to manage the obstacles life throws at you and clearing the path for your true potential to emerge.

It's essential to take inventory of yourself and be open, honest, and genuine about your individual developmental needs. But it's equally vital for you to have compassion for yourself. Don't beat yourself up for being who you are. You developed into the person you are today because of your life's circumstances. The good, bad, and ugly events of your life have shaped who you are today. "Knowledge is important," says Brené Brown in her book *The Gifts of Imperfection: Let Go of Who You Think You're Supposed to Be and Embrace Who You Are,* "but only if we're being kind and gentle with ourselves as we work to discover who we are."[2]

Assess Your Whole Self

To be an emotionally strong leader, you need to take inventory of your emotional composition and how you fare within five composite scales:

- self-perception,

- self-expression,

- interpersonal,

- decision-making, and

- stress management.

As you connect with yourself, it's crucial you look at all aspects of your life, not just work. You are going to take an integrated approach, leaving nothing out and taking a holistic view. It is critical to remember that you bring your entire self to work, not just your career persona.

This step is about taking a good hard look in the mirror, assessing your whole self internally, objectively, and without judgment or criticism, and taking an inventory of your strengths and development opportunities. Here, you will look specifically at five composite scales (and the three EQ competencies within each).

Self-reflective questions pertaining to the competencies are included to get you thinking, and stories to put these competencies into context are highlighted to provide you real-life examples of the competencies in action.

EMOTIONAL & SOCIAL FUNCTIONING

SELF-PERCEPTION

WELL-BEING

SELF-EXPRESSION

PERFORMANCE

STRESS MANAGEMENT

WELL-BEING

Self-Regard
Self-Actualization
Emotional Self-Awareness

Emotional Expression
Assertiveness
Independence

Flexibility
Stress Tolerance
Optimism

Emotional Intelligence

PERFORMANCE

Problem Solving
Reality Testing
Impulse Control

Interpersonal Relationships
Empathy
Social Responsibility

WELL-BEING

DECISION MAKING

WELL-BEING

INTERPERSONAL

EMOTIONAL & SOCIAL FUNCTIONING

There are many measures of EI out there, but only a handful of them have been assessed for reliability and validity. I have found the Emotional Quotient Inventory version 2 (EQ-i 2.0®) developed by Multi-Health Systems Inc.,[3] a leading publisher of scientifically validated assessments, to be the most useful in helping clients assess and understand their EQ as it affects their business relationships and leadership skills.

Self-Perception

Self-perception is the first area that contributes to EI. This is about how we see ourselves. Here, we examine the inner self. The self-perception composite is made up of three competencies:

- self-regard,

- self-actualization, and

- emotional self-awareness.

These three competencies relate to how good you feel about yourself and what you are doing in your life, and how well you understand your emotions.

Ask yourself these questions:

- Are you confident and self-assured?

- Are you fulfilled in your life? Do you set and achieve goals?

- Are you aware of how you are feeling at any given moment? Are you aware of your triggers: the situations, people, or events that quickly lead you to an emotional reaction?

 CLIENT STORY: "ELNAZ"

Elnaz was a winner. When I met her, she had been recently promoted to a regional manager position for a medical equipment company. For years, she had been an individual contributor to the company, and her sales results were the best in the country. She was everyone's best friend on the team; many came to her with their work challenges, and she would help them get the answers they needed to move forward. However, now that she had been given the title "manager," she struggled with the impact she would have on others and the responsibility she might have for them.

Elnaz's EQ results showed that she was high in both self-regard and self-actualization. She knew what her strengths and areas of development were, and she felt very confident in her ability to get the job done and continue to break sales records for the company. Elnaz also felt very fulfilled in her sales role. She garnered a lot of satisfaction knowing that she was making a difference in people's lives because the products she sold were taking care of people's physical well-being. In addition, she was very competitive, and internally, she relished the fact that she kept securing top sales each month.

However, in her new manager role, Elnaz quickly learned that more than managing her team's metrics and outcomes, she was managing their emotions. She had never been trained to be a leader or coach, and now that her team were coming to her with problems—emotional ones—she was becoming frustrated that her people were not "getting on with business" and focusing on results. While she used to like helping others when the obligation was low and she was working with them as a fellow salesperson, she now had little patience for those she managed.

Instead of empathizing with their emotional struggles and supporting them through their challenges, she ended up doing their work for them so her team would continue to be the best in the company. Elnaz was burning the candle at both ends and was burning out. She was no longer fulfilled in her role and simply wanted to go back to the way things were. In short, she'd lost her confidence that she was good at what she did. Instead of leaning into her development opportunity, she doubled down on her righteous sales ability at the sacrifice of being a good leader.

After working with Elnaz for a short while, I helped her realize that she needed to learn and adopt new skills to become competent in her new role. We worked together on some leadership skills, like coaching, leading meetings, having difficult conversations, and providing feedback. Adding these skills to her leadership toolbox gave her back the confidence and fulfillment she needed. She began to lead with EI, focusing on the people and not the results. When she did that, her team felt taken care of, and the results spoke for themselves. What's more: Elnaz loved her job again!

Self-Expression

Self-expression is the second composite scale that contributes to EI. Unlike self-perception, which is about how we view ourselves, this composite scale is about how we show and express ourselves to others. The self-expression composite is made up of three competencies:

- emotional expression,

- assertiveness, and

- independence.

These three competencies relate to how you express your emotions and how you come across to others.

Ask yourself these questions:

- Do you express how you are feeling appropriately and constructively?

- Do you stand up for yourself? If not, why not?

- Do you care too much about what others think?

 CLIENT STORY: "ANDREI"

Andrei was a VP of Finance and Administration for a large transportation company and was being considered for the role of President and CEO. When I first met him, it was evident that emotional expression was one of his lowest competencies. He appeared reserved, stiff, quiet, and even a bit stoic. He was an introvert, and his cautious approach was often misinterpreted as though he were coyly hiding or omitting information. The Board of Directors had a hard time trusting him.

Because Andrei did not openly share or radiate authenticity, the Board simply felt he might not have the chops to be the charismatic leader they needed; his public speaking skills were lacking, and he struggled at matching and mirroring the emotional nonverbal cues in the room so that others felt seen, valued, and understood.

At this stage, why Andrei was even being considered for the CEO role was anyone's guess, but it likely had to do with performance. His personality traits and leadership style worked well for him in his VP role. He rarely needed to divulge company-wide information in a public forum, and his cautious and reserved demeanor made sense given the financial responsibility he was entrusted with. In short, he was good at what he did.

However, to be a CEO, he needed to be an inspiring leader, compelling his followers to exceed their goals. Inspirational leaders are driven by their values, leading from a deep sense of purpose to make a positive difference in the world. This internal drive tends to make these leaders emotionally expressive.

Coaching Andrei for over a year, I saw him make great strides in enhancing his EI deficiencies. He learned to speak with ease and specificity about his emotions. He began to express his feelings, motives, and underlying concerns when making decisions. This step was critical as it helped build trust and create more transparency between Andrei, the team, and the Board. He outwardly showed more emotion when actively listening and became mindful of when he appeared to others as stiff or unapproachable. He smiled and adjusted his body language and tone to gain support from his audience. With practice, Andrei even learned to speak with varying tones when explaining things—a far cry from his previous monotonous droning.

Andrei is a terrific example of how you can enhance your emotional expression. So what happened? A year later, he was promoted to President and CEO. Since then, under his leadership, his company has won multiple awards for being the best in their sector.

Interpersonal

The interpersonal composite is the third area that contributes to EI. This is about how we interact with others. Here, we examine our social graces. The interpersonal composite is made up of three competencies:

- interpersonal relationships,

- empathy, and

- social responsibility.

These three competencies relate to your people skills: how you develop and maintain relationships.

Ask yourself these questions:

- Do you have a difficult time making connections? If so, why? If not, why not?

- Are you able to put yourself in other people's shoes?

- Do you like to give back and be helpful to the greater community?

 CLIENT STORY: "WOLFGANG"

For Wolfgang, interpersonal relationships, social responsibility, and empathy were like three consecutive breaking balls hurled to a batter who had arrived at the plate looking only for a fastball. With each swing, he was unsuccessful at making a connection.

After the law firm where Wolfgang was a senior leader received a recent survey highlighting unacceptably low levels of employee engagement, I was brought in to administer EQ assessments for all the executives and follow up with EI training workshops and private coaching sessions. The VP of HR wanted to improve the culture, and I started at the top, with the senior partners and leaders.

Given his law degree, Wolfgang was a very detailed person and did a lot of research to make sure his decisions were grounded in facts.

Although he was a great lawyer to his clients, he struggled in building interpersonal relationships with some partners in the firm. Wolfgang was uninterested in getting to know people beyond what he needed them to do in the office. This prevented him gaining buy-in on some of his decisions, instilling trust, and garnering the resources he needed.

His low score in the social responsibility competency made it difficult for others to see him as having concern for the greater good and wanting to be helpful. Wolfgang was extremely independent, and many thought he was a poor team player. He based his decisions on what was best for him and put little thought into how his choices affected others.

His lowest competency was empathy. He struggled with seeing things from another person's perspective, especially when he did not think that person worked as hard as he did or had his sense of integrity and authenticity. His standards for others were extremely high, and if a person did not meet them, Wolfgang would write them off and see no value in what they brought to the table. The problem was that Wolfgang felt his view of the world was the correct one, and he had a hard time seeing people from a different lens once they had let him down.

When working with Wolfgang, I isolated each one of his social skills (interpersonal relationships, social responsibility, and empathy) and worked on them, though the common thread was visible: Wolfgang could have high expectations for himself, but he needed to respect others and meet them where they were, not where he wanted them to be. I worked very hard to get him to change his fixed mindset and start to see the value each person brought to the team, even if he would have handled a project differently than said person. I worked hard at teaching him to respect other people's feelings and understand and appreciate what is going on for them, even if he disagreed with them. Finally, I worked on Wolfgang's ability to show his team and colleagues that he cared about others and their initiatives, not just about what he needed for his own client files.

Wolfgang practiced active listening to show others he was there for them if they needed support. He also started to have more check-ins with the partners, soliciting how they were feeling on a regular basis and paying more attention to how his behaviors had an impact on the team.

Wolfgang's courage to get up to the plate and try a different approach still led to several strikeouts before he ended up making a connection on his attempts. He sometimes reverted to his self-centered ways, and when he did, his social interactions with his peers felt insincere and unauthentic. But with continued practice and perseverance, he did connect. He invested his time in building relationships with senior partners, engaged in constructive debate, and leveraged others' skill sets, all of which enabled him to find better solutions to his problems than he could have found independently. He also accepted that interpersonal relationships were a give-and-take proposition, and he began providing help to others where he could.

His working relationships became stronger. The firm was more cohesive and engaged, and the results they achieved were the direct by-product of Wolfgang's ability to respect the alternative points of view and unique perspectives and approaches of his colleagues.

See the value each person **brings to your team.**

Decision-Making

Decision-making is the fourth area that contributes to EI. This is about how we use the information our emotions provide us to make decisions. Here, we examine our decision-making skills. The decision-making composite is made up of three competencies:

- problem-solving,

- reality testing, and

- impulse control.

These three competencies relate to how you use your emotions to solve problems and make better decisions.

Ask yourself these questions:

- Are you aware of your emotional state when making decisions?

- Do you let your emotions cloud your judgment and objectivity?

- Are you able to control your impulses during these times?

 CLIENT STORY: "KELLY"

Jim Collins, author of *Good to Great: Why Some Companies Make the Leap ... and Others Don't*, is famous for his management philosophy of getting the right people in the right seats on the bus.[4] Well, when I met Kelly, she was on the bus all right, but she was driving it right over people who didn't see things her way.

Kelly was a middle manager in a large warehousing company, where she believed she held the best ideas and delivered them with the best intentions. I was brought in to help because she and another manager in the organization were not getting along.

Kelly was not aware of how her reality testing was getting in her way. She was righteous about her perspective to the point that she never once challenged her own assumptions. She drove the bus, and if you wanted on, you'd better agree with her on where it was going.

During one of our sessions, I said to her, "you are not the standard to which everything is judged." This was enough to jostle her from her pedestal of strong opinions. When we dug deeper, she realized that her emotions about how some of the people were choosing to do things at the company were upsetting her. Rather than deal with her emotions, she stuffed them down, and instead of an emotionally intelligent discourse coming out, her strong opinions and beliefs leapt to the fore and clouded her judgment. She assumed that checking her reality with others would slow her down and frustrate her—which, in fairness, it did in the beginning—but by identifying her frustration and choosing to work through it, she felt a weight lifted off her shoulders when she started to share the load.

Working with her colleagues helped her understand that her reality is exactly that—hers. No matter how hard she tried to force her version of reality on others, hers was only one opinion among many, and other opinions were just as valid as hers. Ultimately, she learned that a good leader is one vulnerable enough to ask other people how they see things, instead of telling them what they are supposed to be seeing.

Kelly shared, "I used to be very hesitant about showing my vulnerable side, thinking it was a sign of weakness, but working with you, I've found it to be one of my superpowers."

Kelly is a wonderful example of how our emotions can influence the way we view the world and how we make decisions. Learning to see your emotions as insightful pieces of information allows you to be open to hearing what your feelings are telling you about yourself, others, and how you see the world.

Stress Management

Stress management is the final area that contributes to EI. This is about how well we cope with change, the unfamiliar, and our daily challenges. It's about how we manage when things are not going well. We all know we can't eliminate stress, so the aim should be to boost our ability to cope with our everyday stressors, which helps us face more significant challenges with more self-assurance. Here, we examine how well we handle stress. The stress management composite is made up of three competencies:

- flexibility,

- stress tolerance, and

- optimism.

These competencies relate to how you cope with challenges, remain calm, and see the light at the end of the tunnel.
Ask yourself these questions:

- Do you adapt well to change or uncertainty?

- Do you cope well with stress, and are you resilient in trying times?

- Are you able to remain hopeful about the future?

 CLIENT STORY: "SOFIA"

Sofia was a high-performing event manager for a professional membership association. I was brought in to coach her because she was having significant issues with managing her stress levels, interacting with her superior, and delegating to her team.

Sofia's stumbling block was her inability to express her feelings about the expectations she had of herself, combined with the overwhelming workload she was given and the guilt she felt asking for help from her team. Our work focused on boundary setting, honest and clear communication, and understanding that there is no shame in asking others for help, especially when you're drowning.

Before my intervention, Sofia was always the first into the office and the last to leave. She also had a bad habit of regularly checking in with her team after hours. She didn't pause for lunch, didn't have any recharging rituals, and simply worked herself into the ground.

After months of this behavior, Sofia caught herself feeling irritable and becoming short with colleagues and friends. Her work was making her miserable, yet she couldn't stop herself from doing more and more.

After a few coaching sessions, we worked on ways in which Sofia could delegate and coach some of her high-performing team to help her. Like many new leaders, she felt bad asking for help, and we worked to shed her guilt and establish boundaries that were clear to her and that she could use as guideposts so she didn't slide back into familiar, destructive habits.

We also worked on her ability to express her emotions—especially when she was frustrated or overwhelmed—in a respectful way that invited empathy and compassion. Her team, to no one's surprise, was thrilled to help her, and through her efforts and genuine connection with her colleagues, her emotional resilience grew. Sofia learned to uphold a work-life balance and started to have a more positive outlook because she put her emotional well-being on equal footing with the other aspects of her life.

This is a terrific example of the power that stress management can have on a worker's attitude, performance, and overall happiness.

It's All about Balance

Your EI, like most skills, needs to be balanced. Although we are all striving to have high EI, Dr. Steven Stein, the Founder and Executive Chair of Multi-Health Systems Inc., the company that created the EQ-i2.0® model and assessment, reminds us that "the ideal thing is not just getting all high scores... it's about balance."[5]

Each of your EI competencies is interrelated. You are out of balance when you have wide ranges between your EI levels in different competencies. Learning to increase your EI by narrowing the gap between your EI skills is the key to success. When your competencies are balanced, you enhance your emotional and social functioning and performance, as well as your overall well-being and happiness.

For instance, I have high flexibility, which means I effectively and appropriately manage my emotions when faced with new and unforeseen circumstances. However, sometimes my flexibility rears its ugly head and becomes overplayed; sometimes, I can be too adaptable. I can flip-flop and not know what direction to take or what decision to make, leading others to lose confidence in me. I also have low independence, which sometimes makes me question my judgment and decisions, and I will seek reassurance from others.

These EI competencies (flexibility and independence) are balanced if I can remain open to new ideas and approaches but can remain true to my thoughts, especially when I think something is important, even if it differs from the viewpoint of others. In other words, I need to be receptive to the others' ideas but avoid just going along with the crowd.

Therefore, I need to increase my independence to balance these competencies. I may also need to lower my high flexibility and feel more confident in, and stronger about, my ideas and draw a firm line versus caving in and just going along with the majority. Sometimes, commitment "takes precedence over adaptability."[6] On some issues, I need to take a stand and be strident. My opinions on important matters need to be a priority over being liked or accepted by others.

What you'll discover in the following pages as you learn about your competencies is that we naturally swing back and forth. The trick is to understand when you've swung too far or not far enough. It takes practice to identify the sweet spot and make the needed adjustments. However, to determine where you are on the continuum of your EI competencies, you will first identify your baseline at this moment for each.

High, Medium, Low, or Dark

Before you embark on the exercises in the following pages, I'll give you some context for how to rank yourself on each of the competencies.

One of my high scores in my most current EQ assessment is assertiveness, which means I speak up in meetings, voice my concerns or share my ideas, and set clear boundaries when working with others. One of my low scores is impulse control, which means I have difficulty delaying gratification. I can make rash decisions, like sending an email before thinking it through or making an impulsive purchase at a shopping mall. So for me, assertiveness is a strength, and I would rank myself as high in this area. Impulse control is an area of development, one in which I would rate myself as low.

One of my EI competencies that is neither high nor low is problem-solving, meaning that I am decent at finding solutions to problems when emotions are involved. Sometimes, I am an excellent problem-solver. I research and gather facts first, weighing the pros and cons and drawing on past experiences when I can. But other times, when the problem affects me personally, my emotions can hurt and not help the decision-making process. I can base my decisions on my opinions or impulses, especially when experiencing stress and pressure. Therefore, I would rank myself as medium in problem-solving.

But before we get you to assess your high, medium, and low areas of EI, I want to take a moment to discuss the dark side of EI.

Like any skill, EI can be used for good or evil. A growing body of research has begun to show contexts when EI does not appear helpful and may even be detrimental to a person or those they are in contact with. Very high levels of EI can convey adverse outcomes, suggesting a dark side to the construct.[7]

Having high EI levels isn't always a strength. If your tendencies in areas are overplayed and stack up in ways countering your other predispositions, a strength can quickly become a liability. Have you ever thought about what your strengths look like when overplayed? What impact do these overused strengths have on others?

Take my client "Donna" as an example. She and I have worked together for more than three years. Initially, her impulse control was on the high end, and she concurred that she was not someone who let her temptations guide her decisions. She took her time to develop ideas, narrowed down her options, and looked at the available data. She asked all the right questions to guide her decision, weighing the pros and cons of each choice. Her impulse control was a point of pride for her.

However, with deeper reflection, I asked Donna to consider if her EI was too high in this area. When she investigated things further, she realized that sometimes she took too long to decide. She would contemplate her options over and over, and several times, she just could not pull the trigger on a decision. She would see all the potential dangers that lay around every corner and within every given situation, making her reticent to make changes and take chances. Her indecisiveness was causing her team to lose faith in her competence.

Donna's story is a perfect example of how when a strength is overplayed, it can turn into a liability. I'm happy to report that through Donna's commitment to understanding her emotional makeup and what drives her impulse control, she's been able to slowly come around to making informed decisions more quickly and is no longer paralyzed by the dangers that could be.

* * *

WHAT FOLLOWS IS THE FIRST of six workbooks, but this one is by far the most important. The Step 1: Connect with Yourself exercises (pages 118–22) will set the foundation for your entire journey.

Please have self-compassion as you rate yourself on the competency scales. Trust me, you are the way you are because of your upbringing, education, work, and personal experiences. The moment I stopped blaming my parents for how I turned out was a turning point for me. The moment I had more self-compassion for who I was— that was the moment of truth when I started to make fundamental changes in myself.

As Kristin Neff, author of *Fierce Self-Compassion: How Women Can Harness Kindness to Speak Up, Claim Their Power, and Thrive*, explains, "Self-compassion simply requires being a good friend to ourselves ... treating ourselves with the same kindness we'd naturally show to a good friend."[8]

Be an observer of yourself, looking down from above and objectively analyzing the person you are today, not the person you want or wish to be. Taking a good look in the mirror can be challenging and eye-opening at the same time.

Whatever your EI levels are, don't worry. Instead, look at this as a starting point; your greater self-awareness will help guide you toward continuous improvement in your personal and work relationships. With this self-awareness, you now know that you, like all of us, have areas for improvement. As Sophia Bush says, "You are allowed to be both a masterpiece and work in progress simultaneously."[9]

WORKBOOK

Step 1: Connect with Yourself

Self-Perception Exercise

- Use the descriptions to determine your EI level for self-regard, self-actualization, and emotional self-awareness.

- Are you on the dark side? Or are you high, low, or somewhere in the middle?

COMPETENCY	LOW	HIGH	DARK SIDE
Self-Regard	When you are low in self-regard, you are unsure of yourself. You might fear failure, which can hold you back from succeeding. You lack confidence and self-respect and have low self-esteem. You tend to put little value on your opinions and ideas and believe that others are more capable.	When you are high in self-regard, you accept and respect yourself for who you are. You are confident enough to take your own needs into consideration. You have an accurate view of yourself, understanding and accepting your strengths and weaknesses.	When you have too much self-regard, you risk being overconfident and narcissistic, which can be perceived as rude and self-entitled. You may have an inability to admit your mistakes and cannot see things from another person's perspective.
Self-Actualization	When you are low in self-actualization, you probably feel unfulfilled and think that your life lacks meaning. You might not know which direction to take in life, and you are probably not pursuing enjoyable, meaningful things.	When you are high in self-actualization, you live a life of fulfillment, meaning, and purpose. You focus on self-improvement. You are willing to persistently continue to be the best you can be, improve, and live connected to your passion for a meaningful life.	When you are too self-actualized, you are never satisfied and content with what you have accomplished. You always want bigger, better, more. Too much self-actualization can also lead you to not recognize and, at times, be intolerant when others are dissatisfied and not living up to their potential.
Emotional Self-Awareness	When you are low in emotional self-awareness, you have trouble recognizing or identifying your feelings, leading to a lack of emotional ownership. You are unaware of your triggers and why you are feeling what you are.	When you are high in emotional self-awareness, you can easily recognize and understand your emotions and triggers. You are better at taking the emotional charge out of a situation and just labeling the feeling for what it is without getting too emotionally invested.	When you are too aware of your emotions, it leads to you overthinking situations and focusing on insignificant details. You can spend a lot of time thinking about the hidden meanings in things people say or do, reliving your mistakes, or rehashing conversations.

Determine where you stand by marking an **X** on the continuum for the three self-perception competencies.

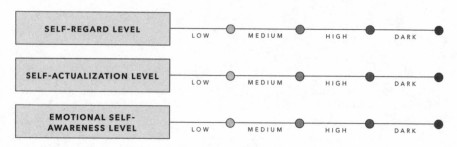

Self-Expression Exercise

- Use the descriptions to determine your EI level for emotional expression, assertiveness, and independence.

- Are you on the dark side? Or are you high, low, or somewhere in the middle?

COMPETENCY	LOW	HIGH	DARK SIDE
Emotional Expression	When you are low in emotional expression, you either do not express how you feel or do so in a non-constructive way. You may be seen as withdrawn, like a closed book and a bit of a mystery. Alternatively, you may have a short fuse and let your emotional responses come out in the wrong way, like yelling or swearing.	When you are high in emotional expression, you can constructively express your emotions and are seen as an open book. You can narrate for others what you are noticing internally. You understand that letting your feelings out respectfully and professionally lets people in.	When you are too expressive with your emotions, others feel uncomfortable, awkward, and pressured to reciprocate. You sometimes share too much information about yourself to gain connection without building trust, which can work against you.
Assertiveness	When you are low in assertiveness, you cannot express yourself and can be quick to compromise to avoid conflict. You can be passive or shy and have a hard time standing up for yourself.	When you are high in assertiveness, you have no problem speaking up respectfully and professionally and saying what you need to say when you need to say it. You are a strong communicator who is forthright and fights constructively for what you deem important.	When you are too assertive, it leads to hurt feelings, damaged relationships, intimidation, and dominating discussions. Your assertiveness can come across as aggressive, adopting a "my way or the highway" stance.
Independence	When you are low in independence, you rely on others for emotional support and often need reassurance. You may lack confidence, are not sure of your ideas, and can be indecisive. You can be needy and rely on others to make decisions for you when you are more than capable of doing it yourself.	When you are high in independence, you are self-directed, confident, and self-reliant. You are self-responsible and can complete daily tasks like decision-making and planning on your own.	When you have too much independence, you can come across as non-collaborative and not a team player. You have a hard time asking for help, making others feel untrustworthy, unneeded, and unwanted.

Determine where you stand by marking an **X** on the continuum
for the three self-expression competencies.

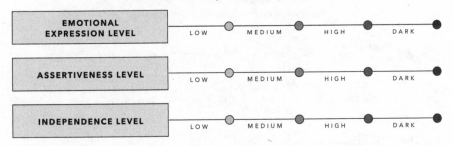

Interpersonal Exercise

- Use the descriptions to determine your EI level for interpersonal relationships, empathy, and social responsibility.

- Are you on the dark side? Or are you high, low, or somewhere in the middle?

COMPETENCY	LOW	HIGH	DARK SIDE
Interpersonal Relationships	When you are low in interpersonal relationships, you are not interested in relationships, are uncomfortable being intimate, and appear aloof and distant. You might have poor social skills and can't interact effectively and appropriately with others.	When you are high in interpersonal relationships, you can nurture, build, and have significant, mutually satisfying relationships. You feel at home in social situations and have no problem building long-term, trust-based connections.	When you are too dependent on your interpersonal relationships, you put yourself last and place your happiness solely on your relationships. You often place others' needs above your own.
Empathy	When you are low in empathy, you might feel surprised by others' reactions. You may not share your feelings and can have difficulty understanding and relating to other people's feelings. Your lack of empathy can come across as uncompassionate to others.	When you are high in empathy, you pay attention to and appreciate the feelings of others. You are very sensitive to what, how, and why people feel the way they do. You can pick up on social cues, anticipate others' reactions, and respond appropriately.	When you are too empathetic, you may coddle the other person, which prevents you from pushing them to excel. Having too much empathy means you do not set clear boundaries and cannot differentiate yourself from others. You get entangled in other people's issues, carry others' emotional burdens on your shoulders, and often put others' needs before your own.
Social Responsibility	When you are low in social responsibility, you can be (or at least appear to be) self-focused and selfish and tend to do what's best for you without thinking about how your actions affect others. You are most likely unwilling to be involved in teams, do not commit to group activities, and are more enthralled with yourself.	When you are high in social responsibility, you like to give back and contribute to the welfare of others. Being socially responsible means you care about others and act responsibly and with concern for the greater community. You may volunteer your time to help others.	When you are too socially responsible, you might help and give too much, which can foster a corporate culture of dependence, where people feel they can't take care of themselves or do their jobs well on their own. When you help too much, your help can sometimes stagnate others and prevent them from developing their skills.

Determine where you stand by marking an **X** on the continuum
for the three interpersonal competencies.

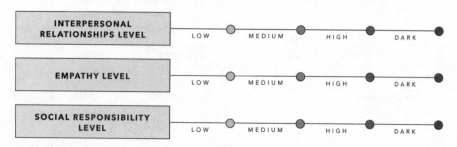

Decision-Making Exercise

- Use the descriptions to determine your EI level for problem-solving, reality testing, and impulse control.
- Are you on the dark side? Or are you high, low, or somewhere in the middle?

COMPETENCY	LOW	HIGH	DARK SIDE
Problem-Solving	When you are low in problem-solving, you often jump to solutions, are often irrational and unstructured, and tend to fly by the seat of your pants. You let the intensity of your emotions get the best of you and have a hard time finding solutions to emotional problems.	When you are high in problem-solving, you can easily find solutions when emotions are involved. You base your decisions on facts versus on your opinions or impulses, and you also draw on past experiences to decipher problems when you can.	When you are too logical with problem-solving, you focus heavily on the task rather than the people the problem impacts. You concentrate on solving the problem but tend to ignore the emotions behind the problem and do not have a lot of empathy, failing to understand what others are going through.
Reality Testing	When you are low in reality testing, you set unrealistic goals, which can be de-motivating to others. You sometimes have biases and preconceived notions about the world, which can cause you to create stories about what is going on.	When you are high in reality testing, you know your biases, keep things in perspective, and do not let your emotions cloud your objectivity. You are rational, grounded, and impartial and can assess situations reasonably and accurately. You live in the present moment rather than ruminating about the past or worrying about the future.	When you are too realistic, you can be too focused on objective evidence, which leads to a lack of optimism and empathy and to over-looking others' viewpoints. You believe what you see is real. But you need to remember that your reality isn't everyone's reality.
Impulse Control	When you are low in impulse control, you can make rash decisions and have trouble controlling your impulses or resisting temptations. You can be unpredictable, aggressive, and reactive.	When you are high in impulse control, you can resist or delay an impulse or temptation to act. You have more self-regulation and control of your emotional responses and tend to be highly tolerant and patient.	When you are too con-trolling of your impulses, you act very slowly and are overly cautious when making decisions. You can be more reticent to make changes and take chances. You tend to be rigid, where everything is deliberate, and for you, spontaneity is scary and dangerous.

Determine where you stand by marking an **X** on the continuum
for the three decision-making competencies.

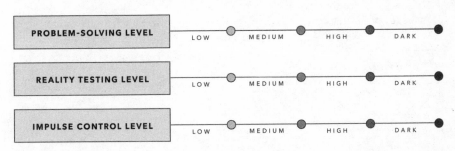

121

Stress Management Exercise

- Use the descriptions to determine your EI level for flexibility, stress tolerance, and optimism.

- Are you on the dark side? Or are you high, low, or somewhere in the middle?

COMPETENCY	LOW	HIGH	DARK SIDE
Flexibility	When you are low in flexibility, you are very rigid and stuck in patterns, preferring the status quo. You do not adapt well to change or the unfamiliar. You do not perform well when conditions are characterized by rapid change.	When you are high in flexibility, you effectively manage your emotions when faced with uncertain, new, or unforeseen circumstances. You adapt to change with ease, are open to new ideas, and go with the flow.	When you have too much flexibility, you can flip-flip too much and not know what direction to take or decision to make, leading others to lose confidence in you. You might not be committed to a strong sense of purpose.
Stress Tolerance	When you are low in stress tolerance, you can have high anxiety levels, feel overwhelmed, and have ineffective coping strategies. Low stress tolerance might leave you feeling fearful and reactive.	When you are high in stress tolerance, you can handle stress without a decrease in performance. You tend to be calm and cope well in difficult situations. You appear optimistic, stable, and relaxed, despite life's drawbacks.	When you are too tolerant of stress, you ask too much of others while not understanding how others cope with stress. If the pressure gets too high for others, their momentum decreases, and stress can immobilize them and stifle their creativity.
Optimism	When you are low in optimism, you may have trouble seeing the good in things. You are pessimistic and very uncertain about your future. You tend to focus on negative outcomes and are more cautious.	When you are high in optimism, you have a positive attitude and outlook on life, remaining hopeful even in the face of adversity. You trust that things will turn out well. You are confident about your future, see a life full of possibilities, and are enthusiastic and hopeful about what lies ahead.	When you are too optimistic, you remain blissfully ignorant of what is going on around you. You filter negative situations and put an optimistic spin on them. You tend not to see things as they are and may not prepare yourself for the future curveballs that life may throw at you.

Determine where you stand by marking an **X** on the continuum
for the three stress management competencies.

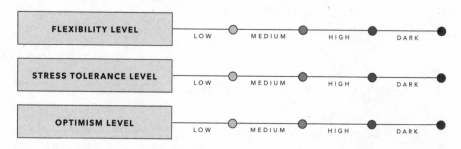

Pause and **Reflect**

When you get to the end of each workbook, you'll be prompted to pause and reflect. The learning and exercises you are completing are deeply personal. Introspection can be rewarding, humbling, and everything in between. Please take a moment to reflect on your journey, your answers, and your feelings. There is no one way to respond, and all your feelings are valid. After you pause and reflect, I invite you to turn the page and complete an emotional check-in. This will help you further identify and understand the things you are feeling. Be kind to yourself and enjoy the journey.

Emotion Check-In

 POSITIVE
 HAPPY
 OPTIMISTIC
 INSPIRED
 EMPATHETIC

 EXCITED
 CONFIDENT
 PROUD
 RELIEVED
 CONTENT

 HOPEFUL
 SURPRISED
 CALM
 STRONG
 PASSIONATE

 JEALOUS
 SAD
 INTIMIDATED
 OFFENDED
 FRUSTRATED

 DISCOURAGED
 AFRAID
 INDIFFERENT
 EMBARRASSED
 DISAPPOINTED

 PESSIMISTIC
 RESENTFUL
 CONFUSED
 INSECURE
 OVERWHELMED

Looking at yourself objectively, without judgment or criticism, and assessing how you show up in the world is powerful. The more you know who you are as a leader, the more you will relate to and connect with others.

Now that you have taken an inventory of your strengths and development opportunities, you can see the areas for improvement.

How do you feel? Use the emotions icons as a guide. The answer can be a combination of any of these feelings or a different emotion altogether.

What is this feeling(s) telling you about yourself?

Whatever you are feeling is okay. This can be a hard journey, but trust me, you are going to a good place.

HETIC DISAPPOINTED INSPIRED PESSIMISTIC EX
RELIEVED JEALOUS CONFUSED STRONG HOPEFU
OSITIVE SAD HAPPY INDIFFERENT EMPATHETIC DI
UD DISCOURAGED CONFIDENT AFRAID CALM REL
TEFUL INTIMIDATED PASSIONATE FRUSTRATED PO
TIC RESENTFUL OVERWHELMED CONTENT PROUD
SURPRISED EMBARRASSED INSECURE GRATEFUL I
INSPIRED PESSIMISTIC EXCITED OPTIMISTIC RE
OUS CONFUSED STRONG HOPEFUL OFFENDED SU
APPY INDIFFERENT EMPATHETIC DISAPPOINTED
RAGED CONFIDENT AFRAID CALM RELIEVED JEAL
IDATED PASSIONATE FRUSTRATED POSITIVE SAD
TFUL OVERWHELMED CONTENT PROUD DISCOURA
EMBARRASSED INSECURE GRATEFUL INTIMIDATE
SSIMISTIC EXCITED OPTIMISTIC RESENTFUL OVE
ONG HOPEFUL OFFENDED SURPRISED EMBARRAS
HETIC DISAPPOINTED INSPIRED PESSIMISTIC EX
RELIEVED JEALOUS CONFUSED STRONG HOPEFU
SITIVE SAD HAPPY INDIFFERENT EMPATHETIC DI
UD DISCOURAGED CONFIDENT AFRAID CALM REL
TEFUL INTIMIDATED PASSIONATE FRUSTRATED PO
TIC RESENTFUL OVERWHELMED CONTENT PROUD
SURPRISED EMBARRASSED INSECURE GRATEFUL I
INSPIRED PESSIMISTIC EXCITED OPTIMISTIC RE
OUS CONFUSED STRONG HOPEFUL OFFENDED SU
APPY INDIFFERENT EMPATHETIC DISAPPOINTED
RAGED CONFIDENT AFRAID CALM RELIEVED JEAL
IDATED PASSIONATE FRUSTRATED POSITIVE SAD
TFUL OVERWHELMED CONTENT PROUD DISCOURA
EMBARRASSED INSECURE GRATEFUL INTIMIDATE
SSIMISTIC EXCITED OPTIMISTIC RESENTFUL OVE
ONG HOPEFUL OFFENDED SURPRISED EMBARRAS
HETIC DISAPPOINTED INSPIRED PESSIMISTIC EX
RELIEVED JEALOUS CONFUSED STRONG HOPEFU
SITIVE SAD HAPPY INDIFFERENT EMPATHETIC DI
UD DISCOURAGED CONFIDENT AFRAID CALM REL
TEFUL INTIMIDATED PASSIONATE FRUSTRATED PO
TIC RESENTFUL OVERWHELMED CONTENT PROUD
SURPRISED EMBARRASSED INSECURE GRATEFUL I
INSPIRED PESSIMISTIC EXCITED OPTIMISTIC RE
OUS CONFUSED STRONG HOPEFUL OFFENDED SU
APPY INDIFFERENT EMPATHETIC DISAPPOINTED

PART V

Get Clarity

THE NEXT PART of the self-coaching model will build upon your self-assessment and push you to a granular understanding of your EI competency levels. By consulting with others and using probing questions to drill down on the data you have, you will come out of Steps 2 and 3 of our self-coaching model with a clear idea of who you are and how you come across to others.

Asking others (and yourself) these thought-provoking questions about how you come across can be hard. But I promise you that knowing the answers will help you move forward on your path to becoming an emotionally strong leader.

Once you intimately connect with your inner iceberg and learn why you do what you do and why you need to change, you will be able to purposefully set an EI goal for yourself. By looking at your areas of development, you will choose the one that has the largest potential for changing your life in the manner you most desire right now.

This goal-setting process is extremely important because you will start to get very clear on what success looks like and think about the benefits of achieving that. Visualizing your goal into reality is important in providing you with a strong mindset and focus while working on your implementation plan.

Chapter 8

Step 2:
Consult with Others

S O YOU NOW have a subjective personal assessment of your EI; this is a great starting point. But it is impossible to assess yourself objectively. You may be unconsciously competent in some areas and unconsciously incompetent in others; you may have blind spots.[1]

We must remember that our emotional experiences influence our self-perception.[2] It is also colored by social and family influences,[3] culture,[4] and the media,[5] which all play a role in shaping how we feel about ourselves and who we think we are.

I have met many successful leaders who have an inflated sense of self. They sometimes buy into how their followers or entourage see them and how they think they compare with others and their role in society. Sometimes, this is a case of the people around them building them up and inflating their egos. Sometimes, it is pure narcissism. In either instance, these individuals likely rank themselves too leniently, therefore placing their EI levels higher than they are.[6]

However, the same is true for those who are too hard on themselves. Some leaders are constantly striving for perfection. They are so tough on themselves that no matter what they do, it never lives up to their expectations. Many times, this is a default reaction,

Your reality isn't everyone's reality.

rooted in their childhood. Perhaps, their parents placed conditions on their affection and expressed love only when their children earned it through particular actions? Or maybe, the parents had high expectations of what their children should accomplish, and they always felt they fell short?[7] Regardless of where this comes from, in these cases, these leaders may rank themselves too harshly, placing their EI levels lower than how others perceive them. When there is a mismatch between how you see yourself and who you wish you were, your self-concept is incongruent, which negatively affects your self-esteem.[8]

Alternatively, some leaders are neither too lenient nor too hard on themselves but simply are not aware of their impact. They might have great intentions on how they show up as a leader but are not aware of how their team experiences their actions and communications. In any of these above cases, your reality may not be everyone else's reality.

After coaching thousands of clients and students, I have seen that many people's perceptions of who they are may not be reality. So we will focus on challenging the assumptions you may have of yourself or the story you have been telling yourself about yourself. We need to separate fact from fiction. It's time to give yourself a reality check.

This next step in the process is getting you to see how your self-perception compares with what others see. Your intentions, the leader you strive to be, may not be leaving the impact you want on others. Others may have a completely different impression or viewpoint of you and your leadership style. It's time to infuse some objectivity into the picture.

Self-Perception Is Inevitably Flawed

For a famous Dove beauty company ad campaign from 2013, several women had their portraits drawn by a forensic artist. The first portrait was based on each subject's self-description. The second was based on descriptions provided by other people. The artist created both portraits for each subject based only on what he had heard. He had never seen the subjects' faces.[9]

The campaign highlighted the bleak reality of how women perceive their physical appearance versus how they are perceived by others. Of course, our perception of our appearance is informed by all sorts of complex emotions. Although this commercial was targeted at women, this idea transcends gender and begs a question: "Why can't we see ourselves as we really are?"[10]

Our sense of self-image develops throughout our life. It is a complicated weaving of societal and cultural expectations and life experiences. This creates a warped reality.[11] Thus, it becomes impossible to see ourselves as we truly are.

According to David Schlundt, a psychologist at Vanderbilt University, self-perception results from a composite of all our life experiences, from childhood to adulthood. "It's not a perceptual thing. It's a combination of emotion, meaning and experience that builds up over our lifetime and gets packaged into a self-schema."[12]

We all have insecurities, and on top of that, the media profoundly influences us and does not make thinking of ourselves in a positive light easier. We live in a culture that bombards us with unrealistic images of beauty, success, and happiness.

For instance, we are blasted with out-of-reach beauty images that are impossible to live up to without Photoshop. Whether it be about beauty or belonging, many of us have that little voice in our heads telling us that we are not good enough. Usually, this voice stems from a childhood experience, and the words and feelings associated with that voice end up getting repeated over and over like a broken record.

In this way, we are our own worst enemies; so many times, our self-limiting beliefs get the best of us. We need to be able to put those aside and get out of our own way. Sometimes, being hard on ourselves can strengthen us, mainly when we've made a bad choice. However, our potential is restricted by an inner voice that won't shut up.[13] All too often, that annoying voice, our inner critic, does not have our best interests in mind.

Be aware of what (and who) you're listening to because not every voice is honest and trustworthy. Those negative voices usually come from inherited legacies or adverse events in your past, and it's essential to identify which are indeed yours and which come from somewhere or someone else.

Listening to our negative thoughts about ourselves is difficult to navigate, especially when life becomes stressful and busy. Sometimes, it can be hard to distinguish between what the inner critics in our head are trying to convince us to believe and our true, authentic, and self-compassionate selves. Our inner critics always find mistakes in everything we do, limiting our potential and affecting our internal motivation. When we give these negative voices too much airtime, making progress on our goals can be challenging.

Therefore, we need to determine if how we see ourselves is based on fact or fiction. Are we listening too much to the cast of inner critics in our heads?[14] Are feelings of self-doubt, worry, frustration, and helplessness taking over? As Susan Jeffers discusses in her book *Feel the Fear ... and Do It Anyway: Dynamic Techniques for Turning Fear, Indecision, and Anger into Power, Action, and Love*, we can overcome these types of feelings—our fears about ourselves. "The real issue has nothing to do with the fear itself, but, rather, how we *hold* the fear. For some, the fear is totally irrelevant. For others, it creates a state of paralysis. The former hold their fear from a position of power (choice, energy and action), and the latter hold it from a position of pain (helplessness, depression and paralysis)."[15]

Self-limiting beliefs can be described as F.E.A.R (False Evidence Appearing Real).[16] Our insecurities about ourselves can appear real, even though they may not be. Arising when we feel threatened or scared, they are urging us to stay in our comfort zone and cling to the familiar.

One of my all-time favorite quotes (which has been attributed to several prominent historical figures) is "watch your **thoughts**, for they become **words**, watch your **words**, for they become **actions**, watch your **actions**, for they become **habits**, watch your **habits**, for they become **character**, watch your **character**, for it becomes your **destiny**."[17]

In other words, it all starts with what goes on underneath the surface, and if we can learn the mental skills to be bigger than what lies beneath and challenge those negative beliefs, we can move mountains.

The Value of External Feedback

Just as some voices in your head you need to ignore and others you need to champion, some external voices will be beneficial and others will be less so. However, sometimes finding the voices that are contributing real value is trickier because we are conditioned to defend ourselves from anything that seems like an attack on our character.

This is precisely why we need to learn how to solicit, assess, and accept external feedback.

Although skipping this step would be easy, as it takes time, energy, and courage, it is one of the most potent steps you can take to becoming emotionally stronger. Please don't cheat yourself and miss this transformational process. I promise it will be worth it.

However, taking this step will be challenging. Hearing others' perception of you can be difficult, especially if it isn't favorable or it runs contrary to how you think of yourself. It may be damaging to your ego. You might even be tempted to argue or get defensive. But before you do, stop yourself from deciding too soon.

In the book *Thanks for the Feedback: The Science and Art of Receiving Feedback Well*, Douglas Stone and Sheila Heen talk about three triggered reactions that are common when we receive feedback (particularly corrective feedback):

- Truth trigger: Is this true or accurate about me?

- Relationship trigger: How do I feel about the person giving me feedback?

- Identity trigger: Does it cause me to question the perception I have about myself?[18]

We need to make sure we are not letting our feelings about what others say lead us to dismiss the feedback too soon. But how do we do that?

One great way is first to manage emotions, take deep breaths, and notice if you are "wrong spotting" by considering the three triggers Stone and Heen discuss:

1. "Challenge to See"—Is this true about me?

   - What is the person giving me feedback trying to tell me?

   - Am I seeing myself accurately? Could this be a blind spot for me?

2. "Challenge of We"—How do I feel about the person giving me the feedback?

   - Am I reacting to the person (the who) or to the message itself (the what)?

   - If someone else were to provide me with this feedback, would I feel different?

3. "Challenge of Me"—Does this hurt my ego?

   - What is my emotional reaction to this feedback?

   - How is this feedback impacting the story I keep telling myself about myself?[19]

If you are relying on family, friends, or coworkers for feedback, it can be a bit easier to ask for feedback. But what if you want candid feedback from your direct reports or subordinates? Sometimes, that can be difficult. How can you get honest feedback from your employees?

A Culture of Feedback

A leading Harvard Business School researcher, Amy Edmondson, coined the term "psychological safety," meaning that "no one will be punished or humiliated for errors, questions, or requests for help, in the service of reaching ambitious performance goals."[20]

As a leader, you are tasked with creating a psychologically safe environment where everyone feels comfortable sharing their opinions and thoughts and feels safe and respected. Creating group norms where each member feels safe to speak freely about themselves, including development opportunities, in front of others is essential.

You also need to show that, as a leader, you are a work in progress. You need to ask for feedback and share openly with others. As everyone on your team should be constantly striving to improve and willing to grow and learn, you must model the way, allowing others to do the same.

Start to cultivate a culture of feedback from all levels. One way I do this is that after every weekly team meeting, I ask my staff several questions: "What am I doing too much of? What am I not doing enough of? What am I doing just right?" I try not to ask closed-ended questions like "can I improve anything?" These types of questions make it too easy for my staff to simply say yes or no and close the conversation.

Another way to get candid feedback from your subordinates is to start critiquing your work and soliciting input from others. Start to make giving and receiving feedback not such a scary thing. Always remember to provide both praise and corrective feedback, not just constructive criticism. If your culture is not ready for honest, open feedback, ask your team for anonymous feedback and make sure you summarize all the feedback you receive from others.

 CLIENT STORY: FEEDBACK IS A GOOD THING

Once while conducting a group coaching session for an industrial company, I noticed some obvious discomfort among employees when they were asked to provide feedback.

The two frontline managers were meeting with their manager from that department and the operations manager, who oversaw their smaller department. After creating a safe environment, I asked the two frontline managers to share their thoughts on the department, what was working well and what wasn't. Both were nervous about providing constructive feedback, so I encouraged them to be brave and share their feelings on their lived experiences. I also offered my feedback to the middle manager and senior manager on how I thought they could better support their team members, including the two frontline managers. We ended the session, all feeling positive about what had come out of the meeting. However, the next day, the middle manager told me that he had a lineup outside his door of staff worried that he would leave, and they all wanted to ensure that he knew he was doing a good job.

Before him, his position had been a revolving door. Over the last few years, many had been hired in his position and either left the company or been fired. Given that context, it was no surprise that his team were nervous he would go, but what the staff's reaction told me more than anything is that they did not have a culture in which sharing feedback was encouraged. They had no problem sharing pats on the back and saying the generic "good job" to each other, but if someone had a different idea or some developmental feedback, that went unsaid.

The bottom line is that employees should feel safe to share their concerns and ideas on improvement. In this case, although the meeting appeared successful to those in the room, I guess the gossip that followed created an alternative reality for many who did not get to witness firsthand how the positive and constructive feedback was given and received; therefore, they were concerned that the middle manager would leave. In a culture that values feedback, this meeting wouldn't raise a single eyebrow, and that is the goal.

Strategies for Soliciting Feedback

Asking others for feedback can feel awkward. But remember, you are doing this to better yourself, and those you are asking have a vested interest in you becoming more emotionally intelligent. So put aside any reservations you have, and be confident that people want to help.

- **Who to Interview**

  Interview at least five people, and make sure you choose people who truly want the best for you. These people can be from any walk of life—family, friends, coworkers—and you also don't have to have known them long. They simply need to be people who have your back.

- **How to Interview**

  Interviews like this are best done in person, and failing that, over a videoconferencing platform; seeing your interviewees' body language is important. Be sure to take notes, and if you get permission, recording your interview can also be helpful.

  If you can't interview in person or over videoconference, ask your interviewees to write their responses down. This approach can be very powerful too, as your interviewee will have more time to consider their answers and they can't be interrupted, as can happen in the natural course of conversation.

  Interview your most trusted person first, and you will find the strength in their answers to interview the rest of your people.

- **What to Expect from Your Interviews**

  During the interview process, you'll be hearing about how you show up and the qualities you bring to a variety of situations. Some of the revelations you'll hear will be pleasing, and others might embarrass or shame you—but fear not! The idea is to learn to recognize both your strengths and your areas for growth. Hopefully, you'll learn a lot about yourself—for better or for worse—in the process.

Strategies for Receiving Feedback

One strategy that works for me when asking for feedback on my performance is acting like I am a journalist who interviews people speaking about someone else, not myself. I try to stay super-objective. I put my ego aside and act as a detective, listening to their feedback as if I were a third party.

Before you ask others about how they see you, please remember some key strategies for receiving feedback, especially constructive feedback, which you may have the urge to dismiss too quickly. The keys to receiving feedback are the following:

1. **Assume Positive Intent**

   When receiving feedback from others, you must put your generous hat on and assume positive intent. You may need to shift your mindset to believe that others actually want the best for you. This can be difficult, especially when your relationship with the feedback giver is strained. However, consider how you will receive feedback differently if you assume the person is rooting for you. Instead of believing that someone just wants to point out what is wrong or wants to be right, assume they want to see you succeed and that they have your professional development in mind.

2. Actively Listen and Ask for Clarification

If the feedback has triggered you, instead of thinking of your rebuttal or defense, actively listen to what your interviewee is really saying. Don't argue with them; get curious about why they feel the way they do. After they are done talking, ask for clarification, as you may describe those same behaviors using different labels or words. Look for the meaning behind their labels, and ask for real-life examples to gain a deeper understanding of how your behaviors affect them. Remember that people experience things differently and have different perceptions. Their reality may not be *the* reality. As such, you want to focus on the facts rather than opinions.

3. Stay Present and Be Open-Minded

Pay attention to how you are feeling when you receive the feedback. It is sometimes difficult to hear feedback, especially constructive feedback. Are you feeling angry? Irritated? Surprised? What is that emotion telling you about yourself? It's critical to pay attention to how you feel after you have received the feedback. Notice your discomfort, and manage your emotional triggers by staying present and being open-minded, no matter what is said, positive or negative. Remember, we all have blind spots, and perhaps the feedback you received may not be something you have considered before. That does not mean the feedback is accurate, but be open and willing to hear and learn from an alternative point of view.

4. Thank Your Feedback Giver

Most importantly, make sure you thank the person for their feedback. Thanking them shows the person you appreciate their input. Remember, they took the time to share with you what was going on for them underneath their surface, which took bravery on their part. Honor that. Right or wrong, their feedback shows you more about how they see you. This insight is invaluable for you to be more other-focused instead of self-focused. You want to cultivate a culture around feedback as worthwhile and generous.

Creating a positive experience for the feedback giver will give them the courage to continue to be honest with you and others.

Although receiving feedback can be unsettling, it provides you with an opportunity to grow and initiate change. It allows you to see yourself in a different light. This will help you understand how others perceive you and how your behavioral style affects them. This can be incredibly insightful for a leader, as it can help you see how you may be coming across to others and help you improve your management skills. Actively listening to others' feedback generates trust and inspires better performance from you, which gets mirrored by your team.[21]

Most people naturally want to succeed at their job and thus are often willing to listen to helpful feedback. According to *Harvard Business Review*, 72 percent of people feel their performance would improve if their managers were to provide corrective feedback. The same survey found that 57 percent of people prefer corrective feedback to purely praise and recognition.[22]

Feedback can also improve working relationships, because giving feedback is an opportunity to get things out in the open so that you can resolve issues and find ways to work together better.[23] In fact, providing regular feedback can actually eliminate the need for a difficult conversation later on. The feedback giver is speaking truthfully and respectfully about what is going on for them. This honesty can either stop discord from occurring or prevent it from escalating.

Feedback can also improve employee engagement.[24] This is especially true as the workforce gets younger. Millennials, for instance, dubbed the most ambitious[25] and growth-driven group out there, want to learn and do better continuously. Therefore, they will need feedback, and plenty of it, as they seek to find a work home where they want to stay for a long time.[26]

According to a Gallup survey, if a manager focuses on an employee's strengths, the odds of that employee becoming actively disengaged at work are only one in a hundred. When a manager ignores an employee, they are roughly twice as likely to be actively disengaged

at work than when the manager focuses on their weaknesses. Therefore, being neglected appears to be more damaging to an employee's
engagement than having to address their weaknesses with their
manager.[27]

Like it or not, feedback is a good thing.

One thing to note: you know yourself best. When it comes to feedback, take what you want and leave the rest, but be open your blind
spots. Remember to show appreciation to the feedback giver for being
so candid with you. Being this honest and vulnerable is hard. If you
don't agree with everything, that's okay, but still, assume positive
intent, actively listen, ask for clarity, stay present and open to their
point of view, and thank them.

SAMPLE INTERVIEW QUESTIONS

Seeking the opinions of others helps to provide a reality check on
your assumptions and beliefs about your strengths and development opportunities. Here are some questions you could ask others
to learn how they see you.

Self-Perception

- **Self-Regard:** In your opinion, when am I at my best? Do you ever
  see me losing confidence in myself or my abilities? Explain.
- **Self-Actualization:** Do you think I am trying to improve myself
  continuously? Explain. Do you think I am fulfilled in my life? If
  not, what do you think I need to do to enjoy my life more?
- **Emotional Self-Awareness:** Do you think I am aware of my emotions and triggers? If so, how do I demonstrate this? If not, what
  do I do that makes you feel I am not aware of my emotions and
  triggers? Please expand.

Self-Expression

- **Emotional Expression:** Do you think I communicate my feelings
  effectively when I am emotional? If so, how? If not, what makes
  you think I do not do this well?

- **Assertiveness:** Am I usually expressing my thoughts, opinions, or beliefs in a conversation, or do I remain silent? Please provide your rationale.
- **Independence:** Do you think I care too much about what others think of me? If so, how do I demonstrate this? If not, why do you believe that?

Interpersonal

- **Interpersonal Relationships:** Do you see me as someone who builds, nurtures, and maintains strong interpersonal relationships? Why or why not?
- **Empathy:** When you or others have a problem, do you see me as someone who can see the situation from another perspective and empathize with others? Explain.
- **Social Responsibility:** Do you think I give back to the greater good and like to be helpful? If so, how? If not, why not?

Decision-Making

- **Problem-Solving:** When I am dealing with an emotional problem, am I able to find sound solutions? Please explain.
- **Reality Testing:** In what area in my life do you think I need to be more realistic? Do you believe I let my emotions cloud my objectivity? Please explain.
- **Impulse Control:** Do you think I can control my impulses? If so, how do I show this? If not, how and when do I demonstrate this? Explain your answer.

Stress Management

- **Flexibility:** Do you think of me as someone who adapts to change with ease? Explain.
- **Stress Tolerance:** Do you think I adequately manage my stress? If so, how? If not, what do you think would be beneficial for me to cope better with stress?
- **Optimism:** Do you consider me a glass half-full or glass half-empty kind of person? Explain.

Compare and Contrast the Self and External

After you have interviewed others, take those fantastic answers you received and compare them with the answers you provided yourself. You might be surprised at what you find.

Did more than two or three people share similar outlooks of you? Were they similar to the outlook you have of yourself? Did any patterns emerge? Did anything catch you off guard?

Sometimes, what you have identified as a self-perceived flaw may be regarded by others as a strength. Or what you thought was a strength may be seen by others as an overplayed competency and a leadership liability.

For me, the most significant aha moment was when I once asked a partner these questions. It was challenging to ask and listen, so I recorded his answers to make sure I truly heard what he said. I was surprised by some of the positive things he saw in me that I failed to see in myself. Akin to the Dove commercial with the sketch artist, I was my own worst critic.

However, it wasn't all roses, and you should be prepared for the same. My then-partner made some observations about me that hurt. He acknowledged those things deep down within myself that I try to keep at bay. While no one likes others to acknowledge their warts, his doing so revealed the depth of my development opportunities and highlighted that some show up more pronounced at home than in the office.

That was a valuable part of the exercise. It revealed to me that, even in my role at my company, where it is okay to be human at work, I had still parked some of my fears and insecurities outside of the office only to let them out when at home. Whoa!

Asking others their perceptions of you can be life-changing. Rarely do we take time to have these intimate conversations with those closest to us. It is a difficult exercise but one that is entirely essential if you are going to discover your inner iceberg and learn to understand and benefit from your emotions.

So take a long hard look at how others see you. Could one of your "weaknesses" be your hidden talent?

CLIENT STORY: "HARPREET"

I had a client named Harpreet, who was told by her boss that she was a slow and overly cautious decision-maker. This was true, but in her case, the feedback just made her feel bad about herself. She didn't like to state her opinions or viewpoints until she had collected all the data.

When coaching her, I spoke about how her high EI levels—reality testing (being objective and seeing things as they really are), empathy (understanding how someone else feels), and emotional self-awareness (being aware of her emotions and triggers)—made her a thorough, analytical, and thoughtful decision-maker. She was precise and deliberate and took her time to make calculated decisions. Harpreet was very strategic and looked at the big picture and the parts making up the picture. She considered how her decisions may impact her team. This was her genius, not her liability. Although her high impulse control (resisting or delaying an impulse or temptation to act) had been, on occasion, overplayed and made her an overly cautious decision-maker, there was a bright side to her dark side. In her role, she had leveraged her ability to control her impulses, avoid making rash decisions, and provide strategic direction for her department.

However, she sometimes needed to make quick decisions at work, and her low assertiveness was getting in her way. She did not always speak up and say what she needed to say when she needed to say it, because she wanted to ensure her opinion was accurate. So we developed an EI strategy for her to use when people wanted an off-the-cuff response; she stated a preamble. "I have not thought this through fully, but if you want my initial thoughts and opinions, they are ..." This forced her to state her opinions and beliefs at the time but also acknowledge that her ideas had not been thoroughly thought out yet.

By working with the feedback she was given on being an overly cautious decision-maker, even though it hurt to hear, Harpreet learned a valuable lesson. She was seen by others as she saw herself—a critical and precise thinker and problem-solver. However, those same people saw these strengths as occasionally limiting her overall potential. Harpreet's ability to internalize, accept, and adapt is exactly why asking for feedback is so valuable.

* * *

AS YOU SET YOUR SIGHTS on conducting your feedback interviews for Step 2: Consult with Others and analyzing the data to answer the questions posed in the workbook that follows, please remind yourself that your feedback givers are doing you a favor. They are on your side. They want you to succeed. Go into your feedback interviews with the aim of limiting your emotional reactions, being brave when confronted with fearful or painful facts, and knowing that by doing this, you will be closer to your goals.

Or as popularly chanted on the television series *Friday Night Lights*, "Clear eyes. Full hearts. Can't lose!"[28]

Step 2: Consult with Others

Interview Theme Analysis

Using the sample questions on pages 140-41, conduct your interviews with five people whom you trust to give you honest and accurate feedback about you and your EI competencies.

After your interviews, analyze the data you collected and answer the following questions. Look for common themes and patterns that emerge from all the answers you gathered:

- What did people say were your strengths?

- What did they say were opportunities for development?

- What surprised you most?

- Did you have blind spots? If so, what were they?

- How do you feel after receiving the feedback?

- What did you learn from completing this activity?

What Is Your New Reality?

Now that you've synthesized all of the data, what do you need to work on? What is keeping you stuck? Are your strengths actually liabilities? Are your weaknesses in reality your genius? What are the three best things about you?

Remember, you can't change everything right away. Don't forget that your high levels of EI may be on the dark side, so make sure your strengths are truly strengths.

Now that you've had hindsight and time to reflect, has this feedback changed your perspective? Do you have a clearer view of yourself and what you want or need to change? Would you feel comfortable saying the commonalities are true? What are the differences?

Take a colored pencil or highlighter and shade in the wheel below with your three EI strengths (the areas you are high). Then, use a different color to mark up the wheel with the three EI competencies you want to improve (the areas where you are low, medium, or on the dark side).

Based on EQ-i 2.0® Model developed by Multi-Health Systems Inc.

Below, based on what you learned, list the three areas you think are your leadership strengths.

1.	
2.	
3.	

What three areas could you improve to most significantly impact your leadership?

1.	
2.	
3.	

You may want to work on areas where you or others rated you low on specific EI competencies. You may want to lower some areas on the dark side. Or you may want to take an EI skill and move it from medium to high.

Pause and **Reflect**

Emotion Check-In

POSITIVE

HAPPY

OPTIMISTIC

INSPIRED

EMPATHETIC

EXCITED

CONFIDENT

PROUD

RELIEVED

CONTENT

HOPEFUL

SURPRISED

CALM

STRONG

PASSIONATE

JEALOUS

SAD

INTIMIDATED

OFFENDED

FRUSTRATED

DISCOURAGED

AFRAID

INDIFFERENT

EMBARRASSED

DISAPPOINTED

PESSIMISTIC

RESENTFUL

CONFUSED

INSECURE

OVERWHELMED

Comparing your self-perception with how others experience you is revealing. It should provide you a clearer picture of who you are and how you lead. Awareness is the first step to any kind of behavioral change. Understanding your external behaviors will enable you to know what to stop doing, start doing, and continue doing.

How do you feel? Use the emotions icons as a guide. The answer can be a combination of any of these feelings or a different emotion altogether.

What is this feeling(s) telling you about yourself?

Chapter 9

Step 3:
Clarify Your Focus

THIS STEP AIMS to re-evaluate what is real and what is the
story you have been telling yourself about yourself. Once this
is done, you can decide what you want to dismiss and what
you want to start paying more attention to. Only when you challenge your assumptions and ask questions about what you see do
you get a clearer picture of what is real.[1] This creates the baseline for
development.

After considering the ideas of all those you've consulted with,
ask yourself whether they identified the same strengths as you did.
Are the areas you identified as your development opportunities truly
the ones you should be focusing on? Is what you or others consider a
development opportunity a weakness? Or is it an area that you should
rely on at particular times? (For example, are you like Harpreet on
page 143, whose analytical skills were a strength when strategizing
but not when needing to make a quick decision?) Are your strengths
being overplayed, and are you on the dark side?

Assessing the internal and external answers from Steps 1 and 2
will clarify your focus. It will provide you a starting point about what
you need to focus on to become an emotionally stronger leader.

Learn Your First *Why*
(Why Do You Do What You Do?)

Now that you know your leadership gaps, both from your perspective and those of others, it's essential to examine, without judgment or criticism, why you do and say what you do. Where did these patterns of behavior come from?

For me, this personal insight was the most critical step in finally dissolving lifelong roadblocks to growth and change. For instance, why do I constantly need to ask for reassurance? Once I understood the underlying reasons for why I behave the way I do, I gained clarity on what I need to do to successfully address my growth opportunities.

It's essential when undergoing this process that you avoid shame, judgment, or guilt. To be an observer of your life, you need to take a step back and view yourself as if you were a director in the film of your life, pondering the motivations for why this "actor" (you) behaves the way they do. Marshall Rosenberg, author of the book *Nonviolent Communication: A Language of Life*, described self-judgments as the "tragic expressions of unmet needs."[2] The tragedy comes from how your self-criticism and judgment diminishes how you perceive your self-worth and inhibits your motivation to change.

My realization that I had relied too much on others because I had never built the skill of being independent allowed me to put a label on some of my struggles and not feel bad about who I was. I came by my reliance honestly. Once I could name it, I started to tame it.[3] I focused on my issues and worked on exercises to make myself more independent.

Acknowledging a leadership gap and understanding why you have this gap provides more insight into why you are the way you are. This enables you to shift your focus from labeling yourself as having an irreparable flaw to recognizing that the root cause of the issue is now within your power to change. Learning your *why* is simply looking at yourself and determining why you are the way you are without assigning any wrongness to it. It is an intellectual self-diagnosis of who you are right now.

Figuring out the *why* can give you a sense of peace and a deeper understanding of yourself. When you look at yourself with compassion

Learning your *why* is simply looking at yourself and determining **why you are the way you are without assigning any wrongness to it.**

and not criticism, you can make peace with and accept the circumstances that helped shape you. As Kristin Neff states, "Self-compassion involves being open to and moved by one's own suffering, experiencing feelings of caring and kindness toward oneself, taking an understanding, nonjudgmental attitude toward one's inadequacies and failures, and recognizing that one's own experience is part of the common human experience."[4] What's more, with this self-awareness and self-compassion, you are now more empowered to make positive changes for yourself. Again, this is about taking 100 percent responsibility for your life and focusing on what you can and will do about it now.

 CLIENT STORY: "MARTINA"

To help my clients learn their *why*, I ask them to describe where they learned or did not learn their EI skills. For example, one of my clients, Martina, had empathy as a strength. In our first coaching session, I asked her where she learned this skill. She said her mother ("Isabella") was an amazing role model for her. Isabella was a senior-care provider, and seeing how much she cared for her elderly patients and how kind she was to everyone she met, Martina tried to adopt that approach in her work and personal life.

As a production manager in a manufacturing plant, Martina demonstrated her empathy by actively listening to her direct reports. She was susceptible to others' feelings, picked up on social cues, and anticipated others' reactions. She knew her employees very well, cared for them deeply, and could put herself in other people's shoes. She understood their perspective in a way that respected their feelings. Martina may have disagreed with them, but she could still recognize and appreciate what was going on for them. Being empathetic meant she could notice someone else's feelings and hold the space for that person to express themselves in a safe environment.

When Martina reviewed her internal assessment and the external feedback she received from others, she found conflicting results. Like many of us, she had blind spots.

Martina's CEO ranked her empathy as her highest EI skill; her direct manager ranked her even higher on this competency than Martina did herself. However, both thought Martina's empathy was becoming a liability. They were worried she did not have clear boundaries with her staff.

In Edwin Friedman's book *A Failure of Nerve: Leadership in the Age of the Quick Fix*, he talked about differentiation, which "means the capacity to become oneself out of one's self, with minimum reactivity to the positions or reactivity of others." He defined this process as knowing the demarcation between oneself and another person. Friedman said that "differentiation is an emotional concept, not a cerebral one; but it does require clear-headedness. And it has enormous consequences for new ways of thinking about leadership."[5]

When you have too much empathy, you take on others' emotions and carry their emotional burdens on your shoulders, and it can emotionally hijack your body and mind, while simultaneously eroding the boundaries necessary for leadership.

Until she examined the roots of her empathetic approach to her leadership, Martina did not realize that her empathy level was too high. The dark side of empathy is that sometimes, as a leader, you can get entangled in your teams' issues and overprotect them, keeping them small and preventing them from stretching outside their comfort zone into their learning zone. Martina got enmeshed in her team's issues and took them home with her at night.

This happens a lot to people; they see a role model and go to the extreme when modeling a quality the role-model possesses. Once Martina started to analyze her *why*, she realized that her mother also took home her patients' issues and struggled with stress. When Martina focused on how she learned empathy, she realized her mother was too empathetic.

Like many parents, Isabella tried to hide her stress—in her case, the toll that the inevitable deaths of many of her patients took on her. So Martina saw only the good of her mother's empathy, not the dark side. Therefore, she tried to model her mother's way of being and adopted the same approach to her own leadership.

After further consideration, Martina realized she had too much compassion for others. This kept her team reliant on her for solutions to problems and prevented her team from reaching their full potential. The work we did together taught her to lower her empathy, push back, and encourage her people to be more self-reliant, and coach them by asking more questions versus telling them what to do.

Connecting with herself and understanding her emotional makeup was essential for Martina's professional development. She was able to compare how she viewed herself and how others saw her. Looking at the perception gaps between her internal and external responses provided her the clarity and focus she needed. Learning her *why* (why she did the things she did) helped her unlearn some deep-rooted behavior patterns and develop into the leader she always knew she could be.

Learn Your Second *Why* (Why Do You Need to Change? What's Your Goal?)

In the workbook that follows, you'll be asked questions that will help you answer your first *why*, and after you do, you'll need to consider your second *why*: Why do you need to change?

Ultimately, this is about determining what your goals are. Where do you want to be?

In what areas in your life are you *not* getting the results you want? What is that costing you? How are you 100 percent responsible for that? These are hard questions, and for many of us, hard to answer.

To turn your vision of the future into reality, you need to set goals as a means to motivate you to achieve more excellence in life. Remember, goal management is tied to the fundamental psychological principles of changing behaviors.[6] You are more likely to succeed if

- you know what you need to do,

- you believe you can do it, and

- you are motivated to do it.

The gap between your current reality and your goals has tension, just like an elastic band. This is the part of our self-coaching model where you will identify your leadership gap, the gap between your current reality and end goal. To reduce the tension, you can do three things:

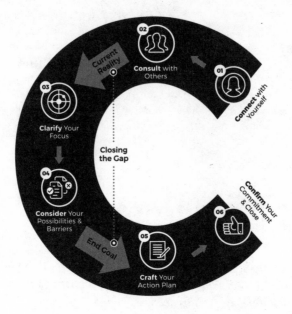

- Change your current reality, and bring it closer to the goal.

- Make your goal easier, and bring it closer to your current reality.

- Use a combination of the first and second approaches.

In his book *The War of Art: Break Through the Blocks and Win Your Inner Creative Battles*, Steven Pressfield states, "Most of us have two lives. The life we live, and the unlived life within us. Between the two stands Resistance."[7] Identifying the gap between your current reality and your end goal allows you to see what is getting in your way of achieving what you want.

Ask yourself why you need to change. Is the goal you've set for yourself truly a priority for you now? Is changing your behavior a wish, or is it linked to one of your core values? Are you blaming your schedule and the time you don't have? As Laura Vanderkam, author of several time management and productivity books, famously once said, "Instead of saying, 'I don't have time' try saying, 'it's not a priority' and see how that feels."[8] I bet you'll look at your goals differently if you do.

On the one hand, learning and development are a value of mine, and if you were to look at my calendar, you'd see that I've made time and space for this in my everyday life. Self-care, on the other hand, is something that I want to be a value, but it is often only a wish. On days that I am busy, I don't make it a priority.

So re-evaluate your goals. Will you make them a focus in your life? Can you fill the gap and be your best self if you work on these goals daily? If so, what is holding you back from starting now?

 CLIENT STORY: "TOBY"

Toby was the CEO of a mid-sized financial firm, and he had an inability to express his feelings around his disappointment in his own performance. He had taken the reins of the company from an outgoing CEO who could only be described as a rock star. Everyone loved this CEO, and he had the company performing remarkably.

These were big shoes for Toby to fill when the CEO decided to retire. As a result, Toby, not wanting to be seen as feeble in comparison with the outgoing CEO, created goals and targets that were unrealistic for him and his executive team. With every missed milestone, Toby felt deflated, the executive team became frustrated, and Toby pushed harder and harder, raising the stakes further and further. Naturally, this set the course for disaster, and as targets kept being missed, the Board was now wondering if Toby and the team were the right ones to be leading the organization.

Thanks to some interventions with the team and some crucial, hard work by Toby (looking at why he needed to change), he came to the understanding that he should not compare himself with the former CEO. He needed to adjust how he saw himself, to shift his self-perception. He needed to re-examine his goal, and not just beat the former CEO's record but be the best leader he could be with his natural talents.

When we worked on him not looking at himself in relation to the former CEO and his record, a reckoning occurred, and slowly but surely, Toby and the team righted the ship. But it could not have happened if Toby had not taken that hard look in the mirror and worked to understand himself emotionally, before trying to fix the problems in the company.

He needed to understand his second *why*. Why did he want to change? What were his goals? What kind of CEO did he want to be? What were his gaps?

The moment he looked inward and took this inside-out approach to his leadership, his viewpoint shifted and so did his impact on the team's and the company's performance.

Toby is a terrific example of the power of connecting with yourself, clarifying your focus (where you are and where you want to go), and understanding your second *why*.

S.M.A.R.T. Goals

A helpful way of making goals more powerful is to use the S.M.A.R.T. mnemonic. S.M.A.R.T. goals should be used when making goals for your personal and professional development.[9] They are Specific, Measurable, Attainable, Realistic, and Time-Bound.

Specific: When goal setting, you should be as specific as possible. You need to clearly define what you will do, why it is important, and how you plan to achieve it.

- What are you going to do? Use action words: "organize," "coordinate," "plan."

- Why is this important to do at this time?

- How are you going to do it?

Measurable: Your goals should be measurable, so you can see the changes occur. "What gets measured gets managed."[10]

- Measurable: "I want to spend 10 percent less on impulsive purchases in October."

- Not measurable: "I want to lower my impulsivity."

Attainable: Your goals should be attainable. Base goals on personal performance, not external factors you cannot control.

- A goal focused on how your manager reacts is something you cannot control. A goal focused on how you are going to handle their reaction is something you can control.

- State each goal as a positive statement—for example, "I will reduce my impulse purchases by 10 percent" rather than "I don't want to spend as much money as I usually do on impulsive purchases."

Realistic: Your goals should be realistic. They should be challenging yet attainable within the given time frame. Goal setting is a balancing act. If your goals are too difficult, you'll surely fail; if they're too easy, you won't be motivated to pursue them.

- Set goals that require the right amount of effort.

- Too easy says you aren't capable of more.

- Too difficult may be discouraging due to slow progress.

- Avoid others' negative influences. Make sure you associate with people who support you in reaching your goals, build you up, and believe in your abilities.

Time-Bound: Your goals should be time-bound to help give a sense of urgency for action. Time should be measurable and realistic. This will allow you to prioritize your goals and prevent you from getting overwhelmed or stressed out.

- Set a target for each goal: one week, three months, one year.

- This gives a sense of urgency to take action.

- Time must be finite and have an end date.

- Prioritize your goals to avoid feeling overwhelmed. You can't do it all, so choose what is most vital for you to focus on.

* * *

AS YOU MOVE TO the workbook for Step 3: Clarify Your Focus, I want you to think about your current reality (where are you now?) and your end goal (what kind of emotionally strong leader do you want to be?).

Sometimes, clarifying your focus takes a while. It's critical that you figure out where you are right now, how you feel about your current reality, and why you do what you currently do. But equally important is understanding what success will look like for you if you reach your goal, why your goal is important to you, and what you want to walk away with when your goal is achieved.

Go into these exercises with the goal of being open-minded, having compassion for yourself, and being curious, not judgmental. You will walk away with a much deeper understanding of yourself and why you lead the way you do.

WORKBOOK

Step 3:
Clarify Your Focus

Learn Your First *Why*

Record what you consider your three highest and three lowest EI competencies from Exercise 3 (pages 148–49) in the tables below. Consider where each of the strengths or development opportunities come from and how they show up in the workplace.

It's incredibly comforting to know where you learned or did not learn a skill. But make sure you don't use this exercise to blame others (like your parents). I get a lot of comfort in knowing that we are all trying to do our best. Your parents, mentors, or whoever did the best they could with the resources they had. Their choices might not have been perfect or been what you would have chosen, but it is what it is and you are who you are right now. However, knowing that you may not have had good role models in certain areas of your life or did not learn how to build these EI muscles (like, for me, independence) can provide you relief.

But here is the good news: EI can be learned, developed, and enhanced. You just need to commit to doing the work while still having compassion for yourself.

Highest EI Competencies	Where did you learn this strength? (Childhood, life experience, parents, mentors, etc.)	How does this strength show up in the workplace?
1.		
2.		
3.		

Lowest EI Competencies	Where does this development opportunity come from in your life? (Childhood, life experience, parents, mentors, etc.)	How does this development opportunity hold you back in the workplace?
1.		
2.		
3.		

What did you learn from completing this activity?

Learn Your Second *Why*

You now know your strengths and development opportunities as a leader. But do you understand why you genuinely need to change? Do you know what you truly want? What is your end goal? Let's figure out your desired outcome now.

Close your eyes for a moment, and imagine yourself as your best self in a life of zero limitations (within reason—I'm not talking about living on the Moon). Now, open your eyes. What did you see?

Describe, in words, the vision of your best self. Your description should be in first person and any length that feels right to you. Outline not just where you are and what you have but also how you feel. Make it detailed; consider all areas of your life, like your health, career, family, and finances; and weave them into a complete picture.

In the chart on the next page, write out one S.M.A.R.T. goal that focuses on one of the EI competencies you jotted down in Exercise 4 (pages 164–65):

- In the EI competency row, list the one competency that, if changed, will have the biggest impact on your leadership.

- In the Specific row, explain what you will do, why doing it is essential, and how you plan to do it. How will attaining your goal benefit your life? What is the benefit of doing all of this self-development work?

- In the Measurable row, list how you will measure your success. This will help you stay accountable and track your progress regularly. How will you know you are making progress? How long will achieving your goal take? What skills are needed for you to achieve it?

- In the Attainable row, list how you can attain this goal. When goal setting, create attainable goals based on performance rather than on external factors you cannot control. Also, list the support and resources you will need to help you along the journey. This is critical. Always ask for help if you need it. Look for books, resources, and people to support you along the way. This will help you stay accountable.

- In the Realistic row, confirm that the goal is realistic: not too difficult but not too easy. Goals need to be meaningful and realistic to the person trying to achieve them. Make sure you are motivated to do the work involved.

- In the Time-Bound row, give a date of completion for the goal. Set milestone dates, and have regular check-ins with yourself to see how you are progressing.

EI Competency:	
Specific: What will you do? Why do you want to do it? How will you do it? How will it benefit your life?	
Measurable: How will you measure whether you achieve your goal?	
Attainable: How will you attain your goal? What support and resources are available to you?	
Realistic: Is this goal attainable given the time frame? Is it too easy? Is it too difficult? Is this a realistic goal that will keep you motivated?	
Time-Bound: When will you achieve this? What will your milestones be?	

Congratulations! Based on your idealized vision for yourself, you have determined why you want to change and have walked away with a meaningful goal to work toward.

Pause and **Reflect**

Emotion Check-In

 POSITIVE

 HAPPY

 OPTIMISTIC

 INSPIRED

 EMPATHETIC

 EXCITED

 CONFIDENT

 PROUD

 RELIEVED

 CONTENT

 HOPEFUL

 SURPRISED

 CALM

 STRONG

 PASSIONATE

 JEALOUS

 SAD

 INTIMIDATED

 OFFENDED

 FRUSTRATED

 DISCOURAGED

 AFRAID

 INDIFFERENT

 EMBARRASSED

 DISAPPOINTED

 PESSIMISTIC

 RESENTFUL

 CONFUSED

 INSECURE

 OVERWHELMED

Learning your first *why* can be heavy. Determining why you do what you do and uncovering how you learned or did not learn a skill may expose you to some challenging memories from your life. This can be an arduous journey.

However, discovering your second *why* enables you to take ownership of who you are and empowers you to chart your own course and become the emotionally strong leader you want to be.

How do you feel? Use the emotions icons as a guide. The answer can be a combination of any of these feelings or a different emotion altogether.

What is this feeling(s) telling you about yourself?

HETIC DISAPPOINTED INSPIRED PESSIMISTIC EX
RELIEVED JEALOUS CONFUSED STRONG HOPEFU
SITIVE SAD HAPPY INDIFFERENT EMPATHETIC DIS
UD DISCOURAGED CONFIDENT AFRAID CALM REL
TEFUL INTIMIDATED PASSIONATE FRUSTRATED PO
TIC RESENTFUL OVERWHELMED CONTENT PROUD
SURPRISED EMBARRASSED INSECURE GRATEFUL I
INSPIRED PESSIMISTIC EXCITED OPTIMISTIC RE
OUS CONFUSED STRONG HOPEFUL OFFENDED SU
APPY INDIFFERENT EMPATHETIC DISAPPOINTED
RAGED CONFIDENT AFRAID CALM RELIEVED JEAL
IDATED PASSIONATE FRUSTRATED POSITIVE SAD
FUL OVERWHELMED CONTENT PROUD DISCOURA
EMBARRASSED INSECURE GRATEFUL INTIMIDATED
SSIMISTIC EXCITED OPTIMISTIC RESENTFUL OVE
ONG HOPEFUL OFFENDED SURPRISED EMBARRAS
HETIC DISAPPOINTED INSPIRED PESSIMISTIC EX
RELIEVED JEALOUS CONFUSED STRONG HOPEFU
SITIVE SAD HAPPY INDIFFERENT EMPATHETIC DIS
UD DISCOURAGED CONFIDENT AFRAID CALM REL
TEFUL INTIMIDATED PASSIONATE FRUSTRATED PO
TIC RESENTFUL OVERWHELMED CONTENT PROUD
SURPRISED EMBARRASSED INSECURE GRATEFUL I
INSPIRED PESSIMISTIC EXCITED OPTIMISTIC RE
OUS CONFUSED STRONG HOPEFUL OFFENDED SU
APPY INDIFFERENT EMPATHETIC DISAPPOINTED
RAGED CONFIDENT AFRAID CALM RELIEVED JEAL
IDATED PASSIONATE FRUSTRATED POSITIVE SAD
FUL OVERWHELMED CONTENT PROUD DISCOURA
EMBARRASSED INSECURE GRATEFUL INTIMIDATED
SSIMISTIC EXCITED OPTIMISTIC RESENTFUL OVE
ONG HOPEFUL OFFENDED SURPRISED EMBARRAS
HETIC DISAPPOINTED INSPIRED PESSIMISTIC EX
RELIEVED JEALOUS CONFUSED STRONG HOPEFU
SITIVE SAD HAPPY INDIFFERENT EMPATHETIC DIS
UD DISCOURAGED CONFIDENT AFRAID CALM REL
TEFUL INTIMIDATED PASSIONATE FRUSTRATED PO
TIC RESENTFUL OVERWHELMED CONTENT PROUD
SURPRISED EMBARRASSED INSECURE GRATEFUL I
INSPIRED PESSIMISTIC EXCITED OPTIMISTIC RE
OUS CONFUSED STRONG HOPEFUL OFFENDED SU
APPY INDIFFERENT EMPATHETIC DISAPPOINTED

PART VI

Ready, Set, Action!

ONGRATULATIONS ON making it through the gauntlet of self-discovery, consulting with others, and clarifying your focus. That level of self-exploration is exceptionally difficult, and you should be proud of yourself for beginning your inside-out journey and charting the course for your future.

When I took "Silas," a Director of Maintenance for a chocolate manufacturer, through this coaching process, he summarized it best when he said, "in my thirty-plus-year career, I have never experienced such profound insight into how and why I act and feel the way I do in the workplace."

So let's review and celebrate how far you have come.

Step 1: Connect with Yourself

- You first connected with yourself and took a good honest look in the mirror. You determined your strengths and the development opportunities that were getting in the way of you being the emotionally strong leader you always dreamed you could be.

Step 2: Consult with Others

- You were even brave enough to have some honest conversations with others to see whether your self-perception matched how others thought of you.

- You looked for patterns and themes that came out of those important conversations, identifying any gaps or mismatches.

- You picked three EI competencies that are your strengths and three that need your attention.

Step 3: Clarify Your Focus

- You clarified your focus by digging deeper and learning your first *why*. Why do you do what you do? You looked at yourself as an observer and without judgment and discovered why you do the things you do for each of your three highest and lowest EI competencies.

- You determined your second *why*: why you need to change. What kind of leader do you want to become and why? You created a S.M.A.R.T. goal as your key focus and are now getting ready to brainstorm how you are going to make that happen.

In the chapters that follow in Ready, Set, Action! (the last three steps of our self-coaching model), I will guide you to choose the one EI competency that, if changed, will have the biggest impact on your leadership and consider all the options to help you get closer to realizing your goal.

You will also contemplate the barriers keeping you stuck and determine a way to dissolve those roadblocks getting in the way of your success. You will then devise an action plan for yourself, taking your leadership to the next level.

Your action plan will review your motivation level and help you find the support you need. You may stumble, like we all do, along the way. But don't worry, you will even put a plan in place in case you fall off track. This part of our self-coaching process will be turning the work you did in Steps 1 through 3 into a solid course of action.

Your journey has already begun, and now, you are going to start working on your plan, which can change your life. Remember to think about what being an emotionally strong leader looks like for you. Make sure that is prominent in your mind. You are about to embark on living your unlived life.[1] How exciting!

Chapter 10

Interlude–
Possibilities to
Enhance Your
Emotional Intelligence

BEFORE WE DIVE INTO Step 4: Consider Your Possibilities and Barriers, I want to provide you some practical strategies to foster your EI skills in the workplace, at home, and in all areas of your life.

Regardless of what EI competency you choose to improve to become emotionally stronger as a leader, you need to have some tips and strategies you can implement right away to enhance your EI.

Strong leaders use their EI to increase their personal and inter-personal effectiveness. Mastering these skills of working with others can increase your efficacy in organizations, and therefore, in tandem, you will be more fulfilled and successful in all aspects of life.

Not all the tactics in the following pages will be relevant for your situation, but undoubtedly, some ideas and strategies will assist you in enhancing your emotional understanding of your-self and help direct you in becoming the emotionally strong leader you're striving to be.

Improve Your Self-Regard

What lies behind us and what lies before us are tiny matters compared to what lies within us. –ALBERT JAY NOCK[1]

Leaders who have high self-regard have an accurate view of their strengths and development opportunities. They are more likely to have a genuine concern for others, share success, and hold themselves accountable when things go wrong. They are confident in themselves and don't shy away from admitting their development opportunities or mistakes.

Tips and Tools for Increasing Self-Regard:
- Surround yourself with supportive people.
- Integrate more positive habits daily.
- Believe in yourself, and until you do, act as if you do.
- Challenge your self-limiting beliefs.

Surround Yourself with Supportive People

Surround yourself with the people in your life who simply "get you" and love you. When you feel bad about yourself, rely on those supportive people to help you counter your self-limiting beliefs or negative thoughts. Solicit feedback about your strengths from your supporters so you can start to appreciate, as much as they do, your natural talents and personality traits.

Integrate More Positive Habits Daily

This need not be an arduous exercise—in fact, that would defeat the purpose of this building block for increasing your self-regard. The best way to add positive daily habits is to keep it simple, especially at first. Identify the areas in which you are looking to grow or change, and find small ways you can incorporate a new habit or routine into an already existing structure. Do you want to improve your outlook on life? Why not incorporate a daily gratitude statement with your family before dinner? Looking to exercise more? Perhaps plan a walk to fetch a coffee after lunch? The possibilities for small positive habits are endless if you plan and tie them to things you already do.

Believe in Yourself, and until You Do, Act as If You Do

You are capable of achieving amazing things. Believe that you can, dedicate yourself to taking steps toward what you want, and work hard. Create a vision in your mind's eye. That vision will help you think through your action plan and how your dreams will materialize. Until you feel confident in yourself, act as if you are. At times, you may believe everyone can see your insecurity. But here's the wonderful truth. It's invisible—it's just a thought. As long as you don't act on that thought, no one can see it. Just act as a confident person would, and start noticing the results.

Challenge Your Self-Limiting Beliefs

Our self-limiting beliefs can control our life choices—what we choose to do and not do. We need to put those negative beliefs aside and work on not letting them rule our life. These destructive beliefs get in your way of being the best version of yourself. With that in mind, think about what you *can* do, and rather than letting your self-limiting beliefs continue to damage you emotionally, learn to reframe a previously negative mindset into a more positive outlook in your life. For instance, are you looking at any situation through a negative lens? How could you turn this around and interpret the same set of events in a more positive framework?

Boost Your Self-Actualization

Your core values provide the compass that keeps you moving in the right direction. —SUSAN DAVID[2]

Leaders practice self-actualization by continuing to improve themselves. Self-actualization enables leaders to bring creativity, innovation, and an open mind into the workplace. It relates to a motivation to optimize both their performance and that of their teams. Leaders who are strong in self-actualization often participate in activities with meaning and are aligned with their own values, which leave them feeling satisfied, energized, and motivated. They are passionate and enthusiastic and strive to be their best.

Tips and Tools for Increasing Self-Actualization:

- Take time to rest.
- Learn something new.
- Exercise your way into happiness.
- Discover your passions.

Take Time to Rest

Technology has made it possible to stay connected with each other 24/7; messages and emails come flooding in at any time, and we feel inclined to respond, even if our workday has ended. But remember, we are humans, not machines. We need time to rest, rejuvenate, and reconnect with ourselves. Getting proper rest requires discipline. So take some much-needed time for yourself and schedule rest.

Learn Something New

Learning something new keeps your mind engaged; you are exercising your brain and improving your memory, concentration, and ability to problem solve. Learning expands your world view and perspectives and helps you gain skill sets, opening more doors for you.

One excellent way to broaden your social circle is to take a class or pursue a new hobby, which will increase your likelihood of making friends with similar interests.

Exercise Your Way into Happiness

Study after study has shown the positive effect being active has on our brains. Exercise produces endorphins and proteins that make us feel happier—it increases our cognitive abilities, helps us sleep better, enhances our self-perception, and improves our whole sense of well-being.[3] It puts more pep in our step every day. On days that you don't feel like exercising, go for a five-minute walk (I mean, if you can't find five minutes, that points to a larger problem, no?). Getting a daily dose of fresh air and activity can help you feel good about yourself.

Discover Your Passions

Ask yourself what fills your bucket and is meaningful to you. Being self-actualized means first discovering and then pursuing what matters to you. That is what fulfillment is all about. Not sure what matters to you or what you are passionate about? Start with determining what you value. Your values are your guiding principles. They determine what you think is important and can dictate how you choose to live your life. See if you can take action and live more congruently with what you value. In essence, that will make you feel more fulfilled.

Enhance Your Emotional Self-Awareness

You've always been what you are. That's not new. What you'll get used to is knowing it. —CASSANDRA CLARE[4]

Leaders who are emotionally self-aware can easily recognize and understand their triggers. Having high emotional self-awareness allows leaders to be in touch with their feelings, take the emotional charge out of situations when triggered, and label an emotion for what it is without getting too emotionally invested. Without emotional self-awareness, leaders may react impulsively, making themselves, and possibly others, victims of their feelings.

Tips and Tools for Increasing Emotional Self-Awareness:

- Identify your triggers.
- Learn to recognize your feelings and pay attention to body sensations.
- Increase your emotional vocabulary, and determine the nuances.
- Be an observer.

Identify Your Triggers

Once you have named the emotion, figure out what provoked that feeling. What might be the underlying root of your emotion? Situations, people, or events that very quickly cause an emotional reaction are known as triggers.[5] Everyone's triggers are different, often based on personal history and experience. Understanding what pushes your buttons allows you to be in the driver's seat of your emotions and is an excellent way to determine how you will respond in advance when triggered.

Learn to Recognize Your Feelings and Pay Attention to Body Sensations

Try to identify your emotions throughout the day and pay attention to your body's response to those feelings—your body's reaction to emotion can have actual physical cues or side effects. A few examples might be a headache from stress, body sweat from anxiety, or a heart racing from fear. If you have a hard time recognizing how you feel, focus on the physical cues your body is telling you, then try to trace back and see if you can identify the emotion you may be feeling.

Increase Your Emotional Vocabulary, and Determine the Nuances

Many people do not have a robust emotional vocabulary. Use the emotions icons at the end of each workbook so you can learn to label how you are feeling at any given point. Tools like this may seem silly, but learning the broad range of feelings beyond happy, sad, and mad will help you uncover the nuances of your many moods. In addition, pay attention to the level of intensity you are feeling. For instance, when feeling happy, you may feel elated when the intensity is high and simply pleased when it is low. When the intensity is somewhere in the middle, you may be satisfied. All these feelings are happiness but at different levels of intensity.

Be an Observer

Imagine watching yourself like a director would be watching the actors in a film. Seeing yourself from an outside perspective enables you to observe your feelings objectively. If you allow yourself to view the feeling separately, you are giving yourself an opportunity to understand what that emotion is trying to tell you about yourself. This emotional self-awareness may help you respond in a manner more fitting to the situation at hand as it helps you separate your emotions from your reactions to said emotions.

Polish Your Emotional Expression

Your emotions are the slaves to your thoughts, and you are the slave to your emotions. —ELIZABETH GILBERT[6]

Leaders who have high emotional expression find that using the right words, tone, facial expressions, and body language effectively conveys their emotions constructively. This helps evoke emotion and passion in others, allows others to feel closer to them, and strengthens and deepens relationships. Using emotive communication ignites a spark in others and drives them to move forward. Leaders with high emotional expression are also mindful not to let their heightened, negative emotions take over and leak into difficult conversations.

Tips and Tools for Increasing Emotional Expression:

- Be specific.
- Describe the behavior first, then your feelings.
- Avoid the word "but."
- Stop and breathe.

Be Specific

It's essential to be very specific when describing how you feel. Don't use vague, one-word descriptors, such as "good" or "bad"; this is not specific enough and is more about a state of being than a feeling. To reduce the chance of being misunderstood, specify the degree or intensity of your feelings—for instance, "I am furious" versus "I am annoyed." When experiencing mixed emotions, express both of them and attempt to separate and explain what each feeling is about. For example, say, "I have mixed feelings. I am grateful that you invited me, but I feel nervous about meeting new people at the party."

Describe the Behavior First, Then Your Feelings

When expressing your feelings, first describe the specific behavior that evoked what you are feeling and then express your feelings. When sharing your feelings, claim the "I." Use "I feel" statements. This can help prevent the person on the receiving end from becoming immediately defensive when they hear, "I am angry with you" versus saying, "when you hung up the phone, I felt angry."

Avoid the Word "But"

Avoid the word "but" as it negates whatever comes before it. Everything you've said before "but" will be diminished and ignored by the person you've told it to—for example, "I love you, but I am moving out." "But" establishes a relationship between two ideas wherein one contradicts the other. A simple replacement for "but" is "and." "And" is also a great alternative because it suggests a positive perspective versus negating what was said before it—for instance, "I love you and

I am moving out." Hearing this still might hurt, but eliminating the "but" eases the pain a little.

Stop and Breathe

Whenever you are overcome with emotion, such as happiness or sadness, stop and breathe through it to ground yourself. Once you have a clear mind, you can start to communicate your emotions. Name the emotion you are feeling but remember to tame it.[7] Say it without the emotional charge behind it. For instance, rather than yelling, "I am furious with you!" simply say calmly, "I feel furious." Don't react and be a victim of your emotions. Be bigger and stronger than your feelings, and control how you express yourself.

Strengthen Your Assertiveness

In business as in life, you don't get what you deserve, you get what you negotiate. —CHESTER KARRASS[8]

In the workplace, assertiveness allows leaders to contribute in meetings by addressing issues directly and effectively. Assertiveness is the quality of being confident and self-assured without being aggressive, being forthright and saying what you need to say when you need to say it. Leaders who have high assertiveness are more likely to respectfully speak up, share ideas, ask questions, challenge opinions, confront negative behavior, and fight for what they deem essential, but in a non-offensive manner.

Tips and Tools for Increasing Assertiveness:
- Show confidence in your body language and tone of voice.
- Remember that clarity is kindness.
- Be honest, and speak your truth.
- Set boundaries.

Show Confidence in Your Body Language and Tone of Voice

Leaders who are high in assertiveness feel confident and show this in their body language. They stand straight, steady, and lean in slightly, are grounded, and directly face the people they speak with while maintaining eye contact. They don't fidget, look down at the ground, or raise their voice and yell. They play around with the inflections of their voice to command attention, get their point across, and appear more reliable. Therefore, watch that your voice pitch does not rise at the end of a sentence. If it does, it sounds like you are asking a question. Slightly altering your pitch can have a powerful effect, and others will have more faith in what you say.

Remember That Clarity Is Kindness

Assertive people are open, direct, and emotionally honest and expressive. Assertive leaders rehearse what they will say and keep it clear, concise, direct, and simple. They don't expect people to read their minds. When expressing their opinion assertively, they state two things: 1) their opinion and 2) an action plan. Use this template for a clear, assertive response: "In my opinion, I think _____. We should do _____." You are stating your opinion and offering an action plan to back it up. Be deliberate and specific, stating your intention behind why you are saying what you are saying. As Brené Brown states in *Dare to Lead: Brave Work. Tough Conversations. Whole Hearts.*, "Clear is kind. Unclear is unkind."[9] So remember, being assertive is being clear and kind.

Be Honest, and Speak Your Truth

Remember the old saying "honesty is the best policy"? If you believe in what you say, being assertive will come naturally. Keep in mind that you do not want to come off as rude, so make sure you're honest but respectful. Have confidence in your beliefs and opinions, and never feel sorry for the way you think. State your assertion by using "I" statements. This "lets others know what you're thinking or feeling without sounding accusatory. For instance, say, 'I disagree,' rather than, 'you're wrong.'"[10] Assertive leaders think before they speak and use honest and accurate information. Being an emotionally strong leader means that you speak your truth respectfully and professionally.

Set Boundaries

Boundaries are the limits you create for yourself which help you determine what is reasonable versus unreasonable behavior. When you are assertive, you have no problem speaking up and stating what you will and won't allow in relationships with others, but you do so respectfully. Setting boundaries empowers you to know when you need to say no to a request or when to disagree with others professionally. Remember to let others know what is okay and what is not okay.

Raise Your Level of Independence

Being brave enough to be alone frees you up to invite people into your life because you want them, not because you need them. –MANDY HALE[11]

Leaders who have high independence are self-directed and able to think for themselves, and generate ideas while still being open to input from others. They know when to be self-reliant, but also know when to ask for help and utilize their team's ideas. Independent leaders are confident, self-assured, and self-responsible. This confidence in themselves translates to feeling certain about their actions and reactions. Instinctually, these people trust their ability to make good decisions.

Tips and Tools for Increasing Independence:

- Resist automatically asking for advice.
- Practice giving yourself reassurance rather than seeking it externally.
- Don't be afraid of failure.
- Schedule some "me" time.

Resist Automatically Asking for Advice

To resist asking others for advice, get your own information. Being well-informed by reading, watching, and listening to the news from various sources will keep you from being a follower and make you a leader with independent thoughts. This allows you to rely on your thoughts rather than being at the mercy of others. Trust your judgments and ideas. Before getting others to weigh in with their ideas and input, try to make your own decisions first.

Practice Giving Yourself Reassurance Rather Than Seeking It Externally

Stop caring about what other people think. Similarly, stop worrying about other people's judgments. People pleasers almost always end up feeling frustrated and taken for granted. By shifting your boundaries to satisfy others, you open yourself up to feelings of resentment when those that you've accommodated don't reciprocate or acknowledge your efforts. When you feel the need for approval, become your own best friend and practice self-validation. Give yourself the reassurance you need rather than seeking it from others. Ask yourself what you want to hear from others and then practice saying those words to yourself.

Don't Be Afraid of Failure

Dependence on others often results from a fear of failure. However, learning from failure helps us to succeed in the future. Failing is unavoidable, but each time we pick ourselves up from failure, we become more emotionally resilient. It also increases the compassion we have for ourselves and others. Don't be afraid to take risks. Never going out on a limb limits you to where you are and shuts out the infinite possibilities and opportunities that await you.

Schedule Some "Me" Time

Plan your day around you. Make a list of what you want to do, need to do, and should have already done. Protect and guard your alone time to do the things most important to you. It's essential to learn to enjoy your own company and feel comfortable handling things on your own. Make yourself a focus and a priority just as you would the other vital things in your life. Drop all the outside influences and proactively block out time for you.

Strengthen Your Interpersonal Relationships

Building and repairing relationships are long-term investments.
—STEPHEN R. COVEY[12]

Successful leaders are able to create strong connections by nurturing, building, and maintaining great, mutually satisfying relationships. They know that by using their interpersonal relationships skills, they can enhance communication in the workplace and build effective and collaborative relationships and associations with all levels across the organization.

Tips and Tools for Increasing Interpersonal Relationships:

- Be willing to open up and share about yourself.
- Be open-minded.
- Ask questions, and practice active listening.
- Schedule time to build relationships.

Be Willing to Open Up and Share about Yourself

By sharing your life experiences, opinions, and challenges, you are creating a psychologically safe place for others to speak up and share theirs. The deeper the conversation, the more of a connection will be built. To build trust, you need to take risks first as a leader and be vulnerable. Taking off your corporate mask and being honest with someone is critical for creating an open and trusting connection.

Be Open-Minded

Every person is different, and they may have different views and opinions than you. Having an open mind and welcoming different views will allow your relationships to grow and become more meaningful. Ask questions, using a friendly tone and smile, to understand where others are coming from, especially those who may be very different from you.

Ask Questions, and Practice Active Listening

Actively listening and asking questions shows others you care. Slow down and let others talk before interjecting about yourself. People respond better to those who truly listen. If you talk less and listen more, you'll quickly become known as trustworthy. Trust bonds are some of the strongest and most crucial when building dynamic, equitable relationships.

Schedule Time to Build Relationships

To develop good workplace relationships, you need to invest the time. When you're able to connect more personally with your colleagues, this investment will pay off in dividends.[13] Devote a portion of your day to build relationships. Even if it's only five minutes, interactions help build the foundation of a good relationship. Building strong, genuine, and trusting relationships needs time and care but goes a long way. Invest the time and energy in getting to know people personally and finding out precisely what makes them tick and what makes them who they are.

Amplify Your Empathy

Empathy is a shared emotional experience. —MARC BRACKETT[14]

Leaders need to display empathy, meaning they need to be sensitive to what, how, and why people feel the way they do. Being empathetic is being able to pick up on emotional cues and respond appropriately. Leaders must "emotionally monitor" others on a moment-by-moment basis. When people feel seen, heard, and cared for, that significantly impacts job satisfaction and the employee experience.

Tips and Tools for Increasing Empathy:

- Have limitless curiosity about others.
- Give others the benefit of the doubt.
- Listen carefully to nonverbal cues.
- Challenge your prejudices and preconceived notions.

Have Limitless Curiosity about Others

Highly empathetic people have a voracious appetite for knowing about others. Make sure that when asking questions, you suspend your judgment so you can truly understand another person's lived experience. EI is about being curious and not judgmental. Ask others questions to help you understand their *why*—why they think, say, or do the things they think, say, or do. By knowing why people are the way they are, you will have more compassion and empathy for others.

Give Others the Benefit of the Doubt

The mind is negatively oriented,[15] so giving others the benefit of the doubt takes intention and effort. In all situations, assuming positive intent and considering an alternative or generous interpretation of the situation will help you feel a little lighter as you learn to accept others with greater ease. Remember, the next time someone cuts you off when driving, put your generous hat on and ask yourself what might be going on for this person. Perhaps, the other person did not realize the lane was ending. The best practice is always to give others the benefit of the doubt.

Listen Carefully to Nonverbal Cues

When you actively listen, you pay attention to what others are saying, what they mean, and the underlying feelings or thoughts behind their words. Try hard not to interrupt others when speaking. This will allow them to talk more and lead the conversation. Besides listening to their words, try to read their gestures, take in their emotions and thoughts, and read between the lines. It's about being present and focused on not only what they say and do but also on what they don't say and do. Remember, 55 percent of what they are saying can be observed in their body language, 38 percent can be heard in their tone of voice, and only 7 percent comes with their words.[16] So when spending time with someone, watch what they are *not* saying in words but are communicating nonverbally.

Challenge Your Prejudices and Preconceived Notions

We all make assumptions and have biased beliefs that prevent us from appreciating what makes others unique. Challenge your preconceived notions and prejudices by focusing on similarities, not differences. Learn to consider other people's point of view, especially those whose beliefs you don't share, and start to see the value others bring. Having an open mind allows you to approach the situation with a growth mindset versus a fixed mindset.[17] In this way, problems become opportunities, assumptions are challenged, and thought-provoking questions come to the fore.

Augment Your Social Responsibility

Again the greatest use of a human was to be useful. Not to consume, not to watch, but to do something for someone else that improved their life, even for a few minutes. –DAVE EGGERS[18]

Leaders active in social responsibility are dependable, have a genuine concern for others, are accommodating and supportive, and contribute to society. Those high in social responsibility like to give back, help others, and positively influence others. By recognizing that their every action and utterance affects those around them, these leaders become more conscious of their words and actions and are therefore more likely to act in a socially responsible way.

Tips and Tools for Increasing Social Responsibility:

- Determine your personal contribution to society.
- Align your values to your actions.
- Volunteer your time.
- Use your genius to help others.

Determine Your Personal Contribution to Society

It's time to define what you see wrong with society. Pick an issue that you are passionate about and want to get involved with. Ask yourself how you will choose to make a difference in the world. After you define your vision of making a difference, set an end goal and make an actionable plan to achieve it. How will you help others? What does that look like?

Align Your Values to Your Actions

The first thing you need to do is evaluate your vision. Who are you, and who do you strive to be? Then, determine what your core values are. Consider where you would fall on a scale of 0 to 10 for each value, with 10 living the value to your fullest potential and 0 not at all. Are you living in alignment with your values? Throughout the day, when you are making decisions, ask yourself if each choice is in alignment with your values. When you know who you want to be, start doing things in alignment with who you want to become. Ask yourself that question often, and if what you're doing is not aligned with becoming a more helpful and better person, don't do it.

Volunteer Your Time

Everybody needs help at some point in their lives. Learning to extend a helping hand is great and brings its own rewards. Anticipating the needs of others and engaging in helping meet those needs is a wonderful way to share your time. As Elizabeth Dove of Imagine Canada explains, make choices and take actions "every day to build a stronger, kinder [world]—making ethical purchases, engaging in causes [you] care about, and greening [your] daily commute. Volunteering ... whether formal or informal, long- or short-term, recurring or one-off activities, build[s] confidence, competence, connections and community."[19]

Use Your Genius to Help Others

Consider your unique talents. How could you be using them to help others? True fulfillment in life comes from being socially aware and engaging in activities that we are passionate about—giving back benefits ourselves and others. When we focus on serving others and not just ourselves, our troubles become smaller as our sense of purpose becomes greater. Where could your talents be helpful outside of your life and benefit others? Winston Churchill said it best: "We make a living by what we get, but we make a life by what we give."

Advance Your Problem-Solving Skills

You don't drown by falling in the water. You drown by staying there!
—EDWIN LOUIS COLE[20]

Leaders with excellent problem-solving skills don't often act rashly when strong feelings surge through their minds. Instead of acting out during an emotional moment, they take a few simple steps to calm themselves. Good problem-solving skills involve quickly sorting through the information emotions provide to develop a course of action to help, not hurt, the process; in many cases, leaders are doing this while experiencing stress and pressure.

Tips and Tools for Increasing Problem-Solving:

- Don't react immediately.
- Share how you feel.
- Think big picture.
- Reframe your thinking.

Don't React Immediately

Emotional triggers are everywhere. Make sure you do not respond right away. If you do, you may regret it. Take a deep breath to alleviate the overpowering impulse. If your emotions are getting the best of you, take yourself out of the problem. Visualize yourself as an observer, not a participant, almost like you are floating out of your body and looking down on the situation from above. As you shift from the participant's role to the observer's, notice the corresponding shift in your emotional state. Seeing the situation from an external point of view can remove the emotion from it and help you know how the situation affects you and how you are affecting others. This can be a very calming exercise to practice to help you think more rationally.

Share How You Feel

When you recognize and understand how your emotions are tied to a problem, make sure you calmly vocalize them so they are not coloring how you should solve the issue. If you don't let people know how you feel about the challenge, the problem can escalate to an even bigger issue. By talking your emotions out with someone or writing them in your journal, you are healthily releasing them.

Think Big Picture

All events in your life—positive and negative—serve a higher purpose. Trust that even in emotionally upsetting moments, there exists a fundamental purpose which you may not understand or appreciate until some time has passed. Try consulting resources and experts when entering new territory, seeing how others view the problem, and asking for their insights and input. Consider these diverse perspectives to stimulate a different way of thinking about the problem you are trying to solve.

Reframe Your Thinking

Negative emotions can trigger other recurring negative thoughts. When you recognize a negative thought, push it from your mind and replace it with a positive one. This reframing will help you find an alternative view of what is happening. When faced with an adverse event, try to actively shift your perspective by considering realities that call into question the story you are telling yourself.[21]

Magnify Your Reality Testing

Get connected to your reality, your real life instead of your emotionally soaked self-talk narrative about your life. —GARY JOHN BISHOP[22]

Reality testing is the act of "tuning into" a moment or situation and looking at it objectively—as it truly is. Leaders must stand back and size up a situation, decreasing emotion and increasing logic. By removing the feeling, they think more rationally, and they are more open to discussions. Removing the emotion from experience can also be calming.

Tips and Tools for Increasing Reality Testing:

- Reflect on your perceptions.
- Check your assumptions with others.
- Press pause when triggered.
- Determine your *why*.

Reflect on Your Perceptions

Eyewitness testimony is well known to be marred by the witness's perceptions. The same goes for our general perceptions. The reality we create based on the perceptions we hold feels very real and true to us, but similar to the testimony from an eyewitness, it isn't necessarily true and factual.[23] Notice whether your perceptions are coloring your interpretations. Ask yourself what story you are telling yourself about this situation or person. Being aware that your reality may not be everyone else's reality is the first step.

Check Your Assumptions with Others

Checking in with others will help free you from your own cycle of thinking and assist you in seeing things from a different perspective. Ask others not only *how* they see something but *why* they see it that way. Challenge your viewpoints, solicit other perspectives, and resist the urge to be defensive or judgmental.

Press Pause When Triggered

Take a deep breath and pause for a few seconds whenever you feel triggered by someone, something, or some situation. This grounding of yourself in the present moment will give you an opportunity to choose how to respond. You do not need to respond immediately either. If you need time, politely say that you will think about things and address the issue at a later time.

Determine Your *Why*

Sakichi Toyoda, the founder of what is now the Toyota Motor Corporation, is popularly referenced today for his critical problem-solving technique, the Five Whys.[24] The basis of this approach is to repeat asking and answering the question "why?" five times. Through this repeated introspection, the nature of the problem, as well as its root cause and potential solution, becomes apparent. Using this approach, ask yourself "why" you think or feel the way you do. A helpful trick is to continually insert the word "because" before every answer. By doing this, you will be digging deeper into your reasoning and rationale, and you can determine the thought process you used to come to that original conclusion.

Heighten Your Impulse Control

For the great doesn't happen through impulse alone, and is a succession of little things that are brought together. —VINCENT VAN GOGH[25]

There is great wisdom in self-control—delaying gratification or hanging in and not reacting immediately often brings great benefit. Hasty actions can be costly. Leaders with high impulse control take the time to stop and think before they act or react. They have more self-regulation and control of their emotional responses, and they tend to be highly tolerant and more patient.

Tips and Tools for Increasing Impulse Control:

- Be emotionally self-aware.
- Create space between your trigger and response.
- Talk to a dependable and compassionate friend.
- Engage in activities that rejuvenate you.

Be Emotionally Self-Aware

When an impulse arises, many of us tend to respond immediately, leaving us no time to stop and think about what we are doing. It is essential to take an inventory of your triggers before they happen and think about how you feel toward the situation before taking action. Identify any prompts that may be causing you to act impulsively. Are you hungry? Tired? Stressed out? Also, remember to look for those physical indicators of a stress reaction. Being mindful about what is going on for you internally can help you react and respond appropriately externally.

Create Space between Your Trigger and Response

You cannot stop yourself from being triggered. Emotions are going to happen. However, your task is not to stop having emotions, but instead to self-regulate and make space for choice before you respond outwardly. The best thing to do is to increase the space between the trigger event and your response. If you can't, you will likely respond impulsively. Creating space can include asking for some time to think, taking deep breaths, or meditating.

Talk to a Dependable and Compassionate Friend

Situations like these are exactly what friends are for. A good vent session is sometimes all you need to reduce the chance your negative thoughts and words will turn into impulsive actions. Friends are also important if you do give in to an impulse. They can help you deal with any disappointment you might feel by having acted impulsively. Find a friend who has compassion for you and can show you how to have the same for yourself.

Engage in Activities That Rejuvenate You

Like a hot towel on an international flight, an activity that freshens us up is needed from time to time. Renewal behaviors rejuvenate us by the sheer fact that they take us out of a stress-inducing head-space and force us to reset. This increases our productivity, energy, and ultimately, emotional resilience.[26] Try taking short walks, stretching, practicing deep breathing exercises, or watching a funny video.

Develop Your Flexibility

A tree that is unbending is easily broken. —LAO TZU[27]

Flexibility allows leaders to quickly adapt when the situation is unfamiliar and unpredictable. Being flexible means dealing effectively and appropriately with emotions when faced with change, uncertainty, and stress. Mentally strong leaders with high flexibility are open to new ideas and tend to go with the flow. They are less judgmental and emotionally uptight and have the stamina to bend their brains. The more ways the mind is stretched, the more flexibility and agility increase.

Tips and Tools for Increasing Flexibility:

- Reflect on areas where you act rigidly, and try something new.
- Open your mind, and explore the alternatives.
- Change the context or environment, and your mind will shift.
- Challenge your thoughts, and watch your words.

Reflect on Areas Where You Act Rigidly, and Try Something New

Do you know where you are highly flexible and where you maintain a rigid stance? Analyze yourself, and in the areas where you are rigid, do your best to be flexible. Keep a diary, jot down your impressions and observations, and then review. How did your attempts to gain flexibility feel? Did adjusting get easier or remain challenging? Making minor adjustments in your life to spice up your daily routine can be novel, and that can contribute to brain growth and development. So try something new.[28]

Open Your Mind, and Explore the Alternatives

Seeking alternative solutions to problems will enable you to discover and act on new ideas, and this is the foundation of flexibility. Being able to pivot when things do not go your way or the future looks bleak allows you to adopt a growth mindset.[29] By turning problems into challenges and seeking alternative solutions to fix what isn't working, you will make your mind agile and increase your ability to think quickly in tough circumstances.

Change the Context or Environment, and Your Mind Will Shift

To help you improve your cognitive flexibility, consider changing where you are physically.[30] Physical perspective can influence how you think and feel, and changing it can help when you are in a negative behavior loop. When speaking with colleagues, try inviting them to sit in your chair while you sit on the other side of your desk. Consider trying new routes to work or switching up your lunchtime routine. Doing so can help you reframe your thoughts and get you unstuck from your negative or unhelpful mindset.[31]

Challenge Your Thoughts, and Watch Your Words

We speak to ourselves internally but don't often listen to what we are telling ourselves when we do. Become aware of what you are thinking and saying to yourself about yourself. If the record in your head is a negative one, flip it. You do not need to be attached to a certain way of thinking. Simply shifting your perspective and listening to what you are saying might be enough to help you realize that changing your thought patterns can change the words you speak.

Hike Up Your Stress Tolerance

Stress is caused by being "here" but wanting to be "there," or being in the present but wanting to be in the future. —ECKHART TOLLE[32]

Life comes with stresses that drain energy. Like everyone else, leaders can't remove stress altogether, so they must aim to boost their ability to cope with stress so that they can face more considerable challenges with more confidence. Stress tolerance assists leaders with managing demanding workloads, establishing clear priorities, meeting deadlines, and performing well under pressure.

Tips and Tools for Increasing Stress Tolerance:

- Prioritize daily tasks, and eliminate nonessentials.
- Build your emotional resilience.
- Leverage your energy.
- Engage in self-care.

Prioritize Daily Tasks, and Eliminate Nonessentials

Organizing your daily priorities can reduce a major source of stress. Creating to-do lists and organizing tasks by priority will help you understand what needs to be done, what can wait, and what can be delegated. It will also show you whether you have too many tasks. If that is the case, be comfortable asking for help.

Build Your Emotional Resilience

When we are busy, we respond by taking on more, not less. This creates situations where we burn out our brains because we have no opportunity to build our emotional resilience. To develop your emotional resiliency, try these ideas:

- Practice relaxation techniques.

  Your body is not a machine. It won't function well if you don't give it time to rest. Try to meditate or practice other deep breathing techniques.

- Be grateful.

  Start a gratitude journal, and every day, write five things you are thankful for.

- Spend quality time with the people you care about.

  Build solid relationships to increase the level of support around you.

Leverage Your Energy

Remember, time is finite (there are only twenty-four hours in a day), but your energy is not. Are you a morning person or a nighthawk? When you have a full workload, it is advantageous to know when you do your best work (when you are most energized) so you can prioritize your schedule to work on the most demanding tasks when you are at your best. Save your downtime for less demanding duties.

Engage in Self-Care

Taking care of your body and mind will enable you to become more stress tolerant. A healthy diet, regular exercise, and solid sleep help mitigate the stress and damage our bodies deal with daily. Also, set boundaries with others by learning to say no to tasks you can't complete. Schedule quiet time between meetings, and make sure you unplug from your workday so the lines between work and home are not blurred.

Lift Your Optimism

We are all in the gutter, but some of us are looking at the stars.
—OSCAR WILDE[33]

When leaders believe anything is possible, they eliminate barriers to achievement. When they model this behavior, it causes others around them to feel that they can also achieve at a high level. Optimistic people tend to expect good things to happen and anticipate the best positive outcomes in any situation. They trust that things will turn out well, which helps ward off stress.

Tips and Tools for Increasing Optimism:

- Set small, realistic goals you can achieve.
- Accept that failures will happen.
- Phone a friend, and talk through your negative thoughts.
- Add positivity practices to your daily routine.

Set Small, Realistic Goals You Can Achieve

To improve your mindset, you must balance realistic and aspirational goals by outlining where you are, where you want to be, and how you plan to get there. When it comes to enhancing optimism, you can dream big but start small. Taking baby steps to larger goals is a simple way to boost your confidence as you achieve the goals you set for yourself.

Accept That Failures Will Happen

You will mess up. However, how you choose to recover from your missteps can lead to an optimistic outlook. Failing is simply part of learning. So when it happens, don't stop! Even if you don't feel optimistic about having failed at something, finding the knowledge contained in the mistake will help boost your feelings of optimism.

Phone a Friend, and Talk through Your Negative Thoughts

Share your ups and downs. Lean on a friend when you find yourself ruminating over the same negative thoughts. By sharing them with your friend, you will be able to let them go. Sometimes, simply speaking your negative thoughts out loud can help you hear them for what they truly are, just thoughts and not facts.

Add Positivity Practices to Your Daily Routine

Positivity can feel hard to come by when you have low optimism. Similar to taking baby steps toward your goals, find small ways to feel good about yourself, because once you do, seeing gloomy things in a brighter light becomes easier. To challenge your negative, self-limiting beliefs, write out positive affirmations, keep a gratitude journal, or share the positive highlights of your day with family.

* * *

NOW THAT YOU HAVE some tips and strategies to help you enhance all fifteen of your EI competencies, let's create an action plan that works for you. In the following pages, you will take definitive steps toward meaningful change that lasts a lifetime.

Chapter 11

Step 4: Consider Your Possibilities and Barriers

THIS PORTION OF our self-coaching model helps you focus on the solution to reach your S.M.A.R.T. goal by considering what is possible and examining what is holding you back or is providing a challenge to be overcome.

Shifting habitual practices is difficult and takes time, dedication, and discipline. It's about getting you ready because the real work is about to begin. Considering your possibilities and barriers is about getting you comfortable with being uncomfortable. It is not going to be easy, but you can be uncomfortable and brave at the same time— and you'll need to try a new way of doing things.

This journey of self-development is hard, but it will be worth it. Trust me. Since having undergone this process numerous times myself, I know that my life is so much better now that I have done the work and I am on the other side. For instance, like some of you, I really don't want to work out in a gym five times a week. That's a lot of time and commitment. However, I'm confident everyone would enjoy the results of great health and more energy from all of that exercise. The same holds true for leadership.

In Step 4, I'll be challenging you to try different approaches, shift your mindset, and build new skills. None of that will be easy, especially if you're used to behaving and communicating in a certain way. But every leader wants the result of this kind of self-development work—to be an exemplary leader who empowers employees to be positive team players, self-motivated, and dependable. Nurturing those kinds of employees creates a profitable, productive organization with happy and engaged employees who are committed to doing meaningful work and making a difference in the world. Who doesn't want that? But it takes work.

An Iterative Process

In my experience, most people don't know what to do or where to start when it comes to fulfilling goals. They know where they want to be but rarely know how they will get there and what the steps look like along the way.

So let's step outside yourself and coach yourself to find out what to do next to close the gap between where you are and where you want to be. Ask yourself what advice you would give your best friend if they had the same goal. When I ask this question, most people can find possibilities to reach their goals, but sometimes, their brain is clouded because they are so engulfed in their personal challenges.

This process is an iterative, two-step cycle consisting of brainstorming the possibilities for action and then outlining the barriers in the way of that action. Discussing the barriers that may be getting in your way of reaching your goal will enable you to discover what real issue(s) is keeping you stuck. It is a constant process as identifying barriers may open up new possibilities, which themselves will likely have barriers. In the end, your barriers provide you the opportunity to brainstorm to dissolve the roadblocks getting in the way of your success.

In the following workbook, you'll start by brainstorming possibilities for action. The best way to do this is to list all of your options that could reduce or even close the gap between where you are and

Barriers =
Real Issues

where you want to go. Identify potential options or courses of action for reaching your goal, weighing the advantages and disadvantages of each. Brainstorm as many options as you can think of, and narrow down what the best solution is to reach your goal. Remember to quiet your mind, listen non-judgmentally, and don't problem solve but simply brainstorm all possible options.

In this step, you're looking to make the lengthiest possible list of different courses of action. Don't look for a "right" answer, and don't worry about the quality of your answers. Quantity rules here.[1] Be careful not to squash ideas or arrive at a conclusion too early. Here, we want to get the creative juices flowing and brainstorm as many options as possible.

Once you have completed that process, it is time to dig deep into what is going to get in your way of realizing each option. What obstacles are preventing you from pursuing your goal and moving forward?

Think of the possible barriers that may get in your way of reaching your goal. Here, you will illuminate what is keeping you stuck, and you'll brainstorm further to find solutions to those problems. Remember that by determining what the barriers are, you are drilling down to the real issues getting in your way of success.

Many of us carry "implicit assumptions, many of which we are barely conscious of."[2] These assumptions restrict us from achieving our goals or limit our thought process to come up with creative solutions.[3] Determining what is keeping us stuck tends to be the key to figuring out how to achieve our wildest dreams.

 CLIENT STORY: "ATHENA"

Athena was a Director of Communications for a large petroleum company. I had privately conducted and debriefed EQ assessments with all senior leaders and was to run a two-day EI retreat, where leadership would come together to gain a deeper understanding about the members of their team.

Athena was anxious. She imagined having to expose all of her "weaknesses" and be critiqued by a group of "perfect people" (her words). What she quickly learned was that each one of those "perfect people" also had shortcomings, even though some of those shortcomings were different from hers.

After the retreat, Athena and I began a six-month private coaching program, where we worked through job-related issues that were keeping her stuck. On the outside, Athena looked like she had it all. But on the inside, she struggled. Her boss had destroyed her self-confidence over the five years they had worked together, and she did not have the courage to speak up and let him know how his comments, feedback, demands, and actions were affecting her.

She had no trouble identifying the problem, but when we reached this step in the coaching model (considering her possibilities), she was frozen with fear. She could not think of one possible solution to resolve the tension between her boss and her until I asked this simple question: "What is it costing you if you do nothing?"

As soon as I asked her that, Athena was motivated to think of possibilities. As scared as she was to confront him, she knew there was a better path forward. Learning about her *why*—why she lacked self-confidence and assertiveness in the first place—helped her understand how she had allowed this person to rule over her for all those years.

In our coaching sessions, we role-played several possibilities, until we landed on a communication model that worked for her and dissolved the barrier around the fear she had of the conversation's consequence. After five years of being under her boss's thumb, Athena had the courage to speak about her feelings with him, making him aware of the impact of his words and actions on her. The result? Her boss had no idea of his effect on her, and Athena felt empowered and an instant sense of freedom as soon as she shared herself.

That day, their relationship changed for the better. He respected her so much for having the courage to speak up, and he made a conscious effort to change his leadership approach with her. That conversation boosted her confidence and changed the way she saw not only their relationship but also herself.

* * *

AS YOU MOVE ON to the workbook for Step 4: Consider Your Possibilities and Barriers, I want you to think back to the EI competency you identified in Exercise 5 (pages 166–67). What EI competency, if changed, would have the biggest impact on your leadership? What benefits will you reap if you do change that EI competency? And what is it costing you if you do nothing? Use that as motivation to propel you forward with generating options.

What follows are brainstorming exercises. Don't judge your ideas or problem solve. Just think of as many ideas as possible, and don't be concerned with the reliability or validity of each. At the same time, start thinking about the obstacles that may get in your way of achieving your goal. That way, you can determine what is needed to overcome these barriers.

Step 4: Consider Your Possibilities and Barriers

Consider Possibilities and Barriers

Consider and answer the following questions to help you explore your options to reach your goal:

• Rewrite the S.M.A.R.T. goal you identified in Exercise 5 (pages 166-67). What EI competency do you want to change that will have the biggest impact on your leadership?

• Have you tried anything previously to improve this competency? If so, what have you tried that either has or hasn't worked to achieve your goal?

• What could you do now? Try to think of at least two or three different ways to get you closer to your goal. If you need a little help, refer to chapter 10 for some tips and strategies for enhancing the EI competency related to your goal.

• Of each of the possibilities you listed above, what are some of the advantages and disadvantages of implementation?

• Now, narrow down your selections to the best possibility or strategy to help you reach your EI goal.

Consider and answer the following questions to help you discover the reasons or barriers that are keeping you stuck from achieving your goal:

- What barriers could stop you from moving forward with this possibility or strategy? How will you overcome them?

- What if those barriers were removed? What might be possible then?

Pause and Reflect

Emotion Check-In

| POSITIVE | HAPPY | OPTIMISTIC | INSPIRED | EMPATHETIC |

| EXCITED | CONFIDENT | PROUD | RELIEVED | CONTENT |

| HOPEFUL | SURPRISED | CALM | STRONG | PASSIONATE |

| JEALOUS | SAD | INTIMIDATED | OFFENDED | FRUSTRATED |

| DISCOURAGED | AFRAID | INDIFFERENT | EMBARRASSED | DISAPPOINTED |

| PESSIMISTIC | RESENTFUL | CONFUSED | INSECURE | OVERWHELMED |

Being clear on what you want to achieve and how you will accomplish it will help you uncover barriers or distractions that may lead you astray. It will also help you determine the possibilities available to you as you move forward on your path of becoming emotionally strong.

Setting clearly defined, measurable goals allows you to see a forward path versus a long pointless grind. Taking pride in achieving goals also helps you raise your self-confidence as you are able to see what you can achieve when you put your mind to it.[4]

How do you feel? Use the emotions icons as a guide. The answer can be a combination of any of these feelings or a different emotion altogether.

What is this feeling(s) telling you about yourself?

Chapter 12

Step 5: Craft Your Action Plan

THE PURPOSE OF this step of our self-coaching model is to move you into action. Here, you will take all the knowledge you gained and use it to inform the action plan you will develop. First, you will pose and answer thought-provoking questions so you can create a specific action plan for your goal. Your action plan will be broken down into bite-sized chunks so you can meticulously plan your course, setting target dates for completion.

As someone who has experienced the transformational impact EI has had on my own leadership development journey, I understand where you are on this self-awakening path. It can feel exhausting and exhilarating at once. Don't worry; I feel you.

However, this action-oriented part of the process will propel you forward. An action plan helps you list all of the tasks you need to finish to realize your goal. Having a plan is essential because it will help you stay motivated and ensure that you are on track to achieve your goal. It will help you overcome procrastination by keeping you driven with a visual goal in mind and a plan of exactly what you need to do and when you need to complete each step.[1]

In Step 5, I'll be asking you to develop a thorough plan listing the steps you need to take to achieve your S.M.A.R.T. goal. Start by thinking of the first step, and end with the last step. Some steps will involve a series of sub-steps.

Let's be honest: you will stumble. We all do. We are human, after all. Don't worry. While you are being strong-willed and working positively toward your EI goal, you will have a plan in place for when you relapse into old patterns of behavior.

Learning is not a straight line but a series of two steps forward, one step back. Regardless of how many steps, sub-steps, or missteps, an action plan gives you direction and helps you to keep moving forward.

Taking One Step at a Time

When you set goals, you envision your optimum future and inspire yourself to attain that future. Setting a S.M.A.R.T. goal (one that is Specific, Measurable, Attainable, Realistic, and Time-Bound) can help you stay focused, driven, and committed to achieving your goal.

Now that you have defined your S.M.A.R.T. goal, you need to create a list of steps to take. In the exercise to come, you will document all of the steps and, if applicable, the sub-steps involved in achieving your goal. You will also indicate how long it will take or when you will complete each step, and what support and resources are available to help you with your plan.

It's important to write out your action plan. In fact, writing down your goal boosts your probability of attaining it by 42 percent.[2] So let's get it out of your head and into this book. You will jot down your action plan, arranging the steps you need to take to realize your goal. Once you complete each step, celebrate by checking it off because you are one step closer to achieving your goal.

You will need to determine how to keep yourself motivated and make sure your end goal is aligned with your values. Your values are your guiding principles for your life, what is important to you. Your decisions about how you spend your time are likely a direct reflection of your values. Roy Disney of Walt Disney Co. said it best: "When your values are clear to you, making decisions becomes easier." [3] If your goals are congruent with your values, you are more likely to make decisions that will help you achieve your goals and stay motivated to chart the course, even during tough times. [4]

Finally, you will need to monitor your progress, whether that be daily, weekly, or monthly. If you need to adjust your plan or tweak your timeline, that's okay. Adjustments and modifications are expected. The key is that you are creating a visual guide that will help you achieve your goals in an effective and timely manner and you are moving toward becoming an emotionally strong leader.

Be Prepared for Roadblocks

Remember what Benjamin Franklin said: "If you fail to plan, you are planning to fail."

However, it is essential to understand that progress is not a straight line. Things won't go perfectly according to plan. We sometimes backslide, or life throws us curveballs that cause us to stop doing what we have been doing and do something else. Sometimes, even though we have taken two steps forward, we can take one or more steps backward and return to old patterns of behavior.

For change to stick, having a relapse prevention plan ahead of time—when you are strong and in the midst of planning—is critical. You need to learn how to recognize a relapse and plan how you will pick yourself up and get back on track. This is an important stage in becoming an emotionally strong leader.

In the past, when I was on a diet and had a slip, I didn't say, "it's okay, Carolyn. We all make mistakes. Just get back on track tomorrow." Instead, I would gorge myself and eat everything in sight. I had no compassion for myself. I hated that I went off my plan, so I sabotaged myself. One bad day turned into two and then three, and that is how I gained one hundred pounds in one year.

When we don't have a plan, we feel bad for failing. Failing discourages us from trying further, because many of us aim for perfection. [5]

But changing behaviors is not a straight line, and we all can relapse.

So how do you create a relapse prevention plan?

Identifying what behaviors or thoughts enter your mind when you are relapsing is critical. I call this relapse recognition. For instance, when I am relapsing and not being independent, I can see that I am asking reassuring questions to my family or employees and seeking validation. My inner belief is that I don't have the answers myself and I need others to help me make a decision.

You might not be aware of the beliefs and feelings associated with your relapse behavior. That's okay. Identify the action first and work backward, figuring out what you were feeling and thinking when the action was provoked.

Regardless of what EI competency you choose to improve, you always need to go back to self-awareness to understand why you behave in the ways that you do. Your inner iceberg holds the secrets for your external responses. Analyzing your internal and external environment for hints is a good first step, and identifying your triggers that lead to relapse is key. Some examples of personal triggers are experiencing miscommunication, being interrupted, having someone not respect your boundaries, being ignored or discounted, witnessing entitlement, being given unreasonable deadlines or requests, listening to people fighting, being kept waiting, and reading or watching upsetting news.

You may not be able to control how a situation makes you feel, but you can control how you react. Identifying how you are feeling about said trigger can empower you to make conscious choices about how you respond. Thinking through your emotions is the key to responding versus reacting. Negative emotions are natural, and feelings will flash before your rational thinking mind—your prefrontal cortex— can kick in. That's why it is critical to understand your triggers and when and how they typically occur.

In every moment, you have a choice: What will you do to respond to the trigger? The choice you make can impact everyone around you. That's why our first practice for developing EI is to become aware of how you are feeling and thinking about what your emotions are telling you about yourself.

Press Pause

Learning to manage our emotions is key to pushing pause long enough to choose a more effective response despite how we are feeling. Emotionally intelligent leaders don't ignore what they are feeling; they deepen their self-awareness by identifying their emotions and look for the information they provide. To leverage the data hidden within our emotions, we need to spend time thinking about, naming, and labeling them.

The more emotions you can identify and label, the stronger your self-awareness and empathy will be and the less likely an emotional reaction will go misunderstood—by you and your team. If you able to accurately articulate your emotional state, you will be better positioned to understand why you are feeling that way and what you should do about it.

Self-awareness enables you to press pause and examine your emotions, thoughts, and triggers before acting. By bringing awareness to your emotions and triggers, you can change your actions.

> **CREATE SPACE FOR CHOICE**
>
> The most helpful thing we can do when experiencing a trigger is to increase the space between the trigger event and our response. If we don't make room for choice, we limit our options to respond to a situation.
>
> "Between stimulus and response, there is a space. In that space lies our freedom and our power to choose our response. In our response lies our growth and our happiness."[6]

Physiological responses, like elevated heartbeat, sweating, pupil dilation, and accelerated breathing, can't be stopped when you have a triggering event. However, when you actively press pause and take a moment to name the emotion you are feeling, you create space between the trigger and the response you are having. Here, you can gain some measure of control over your physiological response and decide how best to form your conscious response to the trigger. The more you practice this pausing and naming, the more your conscious responses become automatic.

CLIENT STORY: "ZANDER"

Zander's inability to create positive connections with those he needed to interact with in his role as an IT Manager for a university was a major strain for his boss, "Clara," as colleagues were avoiding Zander and jumping straight to her. This was causing a lot of problems in the office, and Clara's boss, the VP of IT, was putting a lot of additional demands on her. So Clara's saving the day was neither sustainable nor scalable.

When coaching Zander, I soon noticed that he struggled with interpersonal relationships and was extremely uncomfortable sharing anything personal about himself. To avoid doing so, he made himself appear aloof and distant; that way, he did not have to make deep connections with anyone.

Zander understood that if he could not engender some interpersonal relationships, his job was at stake. So in our coaching, we concluded that to build connections, he would need to get to know his peers on a personal level. We crafted an action plan where he would try to speak to at least one person every day for five minutes about something non-work-related. For Zander, even thinking about enacting this plan felt like torture.

In addition to crafting an action plan, he needed to create a relapse prevention plan. What was Zander going to do when, and if, he reverted to his old patterns of behavior? I also asked him to track his progress and mention not only who he spoke to and what he spoke about but also how he felt after each conversation.

For the first few weeks, Zander felt the plan was very forced and unauthentic. I shared with him that it was not going to feel comfortable, because he was moving out of his comfort zone (hanging out by himself) and into his learning zone (trying to build connections). He needed to get comfortable with the uncomfortable.

Feeling uncomfortable is typical of learning any new skill. How many of us were comfortable getting behind the wheel the first time? How many were instantly good drivers? Probably none of us.

We first needed to learn the mechanics of driving. (Some of us, like me, could not tell the brake from the accelerator and thus needed many extra driving lessons to engage our inner Eeyore and make the learning stick.) Well, Zander needed the same: repeated practice to make his new social skills second nature.

After a few weeks more, he started to get the hang of it, and although sometimes he regressed to his old ways of keeping to himself, his relapse prevention plan showed him a way to get back on track. Little by little, he learned how to have deeper conversations with others.

What will stay with you is creating opportunities to experience an emotional connection to a concept, not rereading your notes from a coaching or training session or reading a book once. When you learn by doing, you gain immediate feedback; you also have a chance for self-examination to decide whether to continue, alter, or jettison a given strategy or technique.[7] Zander learned to work his plan. Reflecting on each interchange allowed him to try different ways of being, think about how he did, pay attention to how he felt, tweak what needed adjusting, and try a new approach. In the end, Zander learned it wasn't the destination that mattered but the journey.

* * *

AS YOU MOVE NOW to the workbook for Step 5: Craft Your Action Plan, I want you to think like Zander. What are the steps you need to take and what are the habits you need to instill to work your emotional muscles for the competency you are looking to change? When you are working to ingrain a behavior as habitual, your inner Eeyore needs feedback, time, practice, and repetition.

Your plan will be only as reliable as you make it. Spend time with the questions that follow, and be honest with yourself about what you need to do and how you will hold yourself accountable for doing it. Will you review your efforts weekly? Monthly? What does success look like for you? Think about how you will be able to let yourself know that your plan is working or when it isn't.

Step 5: Craft Your Action Plan

Plan Your Course of Action

Consider and answer the following questions as you plan your course of action for your S.M.A.R.T. goal:

- Which of the possibilities you previously identified in Exercise 6 (pages 208-9) will you choose to reach your goal?

- How will your plan impact your team? Your organization?

- Clearly outline how many steps you will take to move toward your goal and what each step consists of.

- When and how will you get each step done? How will you know that the step is complete?

- When do you need to review progress? Daily? Weekly? Monthly?

Your Relapse Prevention Plan

So now that you have a solid action plan in hand, highlighting what success looks like, how will you handle any hiccups along the way?

How do you know you are relapsing or about to relapse?

- What triggers do you anticipate you will experience as you attempt to reach your goal? Write down anything you think could trip you up. More is better than less here, to keep your eye on your goal.

- Which of your self-limiting beliefs may get in the way of achieving your goal?

What are you going to do to get yourself back on track and motivated into action again?

- What can you do to avoid these triggers in the future?

- What can you do to challenge these unhelpful beliefs?

Pause and Reflect

Emotion Check-In

 POSITIVE

 HAPPY

 OPTIMISTIC

 INSPIRED

 EMPATHETIC

 EXCITED

 CONFIDENT

 PROUD

 RELIEVED

 CONTENT

 HOPEFUL

 SURPRISED

 CALM

 STRONG

 PASSIONATE

 JEALOUS

 SAD

 INTIMIDATED

 OFFENDED

 FRUSTRATED

 DISCOURAGED

 AFRAID

 INDIFFERENT

 EMBARRASSED

 DISAPPOINTED

 PESSIMISTIC

 RESENTFUL

 CONFUSED

 INSECURE

 OVERWHELMED

Creating an action plan is empowering. Having a road map to future success is a clear indication of your commitment to your leadership development.

Ensuring your action plan is backed up by a reliable relapse prevention plan acknowledges that you may have deeply ingrained habits that will threaten to derail your progress. But being prepared safeguards your efforts and eliminates chances for self-sabotage.

How do you feel? Use the emotions icons as a guide. The answer can be a combination of any of these feelings or a different emotion altogether.

What is this feeling(s) telling you about yourself?

Chapter 13

Step 6: Confirm Your Commitment and Close Your Conversation

IN THIS STEP, you will be committing to the action you planned to take in Step 5. Here, we will determine your motivational level to work your action plan and decide where you can find support for yourself from others.

This final step of our self-coaching model is about establishing accountability. Accountability isn't something you can simply check off a to-do list. It needs constant attention and nurturing. If you let yourself slide on being accountable for reaching your goals, they will become further away and harder to achieve. Think of benchmarks and timelines that you can use to measure your progress. How does each step forward in your EI path fit in with your values and overall strategic objectives or key performance indicators in your leadership role?

When you do fall off the wagon, have compassion for yourself. Remember, instilling new behavioral practices is challenging and creating a habit takes time. Reflect on why you relapsed, and get yourself back on track with your plan. Relapsing can be a slippery slope, so what you do and say the next day and onward can have a huge impact on your results.

Watch the words you use. Are you blaming yourself or others when things don't go according to plan? In the book *Crucial Accountability: Tools for Resolving Violated Expectations, Broken Commitments, and Bad Behavior*, the authors explain the importance of asking "humanizing questions" such as "why would a reasonable, rational, and decent person [you, in this case] do that?" As opposed to asking blaming questions like, "what's the matter with that person [you]?"[1]

This is also where an accountability partner can be extra valuable. A person who can check in with you and your results and call you out if you are using excusatory language—toward yourself or others—is a key piece of staying on track or getting back on it if you've veered off course. Remember that support can come in different forms; a good book on an area you are trying to improve might be all you need until you find the best person to guide you through this journey.

Accountability is incredibly important because it puts you in the driver's seat and empowers you to be in control of your actions. It glues all the steps together and helps you realize your ultimate goal of becoming an emotionally strong leader.

Learn Your Third *Why* (Why Do You Want to Change?)

Surprise! There's a third *why*: Why do you want to change?

Everyone has the choice of self-discovery, whether personally or professionally. If you are going to exercise that choice and realize the full benefit of the journey, you have to answer why you have chosen to commit to a particular development path.

Understanding why you want to change is key to changing, as the knowledge found in your third *why* empowers you to push through the ups and downs you are bound to face as you seek to instill a new way of being. The reason to continue when facing difficult times must come from within you.

Each of us has a different background and holds different values and beliefs. Where we get our genuine drive and inspiration is different for everyone. *Why* comes in many different shapes and sizes.

Once you know your third *why*—your motivation—you will better understand your motives, concerns, and fears.

The underlying drive to change or the motivation to care about something varies from person to person; that reason is always highly personal and emotional. It should be linked to your core values, your guiding principles of how you want to live your life. It should be driven by intrinsic sources (arising from within), not extrinsic (external rewards).[2] Intrinsically motivated people are propelled by the personal joy and satisfaction they take from an activity. The very act of doing satisfies them. Those who are motivated extrinsically need external validation to feel rewarded. External validation involves either a gain (for example, financial) or the avoidance of a loss (for example, of a job).[3]

We are all unique, including our perspectives on rewards. Some people need the external reward: validation and gratification that others can see. Others need the reward of personal satisfaction, and this intrinsic motivation is often more effective for long-term goal setting and achieving.[4] While extrinsic motivation can be powerful, it is limited. A person can take only so much from a job promotion, a new car, or a celebratory dinner. Research suggests that we should use extrinsic rewards sparingly.[5]

I encourage you to change because *you* want to change—not because someone else thinks you should change. Changing for someone else can be short-lived. If *you* are the reason you are changing, that's great. You are committed and motivated to do the hard work. Let's face it; you are with yourself for the rest of your life, and working on your EI is a lifelong journey. We will all spend a lifetime trying to master these skills.

Whatever your motivation for change, naming it is vital. Doing so crystallizes the very reason you are doing the difficult work of self-development. Goals need to be meaningful to the person trying to achieve them for that person to be motivated to do the work involved.[6]

In *Find Your Why: A Practical Guide for Finding Purpose for You and Your Team*, Simon Sinek and his coauthors explain, "once you understand your WHY, you'll be able to clearly articulate what makes you feel fulfilled and to better understand what drives your behavior when you're at your natural best. When you can do that, you'll have a point of reference for everything you do going forward."[7]

 CLIENT STORY: "DAVID"

David was a very successful executive working for a premium consulting firm. His firm worked with top clients in energy and utilities, manufacturing, transportation, government, aerospace, retail, finance, and healthcare, and the firm's ongoing success depended on nurturing a team and culture focused on customer satisfaction.

David's motivation for working with me was initially extrinsic. He wanted to be the CEO, but the Board thought he lacked the requisite EI skills to get the job done. However, he did not enter our engagement with enthusiasm. He was convinced he should simply be given the CEO role as it was a natural progression that he worked so hard for and deserved. Yet his extrinsic, ego-driven focus was preventing him from snagging the top job.

With some deep reflection, David started to ask himself his third *why*: "My transformation truly began when I had an aha moment: Why was I doing this? Why was I going through this process and subjecting myself to all of this scrutiny? Was it for the position, or was it to become a better version of myself? When I came to realize and accept I was choosing to do this to become a better version of myself, regardless of whether I was successful in obtaining the position or not, I was able to truly focus on 'me,' begin the transformation, increase my EQ skills, and further develop as a leader."

You see, like all of us, David needed to understand his third *why*. Why did he want to change? Once he understood his motivation to do this kind of personal and professional development work, which was deeply rooted in his values, he gained the drive he needed to get the work done.

It's critically important to understand your third *why*: Why do you want to pursue this kind of leadership development? The answer will catapult you forward.

Find Your Support

Like making a movie, building yourself into the leader you want to be is a collaborative project requiring several people. Finding a support system that works for you is key. It ties back to you being 100 percent responsible for your life. Finding a person or people who can support you on your EI leadership journey makes you feel more resourceful and empowers you to cope and manage life's daily stressors more positively. It's important to find someone who can provide you emotional support by offering genuine encouragement, reassurance, and compassion.[8] No matter the stressor, peer support helps you process things healthily.

Finding support, however, isn't just about having a shoulder to lean on; it is about building a support network with members who will hold you accountable for trying to be better. When you fail or are feeling weak and want to do that thing that gets in your way, you reach out to your advisor and ask for help and advice. They can guide you to be stronger in areas where you are not. And their age or experience need not be similar to yours. Your advisor simply needs to have your best interests at heart and possess a skill you are trying to acquire or grow.

For instance, Natalie, my Business Development Manager, who is less than half my age, is my independence advisor. When I struggle with caring too much about what people think or I need reassurance when I know the answer already, I pick up the phone, and she walks me away from the ledge.

Natalie is what we call a competency advisor (CA). The cool thing about finding and having CAs in your organization is that everyone is good at something and everyone needs help with something, so it can really eliminate hierarchy because everyone is playing both roles— advisor and advisee. Perhaps, the executive assistant is stronger than the CEO on emotional expression, so when the CEO is struggling being vulnerable and sharing how they feel, they can look to the executive assistant (CA) for guidance and support. Having regular check-ins with people who have qualities you want to emulate provides you a support system to turn to when you are struggling or need a helping hand.

Having CAs inside our company at EI Experience reminds us that skill gaps exist on all sides, regardless of role, age, or background. Each person can address their competency gaps with the help of the other's strengths. All of us are advisors and advisees, students learning from one another. Each day, we show up authentically, flaws and all, and try to learn more, be better, and teach others. We always remember that before we are employees, we are human beings.

Finding CAs is critical in your EI leadership journey as it allows you to start to identify the skills you are trying to gain and master and find other people who already demonstrate those skills. Do not limit yourself to looking for someone who is older than you or has more seniority. You are looking for someone who has an EI competency you want at a level you want it.

Associate with people **you want to emulate.**

How to Find Your Competency Advisors

In choosing a CA, make sure you choose someone who has a skill you want. Remember, if you do what they do, you will probably get the results you want. Associate with people you want to emulate.

What if you don't know anyone who has the EI skill you need and want? I recommend keeping an eye out for that person until you do. In the meantime, find your support in different ways. Perhaps, read a book on the respective skill. I read *Facing Codependence: What It Is, Where It Comes from, How It Sabotages Our Lives* by Pia Mellody[9] until I found my person. Mellody's words helped me during a time when I did not have a CA to help me learn to be more self-reliant and trust in my own talents and decisions.

If you know the person, politely ask them if they would be willing to support you on this leadership development journey. Explain to them what you are looking to achieve, and share with them your S.M.A.R.T. goal and relapse prevention plan. Ask them if they would be willing to check in regularly with you (once a week, every two weeks, or once a month) on your progress. Attach concrete dates, declare what you are committed to doing for that period, and commit to meet your CA to discuss progress. This is an opportunity for your CA to coach and mentor you, recognizing your successes and helping you to remove roadblocks.

If that feels like too much, perhaps ask them for advice only when you need it. If you need more time with the advisor, choose someone who will make sure they hold you accountable more regularly. The arrangement needs to work for you.

Your CA's job is to check in with you and see whether you need any advice on the EI skill you are trying to enhance or reduce (if overplayed), follow up on any progress, celebrate any successes, and discuss any lessons learned. Your CA can be an existing friend, family member, or colleague, but choose someone who will hold you accountable, have open and honest conversations, and if you relapse, not just let you off the hook but encourage you to get back on track. You don't want someone to patronize you or make you feel bad when you screw up or ask questions.

Before choosing a CA, consider the following questions:

- In your opinion, what makes a good CA? What makes a poor CA?

- How do you learn best? What gets in your way of learning?

- What motivates you? What de-motivates you?

- How do you like to receive positive and constructive feedback?

- If you and your CA need to have a difficult conversation, how would you like your CA to approach that?

- What kind of connection and relationship do you want with your CA?

- How do you like to feel appreciated for your efforts in trying to improve your EI skills?

- How can your CA call you out if they see you are reverting to old patterns of thinking or behaving?

- How often do you want to meet?

- What is the best way to get a hold of you?

- Do you want permission to reach out to your CA if you are struggling after hours?

Once you determine your answers to these questions, see if you can get a comfortable level of agreement from your CA. Come to a consensus on each question; you are telling them how you want to be advised and mentored.

When I asked a friend to be my accountability partner to ensure I am exercising, we determined that the best time to connect with each other is when I am on the treadmill. This way, she can hear that I am working out, and if I can talk (and breathe) easily, she will push me to work out harder. That's the kind of person you need: someone who will motivate you, mentor you, and be honest with you, providing candid feedback and suggestions. If you have a CA who will not hold your feet to the fire to stay on track, I suggest finding a different CA.

Closing Your Conversation

You've come a long way from self-discovery to creating an action plan, identifying the cues and triggers that occur when you relapse, and developing a plan to get you back on track from reverting to old patterns of behavior. You have started to think about who to ask to support you, whether that be a CA who has what you want or a book or resource you can refer to for guidance. You also have become aware of the reason you want to change, your motivational driver, by learning your third *why*.

You have done an enormous amount of work toward being the best version of yourself and you are well on the path to becoming an emotionally strong leader.

Breathe.

Reflect.

Savor.

Now, it is time to close your conversation. Here, you highlight the key learning you gained, re-emphasize and recommit to your plan of action, and continue to seek support when needed.

There's not a lot of strategy or advice left to impart to you. Simply, be honest with yourself and approach your development in an open and non-judgmental way. You will succeed.

* * *

AS YOU MOVE NOW to the workbook for Step 6: Confirm Your Commitment and Close Your Conversation, I want you to think about the motivation you have to achieve your S.M.A.R.T. goal. How will you tap into it to ignite the spark that will propel you further? What kind of support will you need to guide you through this work? What needs to happen so that you walk away feeling supported?

Think of yourself like an Olympian who is on the precipice of reaching the podium. An Olympian can't get there by themselves; many hands had to help along the way. Yet no one else can place the Olympian on the podium either. Hold on to your third *why* as you take these final, necessary steps to prepare yourself for success.

WORKBOOK

Step 6: Confirm Your Commitment and Close Your Conversation

Learn Your Third *Why*

Consider the following questions to determine your third *why* (why do you want to change?). Make your third *why* as strong and urgent as you possibly can. Pushing through the status quo is difficult, but that is exactly why you are undertaking all this work to enhance your EI. "No pain, no gain" is a common mantra among athletes, meaning if the work isn't hard, they won't get the results they want. Therefore, something must be urgently pressing them to push themselves to the limit. Examine what that is for you.

- What is driving you to achieve this goal?

- If you achieve this goal, what kind of leader will you be?

- How will you feel if you achieve this goal?

- How can you keep yourself motivated to continue to feel what you listed above?

- What is your level of commitment from 1 to 10? If it's not a 10, what do you need to do bring it to a 10?

In the end, it's all about formulating your inspirational reasons to make a change. So what is your story? If could change anything, what would you like to change right now? Why do you want to make that change now and not somewhere in the future? What could this change bring you?

As we all too often know, our work and home responsibilities can often win over our time and attention and put our personal growth and development plans on the back burner. By putting your third *why* down in writing, you are increasingly focusing on how to become more accountable to yourself. So take a moment and think about why you are choosing to change now, and write it down.

Competency Advisor

It is important to find a CA who can support you through your EI development. Find a person who can commit to supporting you throughout the coming weeks and months. Write their name below.

Competency Advisor	

Schedule at least one follow-up meeting in the next four weeks. Put it in your calendar right now! If you would like more follow-up meetings, schedule them too.

Discuss and identify three ways in which your CA can help and support you in the coming month. Make sure you share this list with them.

1.	
2.	
3.	

Consider these questions when you check in with your CA:

• What strategies have you tried to achieve your goal since the last time you saw your CA? How did it go?

• What worked or is working well? Are you still struggling in any areas? If so, what are they?

• What are you learning about yourself?

• What types of scenarios bring in your exceptional leadership qualities? What situations cause you to revert to your poor leadership behaviors?

• What is one thing you will do differently next time?

Congratulations! You have taken the time and space you need to determine your goals, create a detailed plan, and have the support in place if you need help. Good for you!

Closing Reflections

Take a moment, and reflect on your self-awakening journey. Answer the following questions:

- What did you learn about yourself?

- How will you implement the lessons learned into your leadership and become emotionally strong?

- What was your big takeaway from this self-awakening process?

Pause and **Reflect**

You did it! The last exercise is done. I hope you have been surprised, challenged, and heartened by who you are. Understanding your feelings takes a lot of effort, and by finishing these workbooks you've done yourself a service as you grow to become a leader who is emotionally strong.

Well done!

Emotion Check-In

| POSITIVE | HAPPY | OPTIMISTIC | INSPIRED | EMPATHETIC |

| EXCITED | CONFIDENT | PROUD | RELIEVED | CONTENT |

| HOPEFUL | SURPRISED | CALM | STRONG | PASSIONATE |

| JEALOUS | SAD | INTIMIDATED | OFFENDED | FRUSTRATED |

| DISCOURAGED | AFRAID | INDIFFERENT | EMBARRASSED | DISAPPOINTED |

| PESSIMISTIC | RESENTFUL | CONFUSED | INSECURE | OVERWHELMED |

Pushing yourself to the limit in pursuit of your goal takes discipline, commitment, and the courage of your convictions. The good thing is that you don't have to do it by yourself.

Surrounding yourself with people who will hold you accountable and prop you up will enhance your abilities and enable you to push through on those things you previously thought impossible or improbable.

How do you feel? Use the emotions icons as a guide. The answer can be a combination of any of these feelings or a different emotion altogether.

What is this feeling(s) telling you about yourself?

CONCLUSION

JOURNEYS ARE FUNNY; you never know what you will come across when you travel from one place to another. As you made the passage from cover to cover of this book, you took yourself on a transformational journey that had you dispel myths, check assumptions, understand your triggers, recognize deep-seated habits, develop new skills, discern motivations, and ultimately chart a course for a new horizon that comes from within. The destination is one in which your personal goals, ambitions, and values are honed to be in harmony with your emotional self as you strive to become the best possible you—a leader who leads with EI.

Leading from the inside-out is the key to unlocking your potential. Understanding your emotional makeup and emotional triggers—the contents of your inner iceberg—will allow you to lead authentically. By doing so, you will develop genuine connections that will engender a feeling of emotional safety among your teams, enabling them to communicate, collaborate, and innovate in ways that will transform your workplace culture.

Research has shown that EI is the critical skill exceptional leaders use to get the best results from their teams. Now that you have learned what it takes to lead with EI, you can tap into your leadership superpower and use it to boost productivity, engagement, and overall emotional well-being.

My hope is that you go in to work tomorrow and change the way you lead. Listen to, learn from, and express your emotions constructively. Emotions are not the enemy; they come and go—and you now know you don't have to be afraid of them. Our emotions are filled with wisdom. Only when we are leading from the inside-out can we access the knowledge within.

Learning to lead with EI changed my life. It gave me the road map for how to accept my emotions without judgment. It enabled me to learn how to be bigger than my emotions, not allowing my feelings to rule me but allowing me to rule my feelings. As I learned more and became more aware of my inner iceberg, I became a better leader, partner, family member, and human being.

I want to live in a world with emotionally strong leaders, where tending to emotions in the workplace is not taboo. I want our leaders to model emotionally strong behaviors that their teams and employees can mirror. I want to see leaders who can emotionally mentor the next generation of our workforce so that a decade from today, emotionally connected workplaces are not the exception but the norm.

By taking the inside-out journey that is mapped between the covers of this book, you are becoming part of the solution,

You are turning leadership **on its head.**

future-proofing your leadership, and enabling the emotional growth of those around you.

But employing the self-coaching model in this book is only your first step. Enhancing your EI is a lifelong pursuit. Once you start, you must continue to work your plan and make your actions into habits. In his book *Atomic Habits: An Easy & Proven Way to Build Good Habits & Break Bad Ones*, James Clear discusses how problem-solving lies at the heart of all behavior. Whether it be to close a gap in understanding, achieve something greater than you already have, or lighten your burden by ending a negative relationship or course of action, the purpose of every habit is to solve the problems you face.[1] Whatever you have realized throughout this self-coaching process to become an emotionally strong leader, you need to practice your new mindset shifts and behaviors repeatedly to make them a habit.

When you have maintained your changed behavior long enough and with some success, you will start to get more comfortable with this new version of yourself and get into a rhythm where you can maintain the new behavior change almost automatically and habitually. You'll then continue to build on these successes.

As your life continues to unfold, new EI competencies needing your attention will come to the fore. You'll also identify new habits you want to ingrain. By employing the strategies and repeating the exercises presented in this book, you'll be able to bring further positive changes into your life. Keep this book with you. It can be used again and again and again.

My life's work is to send as many people as possible on the journey you've just completed. Congratulations on the enormous achievement of the transformational self-discovery you've worked to achieve. I know it wasn't easy, but rarely is something worthwhile simple to obtain.

Leading from the inside-out takes guts. By doing so, you are turning leadership on its head. You have it in you to make the world a better place—one EI competency at a time.

Choose to be emotionally strong. Choose to continue your journey. Choose to uncover the depths of your inner iceberg. That is where your leadership superpower lives.

ACKNOWLEDGMENTS

AS IN MY PERSONAL JOURNEY TO EI, so too in my book-writing journey could I not have succeeded without the help of others.

This book has been a huge team effort. I would first like to thank all the dedicated and talented people at Figure 1 Publishing, especially Chris Labonté, Steve Cameron, Mike Leyne, Naomi MacDougall, Teresa Bubela, Mark Redmayne, Lara Smith, and Heidi Waechtler for all their guidance and care through every stage of the publishing process. A special shout-out to my editor and writing partner, Steve Cameron. I can't thank you enough for making my ideas pop off the page like you did. We are an amazing duo. I am forever grateful to you for supporting me throughout this process. Thank you Marnie Lamb, my copy editor, and Alison Strobel, my proofreader, for your incredible attention to detail to make this book an even better read.

Chris Labonté, Mike Leyne, Natalie LeClerc, and Paula Skaper were instrumental early on in pushing me to put my ideas out there. They helped me choose what I was going to write about and coached me on how to structure this book. Thank you. I am forever grateful to you all for supporting me throughout this process. Your suggestions and excitement about this project helped make my dream of writing this book a reality.

Thanks also to those who shared their time and intellect in providing honest feedback on this manuscript: Natalie LeClerc, Kirin Dubois, Lily Yao, Cecilia Jin, and Mia Aleksic. You have a special place in my heart for supporting me on this journey.

I also want to send a special shout-out to Lily Yao, my research assistant. Thank you for all the incredible work you did, sourcing and citing the oodles of research that went into this book. Your countless hours and dedication are a huge reason why this book morphed into the product it is.

Matt Nosworthy, my graphic designer, is responsible for most of the illustrations found in this book. The Self-Coaching to Enhanced Emotional Intelligence Model started off as an idea in my head and has now grown into a solid framework to help thousands of people around the world become emotionally strong. Thank you, Matt, for your dedicated work in helping me communicate these complex ideas visually.

Special thanks to the incredibly brilliant Dr. Claudia Krebs, Professor of Teaching in Neuroanatomy at the University of British Columbia, who helped deepen my learning about the brain and emotions, and taught me that there are fellow professors out there willing to help others and ask nothing in return.

To my entire team at EI Experience and Carolyn Stern & Associates Inc., I'm proud of the work we do together. One person at a time, we are making it okay to be human in the workplace. The work we do goes beyond the four walls of business, and every day, we get to change lives and entire corporate cultures in the process. Thank you.

Thank you to Multi-Health Systems Inc. for allowing me to use the EQ-i 2.0® model as a framework to help my readers break down and measure their EI into fifteen different competencies. Your EQ assessment changed my life and is the reason I wanted to teach others these critical soft skills.

My students, university colleagues, and corporate clients over the last twenty years have made my career a complete joy. My work with all of you has helped me shape my programs, and you motivate me each day to master my craft and try to be the best educator, peer, professional speaker, corporate trainer, and executive coach. Your personal stories and professional triumphs have been peppered into this book and added a lot of color and relatability for others to learn from you. I am forever grateful that you have shared the intimate side of your professional and personal lives with me. This emotional work is hard, but it does change lives. Each of you is modeling the way as an emotionally strong leader and giving others permission to do the same. This book is a tribute to your honesty, courage, and dedication to leading with EI.

I'm deeply indebted to the University of Chicago Medicine, who was the first to adopt our Coaching with Emotional Intelligence model, which stands as a testament to the importance of EI and cultivating a coaching culture in the workplace. The basis for the content of this book is adapted from the work we have done with the university medical center. This transformational change is a groundbreaking beginning for the future of EI in our workplaces, and I am eternally grateful to Wally Smith, who was steadfast in his efforts to bring our Coaching with Emotional Intelligence model to the institution. Thank you!

I want to also thank Cosmo and Velvet (my fur babies), who spent many nights and weekends lying with me as I put pen to paper, keeping me company, and providing me comfort and joy. Your kisses, snuggles, and hugs when I had writer's block meant the world to me.

Above all, I want to thank my mother, Sharyn Stern, for her love and encouragement. Mom, I hold enormous gratitude for all the sacrifices you made in your life for me, and despite having to work three jobs, you provided me with countless opportunities to advance my education, which ultimately led me to find EI. EI was, is, and will always be my lifesaver. It provides me with the emotional skills and mental strategies to be stronger than my feelings. Thank you for the gift of your selflessness.

This book is about personal leadership growth and transformation through unlocking the power emotions bring into our life. Writing it has given me greater insight into my own emotional makeup and inspired me to further enhance my EI competencies, and I hope it has done the same for you.

So last but not least, I thank you, dear reader, for allowing me and this book to guide you through this very personal, inside-out, transformational leadership journey. I hope the lessons learned throughout these pages have ignited a spark in you to be the best version of yourself and become emotionally strong.

—CAROLYN STERN

NOTES

INTRODUCTION

1. Daniel J. Siegel, "Half a Brain in Hiding: Balancing Left and Right," in *Mindsight: The New Science of Personal Transformation* (New York, NY: Bantam Books, 2010), pp. 102–19.
2. Brett Hayes and Beryl Hesketh, "Attribution Theory, Judgmental Biases, and Cognitive Behavior Modification: Prospects and Problems," *Cognitive Therapy and Research* 13, no. 3 (June 1989): pp. 211–30, doi.org/10.1007/bf01173404.
3. Vinky Sharma and Moonis Shakeel, "Illusion versus Reality: An Empirical Study of Overconfidence and Self Attribution Bias in Business Management Students," *Journal of Education for Business* 90, no. 4 (March 16, 2015): pp. 199–207, doi.org/10.1080/08832323.2015.1014458.
4. Hayes and Hesketh, "Attribution Theory, Judgmental Biases, and Cognitive Behavior Modification."
5. Dale Carnegie, "Fundamental Techniques in Handling People," in *How to Win Friends and Influence People*, rev. ed. (1936; New York, NY: Simon and Schuster, 1981).
6. Marjan Boerma et al., "Point/Counterpoint: Are Outstanding Leaders Born or Made?," *American Journal of Pharmaceutical Education* 81, no. 3 (2017): p. 58, doi.org/10.5688/ajpe81358.
7. Travis Bradberry and Jean Greaves, *Emotional Intelligence 2.0* (San Diego, CA: TalentSmart, 2009), p. 25.

SECTION I–TURN LEADERSHIP ON ITS HEAD

1. James K. Harter, Frank L. Schmidt, and Corey L. M. Keyes, "Well-Being in the Workplace and Its Relationship to Business Outcomes: A Review of the Gallup Studies," in *Flourishing: Positive Psychology and the Life Well-Lived*, ed. Corey L. M. Keyes and Jonathan Haidt (Washington, DC: American Psychological Association, 2003), pp. 205–24, doi.org/10.1037/10594-009.

CHAPTER 1: YOUR EMOTIONS ARE NOT THE ENEMY

1. Amy Morin, "The 8 Myths about Emotions That Are Holding Us Back," Forbes, July 18, 2014, forbes.com/sites/amymorin/2014/07/18/the-8-myths-about-emotions-that-are-holding-us-back/?sh=3666902b4eb4.
2. Marc Brackett, *Permission to Feel: Unlocking the Power of Emotions to Help Our Kids, Ourselves, and Our Society Thrive* (New York, NY: Celadon Books, 2019).
3. Joshua K. Hartshorne and Laura T. Germine, "When Does Cognitive Functioning Peak? The Asynchronous Rise and Fall of Different Cognitive Abilities across the Life Span," *Psychological Science* 26, no. 4 (March 13, 2015): pp. 433–43, doi.org/10.1177/0956797614567339.
4. Yasmin Anwar, "Emotional Intelligence Peaks as We Enter Our 60s, Research Suggests," Berkeley News, December 16, 2010, news.berkeley.edu/2010/12/16/agingemotion/.
5. "The Future of Jobs Report 2020," World Economic Forum, October 2020, weforum.org/reports/the-future-of-jobs-report-2020.

6. "The Future of Education and Skills," OECD Future of Education and Skills 2030, May 2018, oecd.org/education/2030/E2030%20Position%20Paper%20 %2805.04.2018%29.pdf.

7. Ronald J. Delamater and J. Regis McNamara, "The Social Impact of Assertiveness," *Behavior Modification* 10, no. 2 (April 1986): pp. 139–58, doi.org/10.1177/01454455860102001.

8. Yusuke Hayashi and Yukiko Washio, "Text-Message Dependency, Executive Function, and Impulsivity in College Students: A Cluster Analysis," *Cyberpsychology, Behavior, and Social Networking* 23, no. 11 (January 2020): pp. 794–99, doi.org/10.1089/ cyber.2019.0743.

9. Andrew J. Martin and Herbert W. Marsh, "Fear of Failure: Friend or Foe?," *Australian Psychologist* 38, no. 1 (March 2003): pp. 31–38, doi.org/10.1080/000500603100017 06997.

10. Habib Yaribeygi et al., "The Impact of Stress on Body Function: A Review," *EXCLI Journal* 16 (July 21, 2017): 1057–72, doi.org/10.17179/excli2017-480.

11. Elia Abi-Jaoude, Karline Treurnicht Naylor, and Antonio Pignatiello, "Smartphones, Social Media Use and Youth Mental Health," *Canadian Medical Association Journal* 192, no. 6 (February 10, 2020), doi.org/10.1503/cmaj.190434.

12. Francisca Catarino et al., "Compassion Motivations: Distinguishing Submissive Compassion from Genuine Compassion and Its Association with Shame, Submissive Behavior, Depression, Anxiety and Stress," *Journal of Social and Clinical Psychology* 33, no. 5 (2014): pp. 399–412, doi.org/10.1521/jscp.2014.33.5.399.

13. Januard D. Dagdag, Hydee G. Cuizon, and Aisie O. Bete, "College Students' Problems and Their Link to Academic Performance: Basis for Needs-Driven Student Programs," *Journal of Research, Policy & Practice of Teachers & Teacher Education* 9, no. 2 (December 2019): pp. 54–65, doi.org/10.37134/jrpptte.vol9.no2.5.2019.

14. Douglas E. Colman et al., "The Efficacy of Self-Care for Graduate Students in Professional Psychology: A Meta-Analysis," *Training and Education in Professional Psychology* 10, no. 4 (2016): pp. 188–97, doi.org/10.1037/tep0000130.

CHAPTER 2: MY JOURNEY TO MY OWN SUPERPOWER

1. Regina Miller and Joan Pedro, "Creating Respectful Classroom Environments," *Early Childhood Education Journal* 33, no. 5 (2006): pp. 293–99, doi.org/10.1007/ s10643-006-0091-1.

2. Marc Brackett, "Part 1," in *Permission to Feel: Unlocking the Power of Emotions to Help Our Kids, Ourselves, and Our Society Thrive* (New York, NY: Celadon Books, 2019).

3. Pamela M. Lee, "Introduction: Aspiration Burnout," *October*, no. 176 (2021): pp. 3–6, doi.org/10.1162/octo_e_00421.

PART II: THE F-WORD

1. Johnmarshall Reeve, *Understanding Motivation and Emotion*, 5th ed. (Hoboken, NJ: Wiley, 2009).

2. Brett Q. Ford et al., "The Psychological Health Benefits of Accepting Negative Emotions and Thoughts: Laboratory, Diary, and Longitudinal Evidence," *Journal of Personality and Social Psychology* 115, no. 6 (2018): pp. 1075–92, doi.org/10.1037/ pspp0000157.

3. John Bradshaw, "The Hiding Places of Toxic Shame," in *Healing the Shame That Binds You* (Deerfield Beach, FL: Health Communications, 1988), p. 108.

4. Da-Yee Jeung, Changsoo Kim, and Sei-Jin Chang, "Emotional Labor and Burnout: A Review of the Literature," *Yonsei Medical Journal* 59, no. 2 (February 5, 2018): p. 187, doi.org/10.3349/ymj.2018.59.2.187.

CHAPTER 3: EMOTIONS MATTER

1. "Sophia the Robot Wants a Baby and Says Family Is 'Really Important,'" BBC, November 25, 2017, bbc.com/news/newsbeat-42122742.
2. Chai M. Tyng et al., "The Influences of Emotion on Learning and Memory," *Frontiers in Psychology* 8 (August 24, 2017), doi.org/10.3389/fpsyg.2017.01454.
3. "State of the Global Workplace 2021 Report," Gallup, June 2021, gallup.com/workplace/349484/state-of-the-global-workplace.aspx.
4. Amy Arnsten, Carolyn M. Mazure, and Rajita Sinha, "This Is Your Brain in Meltdown," *Scientific American* 306, no. 4 (April 2012): pp. 48–53, doi.org/10.1038/scientificamerican0412-48.
5. María Esther Olvera-Cortés et al., "Serotonin/Dopamine Interaction in Learning," *Progress in Brain Research* (2008): pp. 567–602, doi.org/10.1016/s0079-6123(08)00927-8.
6. Claudia Krebs, interview with the author, January 24, 2022.
7. Krebs, interview with the author.
8. Vicki R. LeBlanc, Meghan M. McConnell, and Sandra D. Monteiro, "Predictable Chaos: A Review of the Effects of Emotions on Attention, Memory and Decision Making." *Advances in Health Sciences Education* 20, no. 1 (June 2014): pp. 265–81, doi.org/10.1007/s10459-014-9516-6.
9. Stephen W. Porges, *The Polyvagal Theory: Neurophysiological Foundations of Emotions, Attachment, Communication, and Self-Regulation* (New York: W. W. Norton, 2011).
10. Riccardo Williams, "Anger as a Basic Emotion and Its Role in Personality Building and Pathological Growth: The Neuroscientific, Developmental and Clinical Perspectives," *Frontiers in Psychology* 8 (November 7, 2017), doi.org/10.3389/fpsyg.2017.01950.
11. Lou Solomon, "Two-Thirds of Managers Are Uncomfortable Communicating with Employees," Harvard Business Review, March 9, 2016, hbr.org/2016/03/two-thirds-of-managers-are-uncomfortable-communicating-with-employees.
12. Solomon, "Two-Thirds of Managers Are Uncomfortable."
13. Albert Mehrabian and Susan R. Ferris, "Inference of Attitudes from Nonverbal Communication in Two Channels," *Journal of Consulting Psychology* 31, no. 3 (1967): pp. 248–52, doi.org/10.1037/h0024648.
14. Niklas K. Steffens et al., "A Meta-Analytic Review of Social Identification and Health in Organizational Contexts," *Personality and Social Psychology Review* (July 7, 2016), doi.org/10.1177/1088868316656701.
15. Eduardo B. Andrade and Dan Ariely, "The Enduring Impact of Transient Emotions on Decision Making," *Organizational Behavior and Human Decision Processes* 109, no. 1 (May 2009): pp. 1–8, doi.org/10.1016/j.obhdp.2009.02.003.
16. Gülsüm Ançel and Elif Kabakçi, "Psychometric Properties of the Turkish Form of Codependency Assessment Tool," *Archives of Psychiatric Nursing* 23, no. 6 (December 2009): pp. 441–53, doi.org/10.1016/j.apnu.2008.10.004.
17. Deena Fisher and John Beer, "Codependency and Self-Esteem among High School Students," *Psychological Reports* 66, no. 3 (1990): pp. 1001–2, doi.org/10.2466/pr0.1990.66.3.1001.

18. Stathis Grapsas et al., "The 'Why' and 'How' of Narcissism: A Process Model of Narcissistic Status Pursuit," *Perspectives on Psychological Science* 15, no. 1 (December 5, 2019): pp. 150–72, doi.org/10.1177/1745691619873350.

19. Jeremy A. Yip et al., "Follow Your Gut? Emotional Intelligence Moderates the Association between Physiologically Measured Somatic Markers and Risk-Taking," *Emotion* 20, no. 3 (2020): pp. 462–72, doi.org/10.1037/emo0000561.

20. Karen Pezza Leith and Roy F. Baumeister, "Why Do Bad Moods Increase Self-Defeating Behavior? Emotion, Risk Tasking, and Self-Regulation," *Journal of Personality and Social Psychology* 71, no. 6 (December 1996): pp. 1250–67, doi.org/10.1037/0022-3514.71.6.1250.

21. Jennifer S. Lerner et al., "Emotion and Decision Making," *Annual Review of Psychology* 66, no. 1 (March 2015): pp. 799–823, doi.org/10.1146/annurev-psych-010213-115043.

22. Graham Loomes and Robert Sugden, "Regret Theory: An Alternative Theory of Rational Choice under Uncertainty," *Economic Journal* 92, no. 368 (December 1, 1982): pp. 805–24, doi.org/10.2307/2232669.

23. Johannes Rank and Michael Frese, "Chapter 6: The Impact of Emotions, Moods and Other Affect-Related Variables on Creativity, Innovation and Initiative," in *Research Companion to Emotion in Organizations*, ed. Neal M. Ashkanasy and Cary L. Cooper (Cheltenham, UK: Edward Elgar, 2008), pp. 103–19, doi.org/10.4337/97818484437 78.00015.

24. Peter M. Senge, *The Fifth Discipline: The Art and Practice of the Learning Organization* (New York, NY: Doubleday Currency, 1990).

25. John Bessant and Joseph Tidd, "Chapter 17: Learning to Manage Innovation and Entrepreneurship," in *Innovation and Entrepreneurship*, 3rd ed. (West Sussex, UK: John Wiley & Sons, 2015), pp. 483–500.

26. Md. Hassan Jafri, Chimi Dem, and Sonam Choden, "Emotional Intelligence and Employee Creativity: Moderating Role of Proactive Personality and Organizational Climate," *Business Perspectives and Research* 4, no. 1 (2016): pp. 54–66, doi.org/10.1177/2278533715605435.

27. Jim Clifton, "The Mood of the World," Gallup, May 4, 2021, gallup.com/workplace/349229/mood-world.aspx.

28. Rasmus Hougaard, Jacqueline Carter, and Gillian Coutts, *One Second Ahead: Enhance Your Performance at Work with Mindfulness* (New York, NY: Palgrave Macmillan, 2016).

29. Travis Bradberry and Jean Greaves, "Just the Facts: A Look at the Latest Discoveries in Emotional Intelligence," in *Emotional Intelligence 2.0* (San Diego, CA: TalentSmart, 2009), p. 226.

30. Kirstin Aschbacher et al., "Good Stress, Bad Stress and Oxidative Stress: Insights from Anticipatory Cortisol Reactivity," *Psychoneuroendocrinology* 38, no. 9 (September 2013): pp. 1698–1708, doi.org/10.1016/j.psyneuen.2013.02.004.

31. Bruce S. McEwen, "Physiology and Neurobiology of Stress and Adaptation: Central Role of the Brain," *Physiological Reviews* 87, no. 3 (July 2007): pp. 873–904, doi.org/10.1152/physrev.00041.2006.

32. Myriam N. Bechtoldt, "Chapter 6: Emotional Intelligence, Professional Qualifications, and Psychologists' Need for Gender Research," in *Sexualized Brains: Scientific Modeling of Emotional Intelligence from a Cultural Perspective*, ed. Nicole C. Karafyllis and Gotlind Ulshöfer (Cambridge, MA: MIT, 2008), pp. 117–30.

33. Greg Lewis and Eric Knudsen, "Stressed Employees Browse New Jobs, Unsupported Employees Actually Apply," LinkedIn, June 8, 2021, linkedin.com/business/talent/blog/talent-strategy/stressed-employees-browse-unsupported-employee-apply.

34. Deborah Carr, *Worried Sick: How Stress Hurts Us and How to Bounce Back* (New Brunswick, NJ: Rutgers University Press, 2014).

35. Tarani Chandola, Eric Brunner, and Michael Marmot, "Chronic Stress at Work and the Metabolic Syndrome: Prospective Study," *BMJ* 332, no. 7540 (2006): pp. 521–25, doi.org/10.1136/bmj.38693.435301.80.

36. Mika Kivimäki et al., "Long Working Hours and Risk of Coronary Heart Disease and Stroke: A Systematic Review and Meta-Analysis of Published and Unpublished Data for 603 838 Individuals," *The Lancet* 386, no. 10005 (August 20, 2015): pp. 1739–46, doi.org/10.1016/s0140-6736(15)60295-1.

37. Lukasz D. Kaczmarek et al. "Splitting the Affective Atom: Divergence of Valence and Approach-Avoidance Motivation during a Dynamic Emotional Experience," *Current Psychology* 40 (2021): pp. 3272–83, doi.org/10.1007/s12144-019-00264-3.

38. Seth Kaplan et al., "On the Role of Positive and Negative Affectivity in Job Performance: A Meta-Analytic Investigation," *Journal of Applied Psychology* 94, no. 1 (2009): pp. 162–76, doi.org/10.1037/a0013115.

39. Vicki R. LeBlanc, "The Effects of Acute Stress on Performance: Implications for Health Professions Education," *Academic Medicine* 84, no. 10 (October 2009): s25–s33, doi.org/10.1097/acm.0b013e3181b37b8f.

40. Brett S. Torrence and Shane Connelly, "Emotion Regulation Tendencies and Leadership Performance: An Examination of Cognitive and Behavioral Regulation Strategies," *Frontiers in Psychology* 10 (July 2, 2019), doi.org/10.3389/fpsyg.2019.01486.

41. Kathy Kram, "Foreword," in *Linking Emotional Intelligence and Performance at Work: Current Research Evidence with Individuals and Groups*, ed. Vanessa Urch Druskat, Fabio Sala, and Gerald Mount (Mahwah, NJ: Lawrence Erlbaum, 2006), pp. vii–ix.

42. Susan Sorenson and Keri Garman, "How to Tackle U.S. Employees' Stagnating Engagement," Gallup, June 11, 2013, news.gallup.com/businessjournal/162953/tackle-employees-stagnating-engagement.aspx.

CHAPTER 4: THE BRAIN AND EMOTIONS—IT'S A TEAM EFFORT

1. Aron K. Barbey, Roberto Colom, and Jordan Grafman, "Distributed Neural System for Emotional Intelligence Revealed by Lesion Mapping," *Social Cognitive and Affective Neuroscience* 9, no. 3 (December 6, 2012): pp. 265–72, doi.org/10.1093/scan/nss124.

2. K. Luan Phan et al., "Functional Neuroanatomy of Emotion: A Meta-Analysis of Emotion Activation Studies in PET and FMRI," *NeuroImage* 16, no. 2 (2002): pp. 331–48, doi.org/10.1006/nimg.2002.1087.

3. Claudia Krebs, interview with the author, January 11, 2022.

4. Ewelina Wilkos et al., "Social Cognitive and Neurocognitive Deficits in Inpatients with Unilateral Thalamic Lesions—Pilot Study," *Neuropsychiatric Disease and Treatment* 11 (2015): pp. 1031–38, doi.org/10.2147/NDT.S78037.

5. S. Murray Sherman and R. W. Guillery, *Exploring the Thalamus and Its Role in Cortical Function*, 2nd ed. (Cambridge, MA: MIT, 2006).

6. Lawrence M. Ward, "The Thalamus: Gateway to the Mind," *Wiley Interdisciplinary Reviews: Cognitive Science* 4, no. 6 (2013): pp. 609–22, doi.org/10.1002/wcs.1256.

7. Krebs, interview with the author.

8. Sara E. Morrison and C. Daniel Salzman, "Re-valuing the Amygdala," *Current Opinion in Neurobiology* 20, no. 2 (March 2010): pp. 221–30, doi.org/10.1016/j.conb.2010.02.007.

9. Daniel Goleman, "Self-Mastery," in *The Brain and Emotional Intelligence: New Insights* (Northampton, MA: More Than Sound, 2011), p. 26.

10. Morrison and Salzman, "Re-valuing the Amygdala."

11. Amy F. T. Arnsten, "Stress Signalling Pathways That Impair Prefrontal Cortex Structure and Function," *Nature Reviews Neuroscience* 10, no. 6 (June 2009): pp. 410–22, doi.org/10.1038/nrn2648.

12. Goleman, "Self-Mastery," p. 25.

13. Mauro Luisetto, Naseer Almukhtar, and Farhan Ahmad Khan, "Mindset Kinetics and Crime Behavior—Quantitative Methods? A New Forensic Quantitative Approach. How Biochemistry, Toxicology, Imaging Principle Can Help in Jurisdictional Settings," *Biomedical Journal of Science & Technical Research* 16, no. 2 (2019): pp. 11828–37, doi.org.10.26717/BJSTR.2019.16.002810.

14. Ruud M. Buijs and Corbert G. Van Eden, "The Integration of Stress by the Hypothalamus, Amygdala and Prefrontal Cortex: Balance between the Autonomic Nervous System and the Neuroendocrine System," *Progress in Brain Research* 126 (2000): pp. 117–32, doi.org/10.1016/s0079-6123(00)26011-1.

15. Luisetto, Almukhtar, and Khan, "Mindset Kinetics and Crime Behavior."

16. "Understanding the Stress Response: Chronic Activation of This Survival Mechanism Impairs Health," Harvard Health, July 6, 2020, health.harvard.edu/staying-healthy/understanding-the-stress-response.

17. Chai M. Tyng et al., "The Influences of Emotion on Learning and Memory," *Frontiers in Psychology* 8 (August 24, 2017), doi.org/10.3389/fpsyg.2017.01454.

18. Krebs, interview with the author.

19. Michelle Pugle, "The Anatomy of the Amygdala," Verywell Health, April 1, 2021, verywellhealth.com/amygdala-5112775.

20. Krebs, interview with the author.

21. Bruce S. McEwen, "Physiology and Neurobiology of Stress and Adaptation: Central Role of the Brain," *Physiological Reviews* 87, no. 3 (July 2007): pp. 873–904, doi.org/10.1152/physrev.00041.2006.

22. Daniel Goleman, "Part Four: Windows of Opportunity," in *Emotional Intelligence: Why It Can Matter More Than IQ* (London, UK: Bloomsbury, 2009).

23. Krebs, interview with the author.

24. Krebs, interview with the author.

25. Elizabeth A. Phelps and Joseph E. LeDoux, "Contributions of the Amygdala to Emotion Processing: From Animal Models to Human Behavior," *Neuron* 48, no. 2 (October 2005): pp. 175–87, doi.org/10.1016/j.neuron.2005.09.025.

26. Daniel Goleman, Richard E. Boyatzis, and Annie McKee, "How the Brain Matters," in *Primal Leadership: Unleashing the Power of Emotional Intelligence* (Boston, MA: Harvard Business School, 2002), pp. 102–5.

27. Daniel Goleman, "What Makes a Leader?," Harvard Business Review, November–December 1998, pp. 93–102.

28. F. Gregory Ashby, Benjamin O. Turner, and Jon C. Horvitz, "Cortical and Basal Ganglia Contributions to Habit Learning and Automaticity," *Trends in Cognitive Sciences* 14, no. 5 (March 2010): pp. 208–15, doi.org/10.1016/j.tics.2010.02.001.

29. Krebs, interview with the author.

30. Kyle S. Smith and Ann M. Graybiel, "Habit Formation," *Dialogues in Clinical Neuroscience* 18, no. 1 (March 2016): pp. 33–43, doi.org/10.31887/dcns.2016.18.1/ksmith.

31. Claudio Da Cunha, Alexander Gomez-A, and Charles D. Blaha, "The Role of the Basal Ganglia in Motivated Behavior," *Reviews in the Neurosciences* 23, no. 5–6 (January 2012): pp. 747–67, doi.org/10.1515/revneuro-2012-0063.

32. Krebs, interview with the author.
33. Goleman, "What Makes a Leader?"
34. Krebs, interview with the author.
35. Goleman, "What Makes a Leader?"
36. Goleman, Boyatzis, and McKee, *Primal Leadership*, pp. 104–8.
37. Marilee Sprenger, "Chapter 3: Pieces and Parts: The Anatomy of the Brain," in *Learning and Memory: The Brain in Action* (Alexandria, VA: Association for Supervision and Curriculum Development, 1999), pp. 30–44.
38. Brené Brown, "Section Five: Curiosity and Grounded Confidence," in *Dare to Lead: Brave Work. Tough Conversations. Whole Hearts.* (New York, NY: Random House, 2018).
39. Mary Slaughter and David Rock, "No Pain, No Brain Gain: Why Learning Demands (a Little) Discomfort," Fast Company, April 30, 2018, fastcompany.com/40560075/no-pain-no-brain-gain-why-learning-demands-a-little-discomfort.

CHAPTER 5: WHAT LEADING WITH EMOTIONAL INTELLIGENCE LOOKS LIKE

1. Warren Bennis, "It Ain't What You Know," New York Times, October 25, 1998, archive.nytimes.com/www.nytimes.com/books/98/10/25/reviews/981025.25bennist.html.
2. Carol S. Dweck, *Mindset: The New Psychology of Success* (New York, NY: Random House, 2006).
3. Grant R. Bigg, "Appointment with the Titanic," in *Icebergs: Their Science and Links to Global Change* (Cambridge, UK: Cambridge University Press, 2015), pp. 1–20, doi.org/10.1017/CBO9781107589278.
4. Bigg, "Appointment with the Titanic."
5. Melissa Sloan et al., "Pandemic Emotions: The Extent, Correlates, and Mental Health Consequences of Personal and Altruistic Fear of COVID-19," *SocArXiv*, May 3, 2020, doi.org/10.31235/osf.io/txqb6.
6. "The Future of Jobs Report 2020," World Economic Forum, October 2020, weforum.org/reports/the-future-of-jobs-report-2020.
7. Hillary Anger Elfenbein, "Emotion in Organizations: A Review and Theoretical Integration in Stages," *Academy of Management Annals* 1 (January 2007): pp. 371–457, doi.org/10.2139/ssrn.942383.
8. Arran Caza et al., "How Do You Really Feel? Effect of Leaders' Perceived Emotional Sincerity on Followers' Trust," *Leadership Quarterly* 26, no. 4 (August 2015): pp. 518–31, doi.org/10.1016/j.leaqua.2015.05.008.
9. Caza et al., "How Do You Really Feel?"
10. Brené Brown, "What It Means to Dare Greatly," in *Daring Greatly: How the Courage to Be Vulnerable Transforms the Way We Live, Love, Parent, and Lead* (New York, NY: Gotham Books, 2012).
11. *Emotional Intelligence Superpowers | Marc Brackett | Talks at Google*, YouTube, 2017, youtube.com/watch?v=JcFefehMpz0.
12. Sunita Shukla, Farhat Mohsin, and Vikas Singh, "Relationship between Emotional Intelligence and Employee Engagement: A Study of Leading Printing Press in NCR," *Tecnia Journal of Management Studies* 8, no. 1 (September 2013): pp. 43–50.
13. Marco Nink and Jennifer Robison, "The Damage Inflicted by Poor Managers," Gallup, December 2016, news.gallup.com/businessjournal/200108/damage-inflicted-poor-managers.aspx.

14. Ilios Kotsou et al., "Emotional Plasticity: Conditions and Effects of Improving Emotional Competence in Adulthood," *Journal of Applied Psychology* 96, no. 4 (March 2011): pp. 827–39, doi.org/10.1037/a0023047.

15. Daniel Goleman, "Measuring Leadership's Impact," in *Leadership That Gets Results* (Boston, MA: Harvard Business Review, 2000), pp. 80–82.

16. "Emotional Intelligence (EQ) and Leadership," Norwich University Online, November 2020, online.norwich.edu/academic-programs/resources/ emotional-intelligence-eq-and-leadership.

17. Charles Riborg Mann, "Chapter XVI: The Professional Engineer," in *A Study of Engineering Education: Prepared for the Joint Committee on Engineering Education of the National Engineering Societies,* The Carnegie Foundation for the Advancement of Teaching, bulletin no. 11 (Boston, MA: Merrymount, 1918), pp. 106–13.

CHAPTER 6: IT STARTS WITH YOU BUT IT STAYS WITH THEM

1. Vipula Gandhi and Jennifer Robison, "The 'Great Resignation' Is Really the 'Great Discontent,'" Gallup, July 22, 2021, gallup.com/workplace/351545/great-resignation-really-great-discontent.aspx.

2. Falahat Nejadmahani Mohammad et al., "Emotional Intelligence and Turnover Intention," *International Journal of Academic Research* 6, no. 4 (July 2014): pp. 211–20, doi.org/10.7813/2075-4124.2014/6-4/B.33.

3. Daniel Goleman, Richard E. Boyatzis, and Annie McKee, *Primal Leadership: Unleashing the Power of Emotional Intelligence* (Boston, MA: Harvard Business School, 2002).

4. Susan A. David, *Emotional Agility: Get Unstuck, Embrace Change, and Thrive in Work and Life* (London, UK: Penguin Life, 2016).

5. Ying Lin et al., "Mental Toughness and Individual Differences in Learning, Educational and Work Performance, Psychological Well-Being, and Personality: A Systematic Review," *Frontiers in Psychology* 8 (August 11, 2017), doi.org/10.3389/ fpsyg.2017.01345.

6. "State of the Global Workplace 2021 Report," Gallup, June 2021, gallup.com/ workplace/349484/state-of-the-global-workplace.aspx.

7. John F. Helliwell et al., "World Happiness Report 2021," Sustainable Development Solutions Network, 2021, worldhappiness.report/ed/2021/.

8. John C. Maxwell, "The Definition of Leadership: Influence," in *Developing the Leader within You 2.0* (Nashville, TN: HarperCollins Leadership, 2018).

9. Carol S. Dweck, *Mindset: The New Psychology of Success* (New York, NY: Random House, 2006).

10. Arthur Freeman et al., *Cognition and Psychotherapy,* 2nd ed. (New York, NY: Springer, 2004).

11. *How to Embrace Emotions at Work, The Way We Work* (TED Series, 2020), ted.com/ talks/liz_fosslien_how_to_embrace_emotions_at_work?language=en.

12. Arran Caza et al., "How Do You Really Feel? Effect of Leaders' Perceived Emotional Sincerity on Followers' Trust," *Leadership Quarterly* 26, no. 4 (August 2015): pp. 518–31, doi.org/10.1016/j.leaqua.2015.05.008.

13. Jehangir Bharucha, "Creating an Honest, Transparent and Productive Workplace," *International Journal of Business Excellence* 15, no. 4 (2018): pp. 467–82, doi.org/10.1504/ijbex.2018.093872.

14. Michael Schrage, "Like It or Not, You Are Always Leading by Example," Harvard Business Review, October 5, 2016, hbr.org/2016/10 like-it-or-not-you-are-always-leading-by-example.

15. Dennis S. Reina and Michelle L. Reina, *Trust and Betrayal in the Workplace: Building Effective Relationships in Your Organization* (Oakland, CA: Berrett-Koehler, 2015).

16. Douglas Stone, Bruce Patton, and Sheila Heen, *Difficult Conversations: How to Discuss What Matters Most* (New York, NY: Penguin, 2010).

17. Lilia M. Cortina, "Unseen Injustice: Incivility as Modern Discrimination in Organizations," *Academy of Management Review* 33, no. 1 (2008): p. 62, doi.org/10.5465/amr.2008.27745097.

18. Dean A. Shepherd and Melissa S. Cardon, "Negative Emotional Reactions to Project Failure and the Self-Compassion to Learn from the Experience," *Journal of Management Studies* 46, no. 6 (2009): pp. 923–49, doi.org/10.1111/j.1467-6486.2009.00821.x.

19. Karen Struble Myers, "A 'Little and Big' Start to the New Year," Fred Rogers Center, January 20, 2016, fredrogerscenter.org/2016/01/a-little-and-big-start-to-the-new-year/.

20. James K. Harter, Frank L. Schmidt, and Corey L. M. Keyes, "Well-Being in the Workplace and Its Relationship to Business Outcomes: A Review of the Gallup Studies," in *Flourishing: Positive Psychology and the Life Well-Lived*, ed. Corey L. M. Keyes and Jonathan Haidt (Washington, DC: American Psychological Association, 2003), pp. 205–24, doi.org/10.1037/10594-009.

21. Daniel Goleman, *Leadership That Gets Results* (Boston, MA: Harvard Business Review, 2000).

SECTION II–THE *EI EXPERIENCE* SELF-COACHING TO ENHANCED EMOTIONAL INTELLIGENCE MODEL

1. Maike Neuhaus, "Self-Coaching Model Explained: 56 Questions & Techniques for Self-Mastery," PositivePsychology.com, December 13, 2021, positivepsychology.com/self-coaching-model/.

PART IV: SELF-DISCOVERY

1. Bill George et al., "Discovering Your Authentic Leadership," Harvard Business Review, February 2007, hbr.org/2007/02/discovering-your-authentic-leadership.

CHAPTER 7: STEP 1: CONNECT WITH YOURSELF

1. Brené Brown, "Introduction: Brave Leaders and Courage Cultures," in *Dare to Lead: Brave Work. Tough Conversations. Whole Hearts.* (New York, NY: Random House, 2018).

2. Brené Brown, *The Gifts of Imperfection: Let Go of Who You Think You're Supposed to Be and Embrace Who You Are* (Center City, MN: Hazelden, 2010).

3. *Emotional Quotient Inventory 2.0 (EQ-i 2.0) User's Handbook* (Toronto, ON: Multi-Health Systems Inc., 2011).

4. Jim Collins, *Good to Great: Why Some Companies Make the Leap . . . and Others Don't*, 1st ed. (New York, NY: HarperCollins, 2001).

5. Rich Bellis and Steven J. Stein, "This Emotional Intelligence Test Was So Accurate It Was Creepy," Fast Company, June 27, 2017, fastcompany.com/40434451/this-emotional-intelligence-test-was-so-accurate-it-was-creepy.

6. Jim Heskett, "So We Adapt. What's the Downside?," Harvard Business School, July 7, 2011, hbswk.hbs.edu/item/so-we-adapt-whats-the-downside.

7. Sarah K. Davis and Rachel Nichols, "Does Emotional Intelligence Have a 'Dark' Side? A Review of the Literature," *Frontiers in Psychology* 7 (August 30, 2016), doi.org/10.3389/fpsyg.2016.01316.

8. Kristin Neff, "Chapter 1: The Fundamentals of Self-Compassion," in *Fierce Self-Compassion: How Women Can Harness Kindness to Speak Up, Claim Their Power, and Thrive*, 1st ed. (New York, NY: Harper Wave, 2021), pp. 23–50.

9. Quoted in Tchiki Davis, "Inadequacy: Definition & Overcoming These Feelings," The Berkeley Well-Being Institute, accessed February 10, 2022, berkeleywellbeing.com/inadequacy.html.

CHAPTER 8: STEP 2: CONSULT WITH OTHERS

1. Ronald M. Epstein, "Mindful Practice," *JAMA* 282, no. 9 (January 1999): pp. 833–39, doi.org/10.1001/jama.282.9.833.

2. DNews, "Wrong Reality: Why Our Self-Perception Is So Off," Seeker, April 23, 2013, seeker.com/wrong-reality-why-our-self-perception-is-so-off-1767455982.html.

3. Owen Hargie and David Dickson, *Skilled Interpersonal Communication: Research, Theory and Practice*, 4th ed. (London, UK: Routledge, 2004).

4. Steve Loughnan et al., "Economic Inequality Is Linked to Biased Self-Perception," *Psychological Science* 22, no. 10 (2011): pp. 1254–58, doi.org/10.1177/0956797611417003.

5. Gordon L. Patzer, *Looks: Why They Matter More Than You Ever Imagined* (New York, NY: AMACOM, 2008).

6. Stathis Grapsas et al., "The 'Why' and 'How' of Narcissism: A Process Model of Narcissistic Status Pursuit," *Perspectives on Psychological Science* 15, no. 1 (December 5, 2019): pp. 150–72, doi.org/10.1177/1745691619873350.

7. Jonice Webb and Christine Musello, "Part II: Out of Fuel," in *Running on Empty: Overcome Your Childhood Emotional Neglect* (New York, NY: Morgan James, 2013).

8. Prabhakararao Sampthirao, "Self-Concept and Interpersonal Communication," *International Journal of Indian Psychology* 3, no. 3 (2016): pp. 177–89, doi.org/10.25215/0303.115.

9. *Dove Real Beauty Sketches | You're More Beautiful Than You Think (3mins)*, YouTube, 2013, youtube.com/watch?v=XpaOjMxyJGk.

10. DNews, "Wrong Reality."

11. DNews, "Wrong Reality."

12. Quoted in DNews, "Wrong Reality."

13. Jena E. Pincott, "Silencing Your Inner Critic," Psychology Today, March 4, 2019, psychologytoday.com/us/articles/201903/silencing-your-inner-critic.

14. Barbara McGavin, "Transforming Our Inner Critics: The Power of Presence," *Self & Society* 33, no. 2 (2005): pp. 24–29, doi.org/10.1080/03060497.2005.11083872.

15. Susan Jeffers, *Feel the Fear ... and Do It Anyway: Dynamic Techniques for Turning Fear, Indecision, and Anger into Power, Action, and Love*, rev. ed. (1987; Santa Monica, CA: Jeffers Press, 2007).

16. Céleste Grimard and J. Andrew Morris, "Stepping Up to the Plate: Facing Up to Your Fear of Assuming a Leadership Role," in *Engaged Leadership: Transforming through Future-Oriented Design Thinking*, ed. Joan Marques and Satinder Dhiman (Cham, Switzerland: Springer, 2018), pp. 173–84, doi.org/10.1007/978-3-319-72221-4_9.

17. Quoted in William Donaldson, "In Praise of the 'Ologies': A Discussion of and Framework for Using Soft Skills to Sense and Influence Emergent Behaviors in Sociotechnical Systems," *Systems Engineering* 20, no. 5 (2017): pp. 467–78, doi.org/10.1002/sys.21408. Emphasis in original.

18. Douglas Stone and Sheila Heen, *Thanks for the Feedback: The Science and Art of Receiving Feedback Well* (New York, NY: Viking Penguin, 2014).

19. Stone and Heen, *Thanks for the Feedback*.

20. Amy C. Edmondson, "Managing the Risk of Learning: Psychological Safety in Work Teams," Harvard Business School, 2002, hbs.edu/faculty/Pages/item.aspx?num=12333.
21. Manuel London, "Preface," in *Leadership Development: Paths to Self-Insight and Professional Growth* (Mahwah, NJ: Lawrence Erlbaum Associates, 2002).
22. Jack Zenger and Joseph Folkman, "Your Employees Want the Negative Feedback You Hate to Give," Harvard Business Review, January 15, 2014, hbr.org/2014/01/your-employees-want-the-negative-feedback-you-hate-to-give.
23. M. Eraut et al., "Learning in the Professional Workplace: Relationships between Learning Factors and Contextual Factors," (University of Brighton, AERA 2004 Conference, June 4, 2004), research.brighton.ac.uk/en/publications/learning-in-the-professional-workplace-relationships-between-lear.
24. Jamie A. Gruman and Alan M. Saks, "Performance Management and Employee Engagement," *Human Resource Management Review* 21, no. 2 (2011): pp. 123, doi.org/10.1016/j.hrmr.2010.09.004.
25. Susan Adams, "Forget Self-Centered: Millennials Could Be the Most Ambitious Generation," Bentley University, accessed January 24, 2022, bentley.edu/news/forget-self-centered-millennials-could-be-most-ambitious-generation.
26. Kristin Holmberg-Wright, Tracy Hribar, and J. D. Tsegai, "More Than Money: Business Strategies to Engage Millennials," *Business Education Innovation* 9, no. 2 (2017): pp. 14–23, beijournal.com/images/2_v9n2_final_2-2.pdf.
27. Brian J. Brim and Jim Asplund, "Driving Engagement by Focusing on Strengths," Gallup, Business Journal, November 12, 2009, news.gallup.com/businessjournal/124214/driving-engagement-focusing-strengths.aspx.
28. *Friday Night Lights* | *"Clear Eyes, Full Hearts, Can't Lose,"* YouTube 2020, youtube.com/watch?v=fQPe4RigYmg.

CHAPTER 9: STEP 3: CLARIFY YOUR FOCUS

1. Stephen D. Brookfield, *Becoming a Critically Reflective Teacher*, 2nd ed. (San Francisco, CA: Jossey-Bass, 2017).
2. Marshall B. Rosenberg, "Chapter 9: Connecting Compassionately with Ourselves," in *Nonviolent Communication: A Language of Life*, 3rd ed. (Encinitas, CA: PuddleDancer, 2015).
3. Daniel J. Siegel, "Half a Brain in Hiding: Balancing Left and Right," in *Mindsight: The New Science of Personal Transformation* (New York, NY: Bantam Books, 2010), pp. 102–19.
4. Kristin D. Neff, "The Development and Validation of a Scale to Measure Self-Compassion," *Self and Identity* 2, no. 3 (July 2003): pp. 223–50, doi.org/10.1080/15298860309027.
5. Edwin H. Friedman, *A Failure of Nerve: Leadership in the Age of the Quick Fix*, ed. Margaret M. Treadwell and Edward W. Beal (New York, NY: Church, 2007).
6. Edward L. Deci and Richard M. Ryan, "Facilitating Optimal Motivation and Psychological Well-Being across Life's Domains," *Canadian Psychology/Psychologie Canadienne* 49, no. 1 (2008): pp. 14–23, doi.org/10.1037/0708-5591.49.1.14.
7. Steven Pressfield, *The War of Art: Break Through the Blocks and Win Your Inner Creative Battles* (New York, NY: Warner Books, 2002).
8. Laura Vanderkam, "Are You as Busy as You Think?," Wall Street Journal, February 22, 2012, wsj.com/articles/SB10001424052970203358704577237603853394654.
9. George T. Doran, "There's a S.M.A.R.T. Way to Write Management's Goals and Objectives," *Management Review* 70, no. 11 (1981): pp. 35–36.
10. Quoted in Larry Prusak, "What Can't Be Measured," Harvard Business Review, October 7, 2010, hbr.org/2010/10/what-cant-be-measured.

PART VI: READY, SET, ACTION!

1. Steven Pressfield, *The War of Art: Break Through the Blocks and Win Your Inner Creative Battles* (New York, NY: Warner Books, 2002).

CHAPTER 10: INTERLUDE–POSSIBILITIES TO ENHANCE YOUR EMOTIONAL INTELLIGENCE

1. Henry Stanley Haskins, *Meditations in Wall Street*, introduction by Albert Jay Nock (New York, NY: William Morrow, 1940).
2. Susan A. David, *Emotional Agility: Get Unstuck, Embrace Change, and Thrive in Work and Life* (London, UK: Penguin Life, 2016).
3. Kathleen Mikkelsen et al., "Exercise and Mental Health," *Maturitas* 106 (2017): pp. 48–56, doi.org/10.1016/j.maturitas.2017.09.003.
4. Cassandra Clare, *Clockwork Angel* (New York, NY: Margaret K. McElderry Books, 2010).
5. Michael Caldara et al., "A Study of the Triggers of Conflict and Emotional Reactions," *Games* 8, no. 2 (2017): p. 21, doi.org/10.3390/g8020021.
6. Elizabeth Gilbert, *Eat, Pray, Love: One Woman's Search for Everything across Italy, India and Indonesia* (New York, NY: Viking Penguin, 2006).
7. Daniel J. Siegel, "Half a Brain in Hiding: Balancing Left and Right," in *Mindsight: The New Science of Personal Transformation* (New York, NY: Bantam Books, 2010), pp. 102–19.
8. Chester Louis Karrass, *In Business as in Life, You Don't Get What You Deserve, You Get What You Negotiate* (Stanford, CA: Stanford Street, 1996).
9. Brené Brown, "Section Two: The Call to Courage," in *Dare to Lead: Brave Work. Tough Conversations. Whole Hearts.* (New York, NY: Random House, 2018).
10. "Being Assertive: Reduce Stress, Communicate Better," Mayo Clinic, May 29, 2020, mayoclinic.org/healthy-lifestyle/stress-management/in-depth/assertive/art-20044644?pg=1&reDate=11122020.
11. Mandy Hale, *The Single Woman: Life, Love, and a Dash of Sass* (Nashville, TN: Thomas Nelson, 2013).
12. Stephen R. Covey, *The 7 Habits of Highly Effective People: Powerful Lessons in Personal Change*, infographics ed. (Coral Gables, FL: Mango Publishing Group, 2017).
13. "8 Ways to Build Workplace Relationships," Indeed, June 9, 2021, indeed.com/career-advice/career-development/how-to-build-relationships?aceid=&gclid=CjwK CAiAgvKQBhBbEiwAaPQw3NZ_wBHemZpUS3sV0.
14. Marc Brackett, "Chapter 3: How to Become an Emotion Scientist," in *Permission to Feel: Unlocking the Power of Emotions to Help Our Kids, Ourselves, and Our Society Thrive* (New York, NY: Celadon Books, 2019).
15. Laura G. Kiken and Natalie J. Shook, "Looking Up: Mindfulness Increases Positive Judgments and Reduces Negativity Bias," *Social Psychological and Personality Science* 2, no. 4 (2011): pp. 425–31, doi.org/10.1177/1948550610396585.
16. Albert Mehrabian and Susan R. Ferris, "Inference of Attitudes from Nonverbal Communication in Two Channels," *Journal of Consulting Psychology* 31, no. 3 (1967): pp. 248–52, doi.org/10.1037/h0024648.
17. Carol S. Dweck, *Mindset: The New Psychology of Success* (New York, NY: Random House, 2006).
18. Dave Eggers, *A Hologram for the King* (San Francisco, CA: McSweeney's, 2012).
19. Elizabeth Dove, "How Can You Facilitate Individual Social Responsibility?," Imagine Canada, April 15, 2018, imaginecanada.ca/en/360/how-can-you-facilitate-individual-social-responsibility.

20. Edwin Louis Cole, *Profiles in Courageous Manhood* (Tulsa, OK: Albury, 1998).
21. Yu Song et al., "Effects of Incidental Positive Emotion and Cognitive Reappraisal on Affective Responses to Negative Stimuli," *Cognition and Emotion* 33, no. 6 (2019): pp. 1155–68, doi.org/10.1080/02699931.2018.1541789.
22. Gary John Bishop, *Unfu*k Yourself: Get out of Your Head and into Your Life* (New York, NY: HarperOne, 2017).
23. Thomas D. Albright, "Why Eyewitnesses Fail," *PNAS* 114, no. 30 (2017): pp. 7758–64, doi.org/10.1073/pnas.1706891114.
24. Olivier Serrat, "The Five Whys Technique," in *Knowledge Solutions* (Singapore: Springer, 2017), pp. 307–10, doi.org/10.1007/978-981-10-0983-9_32.
25. Vincent van Gogh to Theo van Gogh, October 22, 1882, in *Vincent van Gogh Letters* (Van Gogh Museum of Amsterdam), vangoghletters.org/vg/letters/let274/letter.html.
26. Christine Carter, *The Sweet Spot: How to Find Your Groove at Home and Work* (New York, NY: Ballantine Books, 2015).
27. Quoted in Yijun Xing, "A Daoist Reflection on Sea-Like Leadership and Enlightened Thinking," *Management and Organization Review* 12, no. 4 (2016): pp. 807–10, doi.org/10.1017/mor.2016.48.
28. Jennifer Moss, "Why It's Important to Stretch and Improve Your Emotional Flexibility: Jennifer Moss," CBC/Radio Canada, November 1, 2020, cbc.ca/news/canada/kitchener-waterloo/happiness-column-jennifer-moss-emotional-flexibility-1.5781721.
29. Dweck, *Mindset*.
30. Linda Connor et al., "Environmental Change and Human Health in Upper Hunter Communities of New South Wales, Australia," *EcoHealth* 1, no. S2 (October 28, 2004): pp. 47–58, doi.org/10.1007/s10393-004-0053-2.
31. Jamie S. Hughes et al., "Stress and Coping Activity: Reframing Negative Thoughts," *Teaching of Psychology* 38, no. 1 (2011): pp. 36–39, doi.org/10.1177/0098628310390852.
32. Eckhart Tolle, *The Power of Now: A Guide to Spiritual Enlightenment* (San Francisco, CA: New World Library, 1999).
33. Oscar Wilde, *Lady Windermere's Fan*, 1892 (Salt Lake City, UT: Project Gutenberg, 1997), gutenberg.org/files/790/790-h/790-h.htm.

CHAPTER 11: STEP 4: CONSIDER YOUR POSSIBILITIES AND BARRIERS

1. John Whitmore, "What Options Do You Have?," in *Coaching for Performance: GROWing Human Potential and Purpose*, 4th ed. (Boston, MA: Nicholas Brealey, 2009), pp. 79–84.
2. Whitmore, "What Options Do You Have?"
3. Robert H. Ennis, "Identifying Implicit Assumptions," *Synthese* 51, no. 1 (April 1982): pp. 61–86, doi.org/http://www.jstor.org/stable/20115734.
4. Edwin A. Locke and Gary P. Latham, "The Application of Goal Setting to Sports," *Journal of Sport Psychology* 7, no. 3 (1985): pp. 205–22, doi.org/10.1123/jsp.7.3.205.

CHAPTER 12: STEP 5: CRAFT YOUR ACTION PLAN

1. Kathrin Krause and Alexandra M. Freund, "How to Beat Procrastination," *European Psychologist* 19, no. 2 (January 2014): pp. 132–44, doi.org/10.1027/1016-9040/a000153.
2. Gail Matthews, "The Impact of Commitment, Accountability, and Written Goals on Goal Achievement," (podium presentation, 87th Convention of the Western Psychological Association, Vancouver, BC, 2007), scholar.dominican.edu/psychology-faculty-conference-presentations/3/.

3. Lee Colan, "A Lesson from Roy A. Disney on Making Values-Based Decisions," Inc., July 24, 2019, inc.com/lee-colan/a-lesson-from-roy-a-disney-on-making-values-based-decisions.html.
4. Liat Levontin and Anat Bardi, "Using Personal Values to Understand the Motivational Basis of Amity Goal Orientation," *Frontiers in Psychology* 9 (January 9, 2019), doi.org/10.3389/fpsyg.2018.02736.
5. Asher R. Pacht, "Reflections on Perfection," *American Psychologist* 39, no. 4 (April 1984): pp. 386–90, doi.org/10.1037/0003-066x.39.4.386.
6. Quoted in Stephen R. Covey, foreword to *Prisoners of Our Thoughts: Viktor Frankl's Principles for Discovering Meaning in Life and Work*, 2nd ed., by Alex Pattakos (Oakland, CA: Berrett-Koehler, 2010), pp. v–xi.
7. Forbes Coaches Council, "Why Experiential Learning Should Be Part of Your Employee Training," Forbes, June 27, 2017, forbes.com/sites/forbescoachescouncil/2017/06/27/why-experiential-learning-should-be-part-of-your-employee-training/?sh=3c86605c585b.

CHAPTER 13: STEP 6: CONFIRM YOUR COMMITMENT AND CLOSE YOUR CONVERSATION

1. Kerry Patterson et al., *Crucial Accountability: Tools for Resolving Violated Expectations, Broken Commitments, and Bad Behavior*, 2nd ed. (New York, NY: McGraw-Hill Education, 2013).
2. Edward L. Deci and Richard M. Ryan, *Intrinsic Motivation and Self-Determination in Human Behavior* (New York, NY: Plenum, 1985).
3. Adrienne Santos-Longhurst, "Intrinsic Motivation: How to Pick Up Healthy Motivation Techniques," Healthline, February 11, 2019, healthline.com/health/intrinsic-motivation.
4. Deci and Ryan, "Extrinsic Motivation and Development," in *Intrinsic Motivation*.
5. Deci and Ryan, "Self-Determination: A Brief History," in *Intrinsic Motivation*.
6. Deci and Ryan, "Constraints and Other Extrinsic Factors," in *Intrinsic Motivation*.
7. Simon Sinek, David Mead, and Peter Docker, "Chapter 1: Start with Why: A Primer," in *Find Your Why: A Practical Guide for Discovering Purpose for You and Your Team* (New York, NY: Portfolio/Penguin, 2017).
8. Crystal Raypole, "How to Be Emotionally Supportive," Healthline, September 10, 2021, healthline.com/health/mental-health/emotional-support.
9. Pia Mellody, *Facing Codependence: What It Is, Where It Comes from, How It Sabotages Our Lives*, with Andrea Wells Miller and J. Keith Miller (New York, NY: Harper & Row, 1989).

CONCLUSION

1. James Clear, *Atomic Habits: An Easy & Proven Way to Build Good Habits & Break Bad Ones* (New York, NY: Avery, 2018).

BIBLIOGRAPHY

Abi-Jaoude, Elia, Karline Treurnicht Naylor, and Antonio Pignatiello. "Smartphones, Social Media Use and Youth Mental Health." *Canadian Medical Association Journal* 192, no. 6 (February 10, 2020). doi.org/10.1503/cmaj.190434.

Adams, Susan. "Forget Self-Centered: Millennials Could Be the Most Ambitious Generation." Bentley University. Accessed January 24, 2022. bentley.edu/news/forget-self-centered-millennials-could-be-most-ambitious-generation.

Albright, Thomas D. "Why Eyewitnesses Fail." *PNAS* 114, no. 30 (2017): 7758–64. doi.org/10.1073/pnas.1706891114.

Ançel, Gülsüm, and Elif Kabakçi. "Psychometric Properties of the Turkish Form of Codependency Assessment Tool." *Archives of Psychiatric Nursing* 23, no. 6 (December 2009): 441–53. doi.org/10.1016/j.apnu.2008.10.004.

Andrade, Eduardo B., and Dan Ariely. "The Enduring Impact of Transient Emotions on Decision Making." *Organizational Behavior and Human Decision Processes* 109, no. 1 (May 2009): 1–8. doi.org/10.1016/j.obhdp.2009.02.003.

Anwar, Yasmin. "Emotional Intelligence Peaks as We Enter Our 60s, Research Suggests." Berkeley News, December 16, 2010. news.berkeley.edu/2010/12/16/agingemotion/.

Arnsten, Amy F. T. "Stress Signalling Pathways That Impair Prefrontal Cortex Structure and Function." *Nature Reviews Neuroscience* 10, no. 6 (June 2009): 410–22. doi.org/10.1038/nrn2648.

Arnsten, Amy, Carolyn M. Mazure, and Rajita Sinha. "This Is Your Brain in Meltdown." *Scientific American* 306, no. 4 (April 2012): 48–53. doi.org/10.1038/scientificamerican0412-48.

Aschbacher, Kirstin, Aoife O'Donovan, Owen M. Wolkowitz, Firdaus S. Dhabhar, Yali Su, and Elissa Epel. "Good Stress, Bad Stress and Oxidative Stress: Insights from Anticipatory Cortisol Reactivity." *Psychoneuroendocrinology* 38, no. 9 (September 2013): 1698–1708. doi.org/10.1016/j.psyneuen.2013.02.004.

Ashby, F. Gregory, Benjamin O. Turner, and Jon C. Horvitz. "Cortical and Basal Ganglia Contributions to Habit Learning and Automaticity." *Trends in Cognitive Sciences* 14, no. 5 (March 2010): 208–15. doi.org/10.1016/j.tics.2010.02.001.

Barbey, Aron K., Roberto Colom, and Jordan Grafman. "Distributed Neural System for Emotional Intelligence Revealed by Lesion Mapping." *Social Cognitive and Affective Neuroscience* 9, no. 3 (December 6, 2012): 265–72. doi.org/10.1093/scan/nss124.

Bechtoldt, Myriam N. "Chapter 6: Emotional Intelligence, Professional Qualifications, and Psychologists' Need for Gender Research." In *Sexualized Brains: Scientific Modeling of Emotional Intelligence from a Cultural Perspective*, edited by Nicole C. Karafyllis and Gotlind Ulshöfer, 117–30. Cambridge, MA: MIT, 2008.

"Being Assertive: Reduce Stress, Communicate Better." Mayo Clinic, May 29, 2020. mayoclinic.org/healthy-lifestyle/stress-management/in-depth/assertive/art-20044644?pg=1&reDate=11122020.

Bellis, Rich, and Steven J. Stein. "This Emotional Intelligence Test Was So Accurate It Was Creepy." Fast Company, June 27, 2017. fastcompany.com/40434451/this-emotional-intelligence-test-was-so-accurate-it-was-creepy.

Bennis, Warren. "It Ain't What You Know." New York Times, October 25, 1998. archive.
    nytimes.com/www.nytimes.com/books/98/10/25/reviews/981025.25bennist.html.
Bessant, John, and Joseph Tidd. "Chapter 17: Learning to Manage Innovation and
    Entrepreneurship." In *Innovation and Entrepreneurship*, 3rd ed., 483–500.
    West Sussex, UK: John Wiley & Sons, 2015.
Bharucha, Jehangir. "Creating an Honest, Transparent and Productive Workplace."
    International Journal of Business Excellence 15, no. 4 (2018): 467–82.
    doi.org/10.1504/ijbex.2018.093872.
Bigg, Grant R. "Appointment with the Titanic." In *Icebergs: Their Science and Links
    to Global Change*, 1–20. Cambridge, UK: Cambridge University Press, 2015.
    doi.org/10.1017/cbo9781107589278.
Bishop, Gary John. *Unfu*k Yourself: Get Out of Your Head and Into Your Life.*
    New York, NY: HarperOne, 2017.
Boerma, Marjan, Elizabeth A. Coyle, Michael A. Dietrich, Matthew R. Dintzner,
    Shannon J. Drayton, Johnnie L. Early, Andrea N. Edginton, et al. "Point/
    Counterpoint: Are Outstanding Leaders Born or Made?" *American Journal of
    Pharmaceutical Education* 81, no. 3 (2017): 58. doi.org/10.5688/ajpe81358.
Brackett, Marc. *Permission to Feel: Unlocking the Power of Emotions to Help Our
    Kids, Ourselves, and Our Society Thrive*. New York, NY: Celadon Books, 2019.
Bradberry, Travis, and Jean Greaves. *Emotional Intelligence 2.0*. San Diego, CA:
    TalentSmart, 2009.
Bradshaw, John. "The Hiding Places of Toxic Shame." In *Healing the Shame That
    Binds You*, 108. Deerfield Beach, FL: Health Communications, 1988.
Brim, Brian J., and Jim Asplund. "Driving Engagement by Focusing on
    Strengths." Gallup. Business Journal, November 12, 2009. news.gallup.com/
    businessjournal/124214/driving-engagement-focusing-strengths.aspx.
Brookfield, Stephen D. *Becoming a Critically Reflective Teacher*. 2nd ed.
    San Francisco, CA: Jossey-Bass, 2017.
Brown, Brené. *Dare to Lead: Brave Work. Tough Conversations. Whole Hearts*.
    New York, NY: Random House, 2018.
Brown, Brené. "Preface." In *The Gifts of Imperfection: Let Go of Who You Think You're
    Supposed to Be and Embrace Who You Are*. Center City, MN: Hazelden, 2010.
Brown, Brené. "What It Means to Dare Greatly." In *Daring Greatly: How the Courage
    to Be Vulnerable Transforms the Way We Live, Love, Parent, and Lead*.
    New York, NY: Gotham Books, 2012.
Buijs, Ruud M., and Corbert G. Van Eden. "The Integration of Stress by the
    Hypothalamus, Amygdala and Prefrontal Cortex: Balance between the Autonomic
    Nervous System and the Neuroendocrine System." *Progress in Brain Research*
    126 (2000): 117–32. doi.org/10.1016/s0079-6123(00)26011-1.
Caldara, Michael, Michael T. McBride, Matthew W. McCarter, and Roman M.
    Sheremeta. "A Study of the Triggers of Conflict and Emotional Reactions."
    Games 8, no. 2 (2017): 21. doi.org/10.3390/g8020021.
Carnegie, Dale. "Fundamental Techniques in Handling People." In *How to Win Friends
    and Influence People*. 1936. Rev. ed. New York, NY: Simon and Schuster, 1981.
Carr, Deborah. *Worried Sick: How Stress Hurts Us and How to Bounce Back*.
    New Brunswick, NJ: Rutgers University Press, 2014.
Carter, Christine. *The Sweet Spot: How to Find Your Groove at Home and Work*.
    New York, NY: Ballantine Books, 2015.
Catarino, Francisca, Paul Gilbert, Kirsten McEwan, and Rita Baião. "Compassion
    Motivations: Distinguishing Submissive Compassion from Genuine Compassion

and Its Association with Shame, Submissive Behavior, Depression, Anxiety and Stress." *Journal of Social and Clinical Psychology* 33, no. 5 (2014): 399–412. doi.org/10.1521/jscp.2014.33.5.399.

Caza, Arran, Gang Zhang, Lu Wang, and Yuntao Bai. "How Do You Really Feel? Effect of Leaders' Perceived Emotional Sincerity on Followers' Trust." *Leadership Quarterly* 26, no. 4 (August 2015): 518–31. doi.org/10.1016/j.leaqua.2015.05.008.

Chandola, Tarani, Eric Brunner, and Michael Marmot. "Chronic Stress at Work and the Metabolic Syndrome: Prospective Study." *BMJ* 332, no. 7540 (2006): 521–25. doi.org/10.1136/bmj.38693.435301.80.

Clare, Cassandra. *Clockwork Angel.* New York, NY: Margaret K. McElderry Books, 2010.

Clear, James. *Atomic Habits: An Easy & Proven Way to Build Good Habits & Break Bad Ones.* New York, NY: Avery, 2018.

Clifton, Jim. "The Mood of the World." Gallup, May 4, 2021. gallup.com/workplace/349229/mood-world.aspx.

Colan, Lee. "A Lesson from Roy A. Disney on Making Values-Based Decisions." Inc., July 24, 2019. inc.com/lee-colan/a-lesson-from-roy-a-disney-on-making-values-based-decisions.html.

Cole, Edwin Louis. *Profiles in Courageous Manhood.* Tulsa, OK: Albury, 1998.

Collins, Jim. *Good to Great: Why Some Companies Make the Leap … and Others Don't.* 1st ed. New York, NY: HarperCollins, 2001.

Colman, Douglas E., Reinalyn Echon, Michelle S. Lemay, Jennifer McDonald, Kathleen R. Smith, Julie Spencer, and Joshua K. Swift. "The Efficacy of Self-Care for Graduate Students in Professional Psychology: A Meta-Analysis." *Training and Education in Professional Psychology* 10, no. 4 (2016): 188–97. doi.org/10.1037/tep0000130.

Connor, Linda, Glenn Albrecht, Nick Higginbotham, Sonia Freeman, and Wayne Smith. "Environmental Change and Human Health in Upper Hunter Communities of New South Wales, Australia." *EcoHealth* 1, no. S2 (October 28, 2004): 47–58. doi.org/10.1007/s10393-004-0053-2.

Cortina, Lilia M. "Unseen Injustice: Incivility as Modern Discrimination in Organizations." *Academy of Management Review* 33, no. 1 (2008): 62. doi.org/10.5465/amr.2008.27745097.

Covey, Stephen R. Foreword to *Prisoners of Our Thoughts: Viktor Frankl's Principles for Discovering Meaning in Life and Work*, 2nd ed., by Alex Pattakos, v–xi. Oakland, CA: Berrett-Koehler, 2010.

Covey, Stephen R. *The 7 Habits of Highly Effective People: Powerful Lessons in Personal Change.* Infographics ed. Coral Gables, FL: Mango Publishing Group, 2017.

Cunha, Claudio Da, Alexander Gomez-A, and Charles D. Blaha. "The Role of the Basal Ganglia in Motivated Behavior." *Reviews in the Neurosciences* 23, no. 5–6 (January 2012): 747–67. doi.org/10.1515/revneuro-2012-0063.

Dagdag, Januard D., Hydee G. Cuizon, and Aisie O. Bete. "College Students' Problems and Their Link to Academic Performance: Basis for Needs-Driven Student Programs." *Journal of Research, Policy & Practice of Teachers & Teacher Education* 9, no. 2 (December 2019): 54–65. doi.org/10.37134/jrpptte.vol9.no2.5.2019.

David, Susan A. *Emotional Agility: Get Unstuck, Embrace Change, and Thrive in Work and Life.* London, UK: Penguin Life, 2016.

Davis, Sarah K., and Rachel Nichols. "Does Emotional Intelligence Have a 'Dark' Side? A Review of the Literature." *Frontiers in Psychology* 7 (August 30, 2016). doi.org/10.3389/fpsyg.2016.01316.

Davis, Tchiki. "Inadequacy: Definition & Overcoming These Feelings." The Berkeley Well-Being Institute. Accessed February 10, 2022. berkeleywellbeing.com/inadequacy.html.

Deci, Edward L., and Richard M. Ryan. "Facilitating Optimal Motivation and Psychological Well-Being across Life's Domains." *Canadian Psychology/Psychologie Canadienne* 49, no. 1 (2008): 14–23. doi.org/10.1037/0708-5591.49.1.14.

Deci, Edward L., and Richard M. Ryan. *Intrinsic Motivation and Self-Determination in Human Behavior.* New York, NY: Plenum, 1985.

Delamater, Ronald J., and J. Regis McNamara. "The Social Impact of Assertiveness." *Behavior Modification* 10, no. 2 (April 1986): 139–58. doi.org/10.1177/01454455860102001.

DNews. "Wrong Reality: Why Our Self-Perception Is So Off." Seeker, April 23, 2013. seeker.com/wrong-reality-why-our-self-perception-is-so-off-1767455982.html.

Donaldson, William. "In Praise of the 'Ologies': A Discussion of and Framework for Using Soft Skills to Sense and Influence Emergent Behaviors in Sociotechnical Systems." *Systems Engineering* 20, no. 5 (2017): 467–78. doi.org/10.1002/sys.21408.

Doran, George T. "There's a S.M.A.R.T. Way to Write Management's Goals and Objectives." *Management Review* 70, no. 11 (1981): 35–36.

Dove, Elizabeth. "How Can You Facilitate Individual Social Responsibility?" Imagine Canada, April 15, 2018. imaginecanada.ca/en/360/how-can-you-facilitate-individual-social-responsibility.

Dove Real Beauty Sketches | You're More Beautiful Than You Think (3mins). YouTube. 2013. youtube.com/watch?v=XpaOjMxyJGk.

Dweck, Carol S. *Mindset: The New Psychology of Success.* New York, NY: Random House, 2006.

Edmondson, Amy C. "Managing the Risk of Learning: Psychological Safety in Work Teams." Harvard Business School Working Paper, 2002. hbs.edu/faculty/Pages/item.aspx?num=12333.

Eggers, Dave. *A Hologram for the King.* San Francisco, CA: McSweeney's, 2012.

"8 Ways to Build Workplace Relationships." Indeed, June 9, 2021. indeed.com/career-advice/career-development/how-to-build-relationships?aceid=&gclid=Cj wKCAiAgvKQBhBbEiwAaPQw3NZ_WBHemZpUS3sV0.

Elfenbein, Hillary Anger. "Emotion in Organizations: A Review and Theoretical Integration in Stages." *Academy of Management Annals* 1 (January 2007): 371–457. doi.org/10.2139/ssrn.942383.

"Emotional Intelligence (EQ) and Leadership." Norwich University Online, November 2020. online.norwich.edu/academic-programs/resources/emotional-intelligence-eq-and-leadership.

Emotional Intelligence Superpowers | Marc Brackett | Talks at Google. YouTube, 2017. youtube.com/watch?v=JcFefehMpz0.

Emotional Quotient Inventory 2.0 (EQ-i 2.0) User's Handbook. Toronto, ON: Multi-Health Systems Inc., 2011.

Ennis, Robert H. "Identifying Implicit Assumptions." *Synthese* 51, no. 1 (April 1982): 61–86. doi.org/http://www.jstor.org/stable/20115734.

Epstein, Ronald M. "Mindful Practice." *JAMA* 282, no. 9 (January 1999): 833–39. doi.org/10.1001/jama.282.9.833.

Eraut, M., F. J. Maillardet, C. Miller, S. Steadman, S. Ali, C. Blackman, and J. Furner. "Learning in the Professional Workplace: Relationships between Learning Factors and Contextual Factors." University of Brighton. AERA 2004 Conference, June 4, 2004. research.brighton.ac.uk/en/publications/learning-in-the-professional-workplace-relationships-between-lear.

Fisher, Deena, and John Beer. "Codependency and Self-Esteem among High School Students." *Psychological Reports* 66, no. 3 (1990): 1001–2. doi.org/10.2466/pr0.1990.66.3.1001.

Forbes Coaches Council. "Why Experiential Learning Should Be Part of Your Employee Training." Forbes, June 27, 2017. forbes.com/sites/forbescoachescouncil/2017/06/27/why-experiential-learning-should-be-part-of-your-employee-training/?sh=3c86605c585b.

Ford, Brett Q., Phoebe Lam, Oliver P. John, and Iris B. Mauss. "The Psychological Health Benefits of Accepting Negative Emotions and Thoughts: Laboratory, Diary, and Longitudinal Evidence." *Journal of Personality and Social Psychology* 115, no. 6 (2018): 1075–92. doi.org/10.1037/pspp0000157.

Freeman, Arthur, Michael J. Mahoney, Paul Devito, and Donna Martin. *Cognition and Psychotherapy*. 2nd ed. New York, NY: Springer, 2004.

Friday Night Lights | "Clear Eyes, Full Hearts, Can't Lose." YouTube, 2020. youtube.com/watch?v=fQPe4RigYmg.

Friedman, Edwin H. *A Failure of Nerve: Leadership in the Age of the Quick Fix*, edited by Margaret M. Treadwell and Edward W. Beal. New York, NY: Church, 2007.

"The Future of Education and Skills." OECD Future of Education and Skills 2030, May 2018. oecd.org/education/2030/E2030%20Position%20Paper%20%2805.04.2018%29.pdf.

"The Future of Jobs Report 2020." World Economic Forum, October 2020. weforum.org/reports/the-future-of-jobs-report-2020.

Gandhi, Vipula, and Jennifer Robison. "The 'Great Resignation' Is Really the 'Great Discontent.'" Gallup, July 22, 2021. gallup.com/workplace/351545/great-resignation-really-great-discontent.aspx.

George, Bill, Peter Sims, Andrew N. McLean, and Diana Mayer. "Discovering Your Authentic Leadership." *Harvard Business Review*, February 2007. hbr.org/2007/02/discovering-your-authentic-leadership.

Gilbert, Elizabeth. *Eat, Pray, Love: One Woman's Search for Everything across Italy, India and Indonesia*. New York, NY: Viking Penguin, 2006.

Gogh, Vincent van. Letter to Theo van Gogh. "Zondag Middag." *Vincent van Gogh Letters*. Van Gogh Museum of Amsterdam, October 22, 1882. vangoghletters.org/vg/letters/let274/letter.html.

Goleman, Daniel. *Leadership That Gets Results*. Boston, MA: Harvard Business Review, 2000.

Goleman, Daniel. "Part Four: Windows of Opportunity." In *Emotional Intelligence: Why It Can Matter More Than IQ*. London, UK: Bloomsbury, 2009.

Goleman, Daniel. "Self-Mastery." In *The Brain and Emotional Intelligence: New Insights*. Northampton, MA: More Than Sound, 2011.

Goleman, Daniel. "What Makes a Leader?" Harvard Business Review (November–December 1998): 93–102.

Goleman, Daniel, Richard E. Boyatzis, and Annie McKee. *Primal Leadership: Unleashing the Power of Emotional Intelligence*. Boston, MA: Harvard Business School, 2002.

Grapsas, Stathis, Eddie Brummelman, Mitja D. Back, and Jaap J. A. Denissen. "The 'Why' and 'How' of Narcissism: A Process Model of Narcissistic Status Pursuit."

Perspectives on Psychological Science 15, no. 1 (December 5, 2019): 150–72. doi.org/10.1177/1745691619873350.

Grimard, Céleste, and J. Andrew Morris. "Stepping Up to the Plate: Facing Up to Your Fear of Assuming a Leadership Role." In *Engaged Leadership: Transforming through Future-Oriented Design Thinking*, edited by Joan Marques and Satinder Dhiman, 173–84. Cham, Switzerland: Springer, 2018. doi.org/10.1007/978-3-319-72221-4_9.

Gruman, Jamie A., and Alan M. Saks. "Performance Management and Employee Engagement." *Human Resource Management Review* 21, no. 2 (2011): 123–36. doi.org/10.1016/j.hrmr.2010.09.004.

Hale, Mandy. *The Single Woman: Life, Love, and a Dash of Sass*. Nashville, TN: Thomas Nelson, 2013.

Hargie, Owen, and David Dickson. *Skilled Interpersonal Communication: Research, Theory and Practice*. 4th ed. London, UK: Routledge, 2004.

Harter, James K., Frank L. Schmidt, and Corey L. M. Keyes. "Well-Being in the Workplace and Its Relationship to Business Outcomes: A Review of the Gallup Studies." In *Flourishing: Positive Psychology and the Life Well-Lived*, edited by Corey L. M. Keyes and Jonathan Haidt, 205–24. Washington, DC: American Psychological Association, 2003.

Hartshorne, Joshua K., and Laura T. Germine. "When Does Cognitive Functioning Peak? The Asynchronous Rise and Fall of Different Cognitive Abilities across the Life Span." *Psychological Science* 26, no. 4 (March 13, 2015): 433–43. doi.org/10.1177/0956797614567339.

Haskins, Henry Stanley. *Meditations in Wall Street*, introduction by Albert Jay Nock. New York, NY: William Morrow, 1940.

Hayashi, Yusuke, and Yukiko Washio. "Text-Message Dependency, Executive Function, and Impulsivity in College Students: A Cluster Analysis." *Cyberpsychology, Behavior, and Social Networking* 23, no. 11 (January 2020): 794–99. doi.org/10.1089/cyber.2019.0743.

Hayes, Brett, and Beryl Hesketh. "Attribution Theory, Judgmental Biases, and Cognitive Behavior Modification: Prospects and Problems." *Cognitive Therapy and Research* 13, no. 3 (June 1989): 211–30. doi.org/10.1007/bf01173404.

Helliwell, John F., Richard Layard, Jeffrey D. Sachs, Jan-Emmanuel De Neve, Lara B. Aknin, and Shun Wang. "World Happiness Report 2021." Sustainable Development Solutions Network, 2021. worldhappiness.report/ed/2021/.

Heskett, Jim. "So We Adapt. What's the Downside?" Harvard Business School, July 7, 2011. hbswk.hbs.edu/item/so-we-adapt-whats-the-downside.

Holmberg-Wright, Kristin, Tracy Hribar, and J. D. Tsegai. "More Than Money: Business Strategies to Engage Millennials." *Business Education Innovation* 9, no. 2 (2017): 14–23. beijournal.com/images/2_v9N2_final_2-2.pdf.

Hougaard, Rasmus, Jacqueline Carter, and Gillian Coutts. *One Second Ahead: Enhance Your Performance at Work with Mindfulness*. New York, NY: Palgrave Macmillan, 2016.

How to Embrace Emotions at Work. The Way We Work. TED Series, 2020. ted.com/talks/liz_fosslien_how_to_embrace_emotions_at_work?language=en.

Hughes, Jamie S., Mary K. Gourley, Laura Madson, and Katya Le Blanc. "Stress and Coping Activity: Reframing Negative Thoughts." *Teaching of Psychology* 38, no. 1 (2011): 36–39. doi.org/10.1177/0098628310390852.

Jafri, Md. Hassan, Chimi Dem, and Sonam Choden. "Emotional Intelligence and Employee Creativity: Moderating Role of Proactive Personality and

Organizational Climate." *Business Perspectives and Research* 4, no. 1 (2016): 54–66. doi.org/10.1177/2278533715605435.

Jeffers, Susan. *Feel the Fear ... and Do It Anyway: Dynamic Techniques for Turning Fear, Indecision, and Anger into Power, Action, and Love.* 1987. Rev. ed. Santa Monica, CA: Jeffers Press, 2007.

Jeung, Da-Yee, Changsoo Kim, and Sei-Jin Chang. "Emotional Labor and Burnout: A Review of the Literature." *Yonsei Medical Journal* 59, no. 2 (February 5, 2018): 187–93. doi.org/10.3349/ymj.2018.59.2.187.

Kaczmarek, Lukasz D., Maciej Behnke, Jolanta Enko, Michał Kosakowski, Przemysław Guzik, and Brian M. Hughes. "Splitting the Affective Atom: Divergence of Valence and Approach-Avoidance Motivation during a Dynamic Emotional Experience." *Current Psychology* 40 (2021): 3272–83. doi.org/10.1007/s12144-019-00264-3.

Kaplan, Seth, Jill C. Bradley, Joseph N. Luchman, and Douglas Haynes. "On the Role of Positive and Negative Affectivity in Job Performance: A Meta-Analytic Investigation." *Journal of Applied Psychology* 94, no. 1 (2009): 162–76. doi.org/10.1037/a0013115.

Karrass, Chester Louis. *In Business as in Life, You Don't Get What You Deserve, You Get What You Negotiate.* Stanford, CA: Stanford Street, 1996.

Kiken, Laura G., and Natalie J. Shook. "Looking Up: Mindfulness Increases Positive Judgments and Reduces Negativity Bias." *Social Psychological and Personality Science* 2, no. 4 (2011): 425–31. doi.org/10.1177/1948550610396585.

Kivimäki, Mika, Markus Jokela, Solja T. Nyberg, Archana Singh-Manoux, Eleonor I. Fransson, Lars Alfredsson, Jakob B. Bjorner, et al. "Long Working Hours and Risk of Coronary Heart Disease and Stroke: A Systematic Review and Meta-Analysis of Published and Unpublished Data for 603 838 Individuals." *The Lancet* 386, no. 10005 (August 20, 2015): 1739–46. doi.org/10.1016/s0140-6736(15)60295-1.

Kotsou, Ilios, Delphine Nelis, Jacques Grégoire, and Moïra Mikolajczak. "Emotional Plasticity: Conditions and Effects of Improving Emotional Competence in Adulthood." *Journal of Applied Psychology* 96, no. 4 (March 2011): 827–39. doi.org/10.1037/a0023047.

Kram, Kathy. "Foreword." In *Linking Emotional Intelligence and Performance at Work: Current Research Evidence with Individuals and Groups*, edited by Vanessa Urch Druskat, Fabio Sala, and Gerald Mount, vii–ix. Mahwah, NJ: Lawrence Erlbaum Associates, 2006.

Krause, Kathrin, and Alexandra M. Freund. "How to Beat Procrastination." *European Psychologist* 19, no. 2 (January 2014): 132–44. doi.org/10.1027/1016-9040/a000153.

Krebs, Claudia, and Carolyn Stern. Interview with Dr. Claudia Krebs. Personal, January 11, 2022.

Krebs, Claudia, and Carolyn Stern. Interview with Dr. Claudia Krebs. Personal, January 24, 2022.

LeBlanc, Vicki R. "The Effects of Acute Stress on Performance: Implications for Health Professions Education." *Academic Medicine* 84, no. 10 (October 2009): S25–S33. doi.org/10.1097/acm.0b013e3181b37b8f.

LeBlanc, Vicki R., Meghan M. McConnell, and Sandra D. Monteiro. "Predictable Chaos: A Review of the Effects of Emotions on Attention, Memory and Decision Making." *Advances in Health Sciences Education* 20, no. 1 (June 2014): 265–81. doi.org/10.1007/s10459-014-9516-6.

Lee, Pamela M. "Introduction: Aspiration Burnout." *October*, no. 176 (2021): 3–6. doi.org/10.1162/octo_e_00421.

Leith, Karen Pezza, and Roy F. Baumeister. "Why Do Bad Moods Increase Self-Defeating Behavior? Emotion, Risk Tasking, and Self-Regulation." *Journal of Personality and Social Psychology* 71, no. 6 (December 1996): 1250–67. doi.org/10.1037/0022-3514.71.6.1250.

Lerner, Jennifer S., Ye Li, Piercarlo Valdesolo, and Karim Kassam. "Emotion and Decision Making." *Annual Review of Psychology* 66 (March 2015): 799–823. doi.org/10.1146/annurev-psych-010213-115043.

Levontin, Liat, and Anat Bardi. "Using Personal Values to Understand the Motivational Basis of Amity Goal Orientation." *Frontiers in Psychology* 9 (January 9, 2019). doi.org/10.3389/fpsyg.2018.02736.

Lewis, Greg, and Eric Knudsen. "Stressed Employees Browse New Jobs, Unsupported Employees Actually Apply." LinkedIn, June 2021. linkedin.com/business/talent/blog/talent-strategy/stressed-employees-browse-unsupported-employee-apply.

Lin, Ying, Julian Mutz, Peter J. Clough, and Kostas A. Papageorgiou. "Mental Toughness and Individual Differences in Learning, Educational and Work Performance, Psychological Well-Being, and Personality: A Systematic Review." *Frontiers in Psychology* 8 (August 11, 2017): 1–15. doi.org/10.3389/fpsyg.2017.01345.

Locke, Edwin A., and Gary P. Latham. "The Application of Goal Setting to Sports." *Journal of Sport Psychology* 7, no. 3 (1985): 205–22. doi.org/10.1123/jsp.7.3.205.

London, Manuel. "Preface." In *Leadership Development: Paths to Self-Insight and Professional Growth*. Mahwah, NJ: Lawrence Erlbaum Associates, 2002.

Loomes, Graham, and Robert Sugden. "Regret Theory: An Alternative Theory of Rational Choice under Uncertainty." *Economic Journal* 92, no. 368 (December 1, 1982): 805–24. doi.org/10.2307/2232669.

Loughnan, Steve, Peter Kuppens, Jüri Allik, Katalin Balazs, Soledad de Lemus, Kitty Dumont, Rafael Gargurevich, et al. "Economic Inequality Is Linked to Biased Self-Perception." *Psychological Science* 22, no. 10 (2011): 1254–58. doi.org/10.1177/0956797611417003.

Luisetto, Mauro, Naseer Almukhtar, and Farhan Ahmed Khan. "Mindset Kinetics and Crime Behavior—Quantitative Methods? A New Forensic Quantitative Approach. How Biochemistry, Toxicology, Imaging Principle Can Help in Jurisdictional Settings." *Biomedical Journal of Scientific & Technical Research* 16, no. 2 (March 2019): 11828–37. doi.org/10.26717/bjstr.2019.16.002810.

Mann, Charles Riborg. "Chapter XVI: The Professional Engineer." In *A Study of Engineering Education: Prepared for the Joint Committee on Engineering Education of the National Engineering Societies*, The Carnegie Foundation for the Advancement of Teaching, bulletin no. 11: 106–13. Boston, MA: Merrymount, 1918.

Martin, Andrew J., and Herbert W. Marsh. "Fear of Failure: Friend or Foe?" *Australian Psychologist* 38, no. 1 (March 2003): 31–38. doi.org/10.1080/00050060310001706997.

Matthews, Gail. "The Impact of Commitment, Accountability, and Written Goals on Goal Achievement." Podium presentation at the 87th Convention of the Western Psychological Association, Vancouver, BC, 2007. scholar.dominican.edu/psychology-faculty-conference-presentations/3/.

Maxwell, John C. "The Definition of Leadership: Influence." In *Developing the Leader within You 2.0*. Nashville, TN: HarperCollins Leadership, 2018.

McEwen, Bruce S. "Physiology and Neurobiology of Stress and Adaptation: Central Role of the Brain." *Physiological Reviews* 87, no. 3 (July 2007): 873–904. doi.org/10.1152/physrev.00041.2006.

McGavin, Barbara. "Transforming Our Inner Critics: The Power of Presence." *Self & Society* 33, no. 2 (2005): 24–29. doi.org/10.1080/03060497.2005.11083872.

Mehrabian, Albert, and Susan R. Ferris. "Inference of Attitudes from Nonverbal Communication in Two Channels." *Journal of Consulting Psychology* 31, no. 3 (1967): 248–52. doi.org/10.1037/h0024648.

Mellody, Pia. *Facing Codependence: What It Is, Where It Comes from, How It Sabotages Our Lives*. With Andrea Wells Miller and J. Keith Miller. New York, NY: Harper & Row, 1989.

Mikkelsen, Kathleen, Lily Stojanovska, Momir Polenakovic, Marijan Bosevski, and Vasso Apostolopoulos. "Exercise and Mental Health." *Maturitas* 106 (2017): 48–56. doi.org/10.1016/j.maturitas.2017.09.003.

Miller, Regina, and Joan Pedro. "Creating Respectful Classroom Environments." *Early Childhood Education Journal* 33, no. 5 (2006): 293–99. doi.org/10.1007/s10643-006-0091-1.

Mohammad, Falahat Nejadmahani, Lau Teck Chai, Law Kian Aun, and Melissa W. Migin. "Emotional Intelligence and Turnover Intention." *International Journal of Academic Research* 6, no. 4 (July 2014): 211–20. doi.org/10.7813/2075-4124.2014/6-4/B.33.

Morin, Amy. "The 8 Myths about Emotions That Are Holding Us Back." Forbes, July 18, 2014. forbes.com/sites/amymorin/2014/07/18/the-8-myths-about-emotions-that-are-holding-us-back/?sh=3666902b4eb4.

Morrison, Sara E., and C. Daniel Salzman. "Re-valuing the Amygdala." *Current Opinion in Neurobiology* 20, no. 2 (March 2010): 221–30. doi.org/10.1016/j.conb.2010.02.007.

Moss, Jennifer. "Why It's Important to Stretch and Improve Your Emotional Flexibility: Jennifer Moss." CBC/Radio Canada, November 1, 2020. cbc.ca/news/canada/kitchener-waterloo/happiness-column-jennifer-moss-emotional-flexibility-1.5781721.

Myers, Karen Struble. "A 'Little and Big' Start to the New Year." Fred Rogers Center, January 20, 2016. fredrogerscenter.org/2016/01/a-little-and-big-start-to-the-new-year/.

Neff, Kristin. "Chapter 1: The Fundamentals of Self-Compassion." In *Fierce Self-Compassion: How Women Can Harness Kindness to Speak Up, Claim Their Power, and Thrive*, 1st ed., 23–50. New York, NY: Harper Wave, 2021.

Neff, Kristin D. "The Development and Validation of a Scale to Measure Self-Compassion." *Self and Identity* 2, no. 3 (July 2003): 223–50. doi.org/10.1080/15298860309027.

Neuhaus, Maike. "Self-Coaching Model Explained: 56 Questions & Techniques for Self-Mastery." PositivePsychology.com, December 13, 2021. positivepsychology.com/self-coaching-model/.

Nink, Marco, and Jennifer Robison. "The Damage Inflicted by Poor Managers." Gallup, December 2016. news.gallup.com/businessjournal/200108/damage-inflicted-poor-managers.aspx.

Olvera-Cortés, María Esther, Patricia Anguiano-Rodríguez, Miguel Ángel López-Vázquez, and José Miguel Cervantes Alfaro. "Serotonin/Dopamine Interaction in Learning." *Progress in Brain Research* (2008): 567–602. doi.org/10.1016/s0079-6123(08)00927-8.

Pacht, Asher R. "Reflections on Perfection." *American Psychologist* 39, no. 4 (April 1984): 386–90. doi.org/10.1037/0003-066x.39.4.386.

Patterson, Kerry, Joseph Grenny, David Maxfield, Ron McMillan, and Al Switzler. *Crucial Accountability: Tools for Resolving Violated Expectations, Broken*

Commitments, and Bad Behavior. 2nd ed. New York, NY: McGraw-Hill Education, 2013.

Patzer, Gordon. *Looks: Why They Matter More Than You Ever Imagined.* New York, NY: AMACOM, 2008.

Phan, K. Luan, Tor Wager, Stephan F. Taylor, and Israel Liberzon. "Functional Neuroanatomy of Emotion: A Meta-Analysis of Emotion Activation Studies in PET and FMRI." *NeuroImage* 16, no. 2 (2002): 331–48. doi.org/10.1006/nimg.2002.1087.

Phelps, Elizabeth A., and Joseph E. LeDoux. "Contributions of the Amygdala to Emotion Processing: From Animal Models to Human Behavior." *Neuron* 48, no. 2 (October 2005): 175–87. doi.org/10.1016/j.neuron.2005.09.025.

Pincott, Jena E. "Silencing Your Inner Critic." Psychology Today, March 4, 2019. psychologytoday.com/us/articles/201903/silencing-your-inner-critic.

Porges, Stephen W. *The Polyvagal Theory: Neurophysiological Foundations of Emotions, Attachment, Communication, and Self-Regulation.* New York, NY: W. W. Norton, 2011.

Pressfield, Steven. *The War of Art: Break Through the Blocks and Win Your Inner Creative Battles.* New York, NY: Warner Books, 2002.

Prusak, Larry. "What Can't Be Measured." Harvard Business Review, October 7, 2010. hbr.org/2010/10/what-cant-be-measured.

Pugle, Michelle. "The Anatomy of the Amygdala." Verywell Health, April 1, 2021. verywellhealth.com/amygdala-5112775.

Rank, Johannes, and Michael Frese. "Chapter 6: The Impact of Emotions, Moods and Other Affect-Related Variables on Creativity, Innovation and Initiative." In *Research Companion to Emotion in Organizations,* edited by Neal M. Ashkanasy and Cary L. Cooper, 103–19. Cheltenham, UK: Edward Elgar, 2008. doi.org/10.4337/9781848443778.00015.

Raypole, Crystal. "How to Be Emotionally Supportive." Healthline, September 10, 2021. healthline.com/health/mental-health/emotional-support.

Reeve, Johnmarshall. *Understanding Motivation and Emotion.* 5th ed. Hoboken, NJ: Wiley, 2009.

Reina, Dennis S., and Michelle L. Reina. *Trust and Betrayal in the Workplace: Building Effective Relationships in Your Organization.* Oakland, CA: Berrett-Koehler, 2015.

Rosenberg, Marshall B. "Chapter 9: Connecting Compassionately with Ourselves." In *Nonviolent Communication: A Language of Life,* 3rd ed. Encinitas, CA: PuddleDancer, 2015.

Sampthirao, Prabhakararao. "Self-Concept and Interpersonal Communication." *International Journal of Indian Psychology* 3, no. 3 (2016): 177–89. doi.org/10.25215/0303.115.

Santos-Longhurst, Adrienne. "Intrinsic Motivation: How to Pick Up Healthy Motivation Techniques." Healthline, February 11, 2019. healthline.com/health/intrinsic-motivation.

Schrage, Michael. "Like It or Not, You Are Always Leading by Example." Harvard Business Review, October 5, 2016. hbr.org/2016/10/like-it-or-not-you-are-always-leading-by-example.

Senge, Peter M. *The Fifth Discipline: The Art and Practice of the Learning Organization.* New York, NY: Doubleday Currency, 1990.

Serrat, Olivier. "The Five Whys Technique." In *Knowledge Solutions,* 307–10. Singapore: Springer, 2017. doi.org/10.1007/978-981-10-0983-9_32.

Sharma, Vinky, and Moonis Shakeel. "Illusion versus Reality: An Empirical Study of Overconfidence and Self Attribution Bias in Business Management Students." *Journal of Education for Business* 90, no. 4 (March 16, 2015): 199–207. doi.org/10.1080/08832323.2015.1014458.

Shepherd, Dean A., and Melissa S. Cardon. "Negative Emotional Reactions to Project Failure and the Self-Compassion to Learn from the Experience." *Journal of Management Studies* 46, no. 6 (2009): 923–49. doi.org/10.1111/j.1467-6486.2009.00821.x.

Sherman, S. Murray, and R. W. Guillery. *Exploring the Thalamus and Its Role in Cortical Function.* 2nd ed. Cambridge, MA: MIT, 2006.

Shukla, Sunita, Farhat Mohsin, and Vikas Singh. "Relationship between Emotional Intelligence and Employee Engagement: A Study of Leading Printing Press in NCR." *Tecnia Journal of Management Studies* 8, no. 1 (September 2013): 43–50.

Siegel, Daniel J. "Half a Brain in Hiding: Balancing Left and Right." In *Mindsight: The New Science of Personal Transformation,* 102–19. New York, NY: Bantam Books, 2010.

Sinek, Simon, David Mead, and Peter Docker. "Chapter 1: Start with Why: A Primer." In *Find Your Why: A Practical Guide for Discovering Purpose for You and Your Team.* New York, NY: Portfolio/Penguin, 2017.

Slaughter, Mary, and David Rock. "No Pain, No Brain Gain: Why Learning Demands (a Little) Discomfort." Fast Company, April 30, 2018. fastcompany.com/40560075/no-pain-no-brain-gain-why-learning-demands-a-little-discomfort.

Sloan, Melissa, Murat Haner, Amanda Graham, Francis T. Cullen, Justin Pickett, and Cheryl Lero Jonson. "Pandemic Emotions: The Extent, Correlates, and Mental Health Consequences of Personal and Altruistic Fear of COVID-19." *SocArXiv,* Working Paper, May 3, 2020. doi.org/10.31235/osf.io/txqb6.

Smith, Kyle S., and Ann M. Graybiel. "Habit Formation." *Dialogues in Clinical Neuroscience* 18, no. 1 (March 2016): 33–43. doi.org/10.31887/dcns.2016.18.1/ksmith.

Solomon, Lou. "Two-Thirds of Managers Are Uncomfortable Communicating with Employees." Harvard Business Review, March 9, 2016. hbr.org/2016/03/two-thirds-of-managers-are-uncomfortable-communicating-with-employees.

"Sophia the Robot Wants a Baby and Says Family Is 'Really Important.'" BBC, November 25, 2017. bbc.com/news/newsbeat-42122742.

Sorenson, Susan, and Keri Garman. "How to Tackle U.S. Employees' Stagnating Engagement." Gallup, June 11, 2013. news.gallup.com/businessjournal/162953/tackle-employees-stagnating-engagement.aspx.

Sprenger, Marilee. "Chapter 3: Pieces and Parts: The Anatomy of the Brain." In *Learning and Memory: The Brain in Action,* 30–44. Alexandria, VA: Association for Supervision and Curriculum Development, 1999.

"State of the Global Workplace 2021 Report." Gallup, June 2021. gallup.com/workplace/349484/state-of-the-global-workplace.aspx.

Steffens, Niklas K., S. Alexander Haslam, Sebastian C. Schuh, Jolanda Jetten, and Rolf van Dick. "A Meta-Analytic Review of Social Identification and Health in Organizational Contexts." *Personality and Social Psychology Review* (July 7, 2016). doi.org/10.1177/1088868316656701.

Stone, Douglas, Bruce Patton, and Sheila Heen. *Difficult Conversations: How to Discuss What Matters Most.* New York, NY: Penguin, 2010.

Stone, Douglas, and Sheila Heen. *Thanks for the Feedback: The Science and Art of Receiving Feedback Well.* New York, NY: Viking Penguin, 2014.

Tolle, Eckhart. *The Power of Now: A Guide to Spiritual Enlightenment.* San Francisco, CA: New World Library, 1999.

Torrence, Brett S., and Shane Connelly. "Emotion Regulation Tendencies and Leadership Performance: An Examination of Cognitive and Behavioral Regulation Strategies." *Frontiers in Psychology* 10 (July 2, 2019). doi.org/10.3389/fpsyg.2019.01486.

Tyng, Chai M., Hafeez U. Amin, Mohamad N. M. Saad, and Aamir S. Malik. "The Influences of Emotion on Learning and Memory." *Frontiers in Psychology* 8 (August 24, 2017). doi.org/10.3389/fpsyg.2017.01454.

"Understanding the Stress Response: Chronic Activation of This Survival Mechanism Impairs Health." Harvard Health, July 6, 2020. health.harvard.edu/staying-healthy/understanding-the-stress-response.

Vanderkam, Laura. "Are You as Busy as You Think?" Wall Street Journal, February 22, 2012. wsj.com/articles/SB10001424052970203358704577237603853394654.

Ward, Lawrence M. "The Thalamus: Gateway to the Mind." *Wiley Interdisciplinary Reviews: Cognitive Science* 4, no. 6 (2013): 609–22. doi.org/10.1002/wcs.1256.

Webb, Jonice, and Christine Musello. "Part II: Out of Fuel." In *Running on Empty: Overcome Your Childhood Emotional Neglect.* New York, NY: Morgan James, 2013.

Whitmore, John. "What Options Do You Have?" In *Coaching for Performance: GROWing Human Potential and Purpose,* 4th ed., 79–84. Boston, MA: Nicholas Brealey, 2009.

Wilde, Oscar. *Lady Windermere's Fan.* 1892. Salt Lake City, UT: Project Gutenberg, 1997. gutenberg.org/files/790/790-h/790-h.htm.

Wilkos, Ewelina, Timothy J. B. Brown, Ksenia Slawinska, and Katarzyna A. Kucharska. "Social Cognitive and Neurocognitive Deficits in Inpatients with Unilateral Thalamic Lesions—Pilot Study." *Neuropsychiatric Disease and Treatment* 11 (2015): 1031–38. doi.org/10.2147/NDT.S78037.

Williams, Riccardo. "Anger as a Basic Emotion and Its Role in Personality Building and Pathological Growth: The Neuroscientific, Developmental and Clinical Perspectives." *Frontiers in Psychology* 8 (November 7, 2017). doi.org/10.3389/fpsyg.2017.01950.

Xing, Yijun. "A Daoist Reflection on Sea-Like Leadership and Enlightened Thinking." *Management and Organization Review* 12, no. 4 (2016): 807–10. doi.org/10.1017/mor.2016.48.

Yaribeygi, Habib, Yunes Panahi, Hedayat Sahraei, Thomas P. Johnston, and Amirhossein Sahebkar. "The Impact of Stress on Body Function: A Review." *EXCLI Journal* 16 (July 21, 2017): 1057–72. doi.org/10.17179/excli2017-480.

Yip, Jeremy A., Daniel H. Stein, Stéphane Côté, and Dana R. Carney. "Follow Your Gut? Emotional Intelligence Moderates the Association between Physiologically Measured Somatic Markers and Risk-Taking." *Emotion* 20, no. 3 (2020): 462–72. doi.org/10.1037/emo0000561.

Yu Song, Jessica I. Jordan, Kelsey A. Shaffer, Erik K. Wing, Kateri McRae, and Christian E. Waugh. "Effects of Incidental Positive Emotion and Cognitive Reappraisal on Affective Responses to Negative Stimuli." *Cognition and Emotion* 33, no. 6 (2019): 1155–68. doi.org/10.1080/02699931.2018.1541789.

Zenger, Jack, and Joseph Folkman. "Your Employees Want the Negative Feedback You Hate to Give." Harvard Business Review, January 15, 2014. hbr.org/2014/01/your-employees-want-the-negative-feedback-you-hate-to-give.

INDEX

relationships and, 45–46; resilience and, 185, 196, 199; sharing how you feel, 192; strength and, 1; stress management and, 49–50; as superpower, 13–14; vocabulary for, 179–80; wisdom from, 17. *See also* emotional intelligence

empathy: about, 28, 187–88; Harpreet's story, 143; within interpersonal, 106; Martina's story, 155–56; sample interview questions, 141; self-assessment, 120, 148; Shawn's story, 85; tips and tools, 188–89; Wolfgang's story, 107

employees: employee experience, 72; engagement, 52, 72, 139–40; labor force complexity, 13; leadership's impact on, 73–75; retention and turnover, 71, 73; stress, worry, sadness, and anger among, 76. *See also* workplace

energy, 199

environment, changing, 197–98

exercise, 178

expression. *See* emotional expression; self-expression

failure, 23, 87, 185, 201

feedback: analyzing responses, 142, 146–47; client story, 135–36; common reactions to, 132–34; culture of, 134–35; discomfort with, 44; Harpreet's story, 143, 152; sample interview questions, 140–41; strategies for receiving, 137–39, 140; strategies for soliciting, 136–37; value of, 132, 139–40. *See also* Consult with Others

feelings, 39–41. *See also* emotions

fight-or-flight response, 55

flexibility: about, 196; author's experience, 113; sample interview questions, 141; self-assessment, 122, 148; within stress management, 111; tips and tools, 197–98

Franklin, Benjamin, 214

Friedman, Edwin, 156

Future of Education and Skills (OECD), 22

Future of Jobs Report 2020 (World Economic Forum), 22, 69

Gallup, 48, 52, 73, 139; *State of the Global Workplace 2021 Report*, 43, 76, 76

Gilbert, Elizabeth, 180

goals: introduction, 127; aligning with values, 213–14; closing the gap, 157–59; crafting your action plan, 213, 220; exploring options for reaching, 208–9, 211; optimism and, 200; S.M.A.R.T. goals, 160–61, 166–67

Goleman, Daniel, 55, 56, 74

Greaves, Jean, 6

growth mindset, 67, 77, 189, 197

habits: development and practice, 57–60, 60–61, 242; positive daily habits, 175–76, 201

Hale, Mandy, 184

Harpreet (feedback story), 143, 152

health, 48–49, 50

Heen, Sheila, 133

hippocampus, 53, *54*, 56

honesty, 183–84

humility, 67

hustle culture, 34

hypothalamus, 53, *54*, 55, 56

impacts, vs. intentions, 81–83

implicit assumptions, 204–5

impulse control: about, 195; author's experience, 114; within decision-making, 109; Donna's story, 115; Harpreet's story, 143; sample interview questions, 141; self-assessment, 121, 148; tips and tools, 195–96

independence: about, 184; author's experience, 113, 153; sample interview questions, 141; self-assessment, 119, 148; within self-expression, 104; tips and tools, 184–86

Congratulations on undertaking your own inside-out journey to becoming an emotionally strong leader.

To help you build on what you've learned in these pages, you can now access exclusive content, such as video and audio lessons, additional exercises and resources, as well as an EI Guide that complements the learning in this book.

Kick-start your transformation in life and leadership, all with the power of your own emotions. Scan the QR code below to harness your emotional superpower.